That Reminds Me of the Time...
Volume 2

An anthology

by the

Arizona Highway Patrol
Coalition of DPS Retirees

CLC Publishing
Books with Purpose

Published by CLC Publishing, LLC
Mustang, OK 73064

Photographs used with permission.

Printed in the United States of America

Book Design by Shannon Whittington
Cover Design by Shannon Whittington

ISBN 978-1-0879-0270-8

Biography/Autobiography/Law Enforcement
Biography/Autobiography/Personal Memoir

Coalition of DPS Retirees, Inc.

The Coalition of DPS Retirees proudly presents this book for your reading pleasure. It is comprised of true stories and experiences written and compiled by members and their families of our Coalition.

Colin Peabody, Chairman
Ed Felix, Vice Chairman
Norma Risch, Secretary
James Gentner, Comptroller
Ardith Hundley, Member Services

ACKNOWLEDGEMENTS

The Coalition of DPS Retirees, Inc. wishes to thank the following DPS retirees and their families for contributing their stories to this book. Without their experiences and their humor, Volumes 1 and 2 would not have been possible. Many of the authors' stories were written prior to their passing and kept for this book.

Harley Thompson, Don Uhles, Lee Patterson, Willie Hall, Jeff Trapp, John Gantt, John Kennedy, Paul Palmer, Colin Peabody, Ron Cox, Dennis McNulty, Tom Clinkenbeard, Ron Young, Rich Richardson, Rick Ulrich, Bill Rogers, Dick Lewis, Frank Glenn, Bob Singer, Barry Allen, Lannie Van Tassel, Jim Chilcoat, Loma Jenkins, T. K. Waddell, Bob Mitchell, Jay Atwater, Don Barcello, C.B. Fletcher, John Underwood, Jim Heflin, Tom Ticer, Gregg Girard, Tim Hughes, Larry Jensen, Steve Gendler, Lyn Diehl, Vern Andrews, Jim Phillips, Peg Kennedy, Alex Carrillo, J.R. Ham, Ric Miller, Jim Gentner, Doug Kluender, Bob Osborn, Steve Mason, Bernie Gazdzik, Heber John Davis, Gary Ciminski, Tom Gosch, John Fink, Bob Pierce, Jack Grant, Gamble Dick, Allan Wright, Terry Johnson, Art Coughanour, Frank Root, Rick Ayars, Jack Bell, Brian Frank, Greg Eavenson, Charley Ruiz, Ralph Shartzer, Larry Thompson, Martin Marquez, Randy Strong, Tom Armstrong, Clarence Forbey, Jerry Foster, Gail Mosher, Frank Gillette

Those contributing their stories especially wish to thank the Coalition of DPS Retirees for their full support of this book.

DEDICATION

This book would not have been possible without the input from some of the finest people you could ever meet. These people are the men and women of the Arizona Highway Patrol/Department of Public Safety who have honorably served and retired from this great agency.

This book is dedicated to our current retirees, retirees who have passed, and to future retirees. You are a fantastic group, and it is an honor to have served with you.

INTRODUCTION

When we first began asking our retirees to send us stories we got a great response. It wasn't long before we had enough stories for a book. Yet some said that they didn't have any stories anyone would be interested in.

When "That Reminds Me Of The Time" was published and distributed, after reading the stories, folks decided that yes, just like the retirees who submitted stories, they too had a story to tell. And the stories started coming in.

Some stories came in with a format incompatible with what we were working with. The formats were changed where we could work with them. Some stories were oral and we received some hand written stories. No matter what format we received, we made it work. In Volume 2, Paul Palmer deserves the credit for compiling all the stories and getting them in a workable format.

This book, "That Reminds Me Of The Time Volume 2" is in the same format as the original. Some stories will have you laughing and some will bring a tear to your eye. But also in this book you will read stories about arrests and shootings you have heard about over the years, but never got the whole story. Some of what you heard may not have been entirely correct, but in this book we hear from the officers involved and you will think, "so that's why he did that."

Our retirees are recording our history for future generations and for that, everyone is grateful. So, once again, grab a cup, kick back and enjoy these stories.

Paul Palmer #342
Colin Peabody #481

Arizona, geographically, is a bold state.

Jagged mountains, isolated mesas, gaping canyons, wind-swept plateaus, lonesome valleys, alpine peaks and searing deserts are rolled like dice across her landscape.

Within this jumbled topography, freeways and highways crisscross the state from east to west and south to north. They emerge from major metropolitan centers like Phoenix and Tucson and stretch to tiny hamlets like Mexican Water and Why. These bustling superhighways and desolate two-lane highways link us to each other across great spans of distance.

But these roadways do more than physically connect us. They tie together our past and present and will carry us into our future. Through time they have provided the underpinning that forged our history and spirit into a common Arizona heritage.

Yet more than the concrete, asphalt and steel guardrails that bind and shape our highways, there is a stronger, transcendent human element of bravery, compassion, humor, loyalty, and camaraderie that tick by like centerline strips down each and every mile of Arizona highway.

In the following pages the reader will meet, perhaps for the first time, the men and women of the Arizona Highway Patrol and Department of Public Safety.

Like Arizona's geography, the personalities and actions of these men and women are bold. Often alone in remote locations, emergency situations demand quick decisions. Jumping into action, they make them, by themselves, on the spot, without hesitation. In other cases, they display great compassion for their fellow man, fiercely loyal to the ideal that first and foremost, they patrol our highways to keep us, the public, safe. In so many stories we see their selfless action charge into action without regard to their own well-being. Not reckless, but well-trained. Through the pages and stories the reader will envy their departmental camaraderie and esprit de corps. While many stories recount humorous antics and lighthearted mischief amongst their ranks, in case after case we see how deadly serious these men and woman regard their public service. I believe they inherently understand the importance of their service to a cause greater than themselves. In times of crises, hardship and danger, they embrace their duty to serve humankind.

As I read these stories, I reflected on an experience I had with the DPS as a young man more than four decades ago.

In my early 20s my brother and I hiked with two mules 810 miles across the entire state of Arizona from south to north. Deep in the Bradshaw mountains, record-breaking rains and floods stopped us in our tracks. Two weeks of pounding rain had transformed normally dry creek beds into raging maelstroms capable of sweeping us and our mules to our doom. Though we were stopped this morning within a steep desert canyon, we were high above the roiling waters. We had plenty of food, and we had the time to wait for the flooding to subside.

Suddenly above the roar of howling winds and hammering rains, we heard the whock-whock of helicopter blades. To our astonishment, through the clouds a DPS helicopter was descending into the canyon directly above us. How we were spotted, we never knew. We winced as we watched devilish winds buffeting the chopper dangerously close to the canyon walls.

My brother and I waved our arms furiously, attempting to signal that we were okay and they need not risk their lives trying to "save" us. By this time the helicopter was so close that we could clearly see the pilot and an accompanying officer. Though the pilot was unable to land, he was able to place one skid on a rock promontory. The officer climbed out and jumped to the ground, crouching low. My brother and I scrambled up the slope to meet him, ducking our heads as well.

I remember seeing his pressed uniform and badge getting doused in the cold rain.

Communication because of the thudding rotor was nearly impossible. The officer first asked if we were okay. We nodded. Did we need his help, he asked. We shook our heads back and forth. We leaned in closer and shouted that we were hiking across the state, but as soon as we spoke our words were whisked away. We had to repeat ourselves several times before the officer was able to hear and understand us. Hunched beneath the rotating helicopter blades, he gripped our hands firmly, looked us in the eyes and assured us that they would be watching out for us.

Seconds later, with a whoosh, he and the chopper disappeared into the clouds. Stunned, my brother and I looked at each other. What just happened? How did they know we were here? How brave could they possibly be?

Since that wet and windy morning so many years ago, I have reminisced over the bravery of those two men who clearly risked their lives to ensure our safety – complete strangers to them. To me, their actions inside that narrow canyon that easily could have become their coffin, epitomize the will, strength and courage of those who serve to protect.

In a recent enjoyable twist of fate, while hiking in the seldom visited Cabeza Prieta National Wildlife Refuge on the US/Mexican border, I encountered US Border Patrol agent Oran Kennedy. I thanked him for his service. He retorted that was in his blood, and that his grandfather John Kennedy served on the Arizona Highway Patrol many years ago. In fact, he said, there is a book entitled "That Reminds Me Of The Time", an anthology of early Arizona Highway Patrol stories. As soon as I returned, I immediately read it.

If you're interested in Arizona history from all corners of the state, you will enjoy these stories you're about to read. At the end, I'm sure you will feel the same way I do about the Arizona Highway Patrol and Department of Public Safety.

Troy Gillenwater

Troy Gillenwater has volunteered at the Arizona Historical Society and serves today as the Museum of Northern Arizona board chairman.

US66 GAMBLING
Harley Thompson #6

The Arizona Highway Patrol was first formed of course in 1931 and was a political law enforcement organization. Officers had no tenure and worked at the pleasure of the governor. There was really not a lot of pride nor unity since no one could be certain that he had a job after the next election. And so it was, up through the war years, 1941-45.

In late 1946 while I was stationed in Williams, Captain Jack Powell told me and Patrolman Dick Raymond that he was picking up some rumors of gambling at different tourist attractions along US66 and asked us to be aware of the possibility and keep our ears open for any complaints that are brought to our attention.

The winter months rolled on by with the usual problems found on highways with black ice. Too much snow and drivers who never learned how to function in the high country.

It wasn't until late February or the first of March 1947 when the real problem with gambling along US66 reared its ugly head.

Patrolman Dick Whitlow who was stationed in Holbrook was offered a bribe of $75.00 by a man who claimed to be an undercover officer working for the Attorney General of the state of Arizona.

The following excerpts are from several different news services:

Phoenix, Arizona March 22, 1947 --- Rumors persisted this week that a scandal is looming which may shake virtually the entire state of Arizona. The rumors gained their impetus after the arrest of Harry Hendricks, identified by John L. Sullivan, state attorney general, as a special investigator for his office.

Hendricks is charged in Holbrook with attempting to bribe Dick Whitlow, a state highway patrolman. Whitlow charged that Hendricks dropped $75.00 in currency on the seat of his

(Whitlow's automobile) with the "suggestion" that if the patrolman received any complaints concerning tourists losing their money in gambling games at a so-called Indian trading post on US66, he advise the complainants to return to the trading post and their money would be refunded.

Holbrook Tribune News --- The attorney general said tourists were being attracted by exhibits of snakes or reptiles along main highways in Apache, Pima, Pinal, Yavapai and Yuma counties and then lured into confidence games. Apache County Attorney Marion Gibbons charged that Hendricks had offered him a $300.00 bribe which was later raised to $800.00 to keep "hands off" of a so called "trading post". This offer was made after Gibbons prosecuted A.J. Berry, operator of one of the establishments along US66 and he was fined $300.00.

Holbrook (by the Sun's own service) Hendricks found guilty and sentenced to 6 to 10 years. (March 29 1947)

As part of the aftermath of this sensational trial and conviction of bribery, John L. Sullivan, state attorney general, was arrested and accused on a charge of attempting to bribe Marion Gibbons, county attorney for Apache County. The attorney general was later convicted of this charge and was removed from office.

1947 rolled into the new year with many people in state government now actively promoting the Arizona Highway Patrol a force to be reckoned with and were suggesting it be taken out of politics and placed under a Merit System body in order that good officers may be able to keep their jobs and go forth with a real career in mind. Petitions were drawn up and distributed throughout the state in order to gather enough valid signatures and have an initiative referendum placed on the ballot and let the people of Arizona decide.

More than enough signatures were gathered, the bill was placed on the ballot and the result was that on November 2, 1948 during the regular general election, the removal of the Highway Patrol from politics became a reality.

TAN HIGHWAY PATROL UNIFORMS
AND OTHER MEMORIES
Colin Peabody #481

In the AHP Academy Class #10, in January 1968, cadet patrolmen were issued tan khaki long sleeved uniform shirts with one AHP shoulder patch and trousers, a black leather gun belt with only a handcuff case, a pair of handcuffs and the crupper strap, but no holster or weapon. A paper name tag with our badge number and name was pinned on the left chest above the pocket. When we went out on OJT midway through the academy, we had completed firearms training, however we were not authorized to carry a sidearm. We had to provide our own sidearms back then.

Once out on OJT, now called FTO, my coach was Patrolman Bob Varner. During the first or second shift with Bob, he was troubled by the fact that I was unarmed, so we made an unofficial visit to a local trading post west of Winslow and he borrowed a Smith and Wesson .38 caliber snub nosed revolver for me just in case. We had to keep it in the glove compartment of the patrol car, so that our sergeant or class counselors who would be riding with us wouldn't know it was there. Accessibility was a factor, but at least we had it if necessary.

We had stopped a violator for some traffic violation and as I was writing out the paperwork, the driver noticed that I didn't have a weapon and he asked Bob if I had forgotten my gun that morning. Bob, never at a loss for words, was quick with his reply, "He is so damn tough, he doesn't need a gun!" To my surprise, the violator accepted that explanation!

Once we graduated from the academy, we were issued our new silver tan, dry clean only, long sleeved uniforms with the AHP shoulder patches on each sleeve and an American Red Cross First Aid patch on the lower right sleeve. A black lanyard was attached under the epaulet on the left or right shoulder, depending if you were left or right handed with a clip that held your handcuff key and maybe even your Acme Thunderer whistle. The 7-point star of the Arizona Highway Patrol was pinned above the left breast pocket and had your badge number on it. Your name tag was attached above the right chest pocket. Black necktie required for winter shirt. Our duty belt then included a Border Patrol style holster for our new duty weapon, my choice being a new Smith and Wesson Model 19, .357 Magnum 6 shot revolver with 4-inch barrel. We were also issued a belt loop carrier that held 6 rounds of authorized .38 caliber (only) ammunition as well as a belt loop for our issued nightstick. We no longer had to wear the Sam Brown crupper strap, but we had it for dress uniform occasions. Veteran officers with more than 5 years of service wore a star on the lower left sleeve for each 5 years of service.

The belt loops held our extra ammo, but the problem was, the lead tips of the bullets rubbed against our trousers when we were seated in the car, leaving 6 gray smudges on our pants. Some guys coated the tips of their bullets with clear nail polish to avoid that smudging, but I wasn't sure how that stuff would react once the bullet was fired through the barrel. I sure didn't want it clogging up a perfectly well rifled barrel. My solution was to use a small towel tucked between the cartridge holder and my trousers and kept in place by the seat belt. Barring unforeseen circumstances, I could get an extra day out of a pair of pants by doing that and dry cleaning was expensive back in those days. Summer uniforms were of a lighter material and short sleeved, but dry cleaning was still required.

Our headgear consisted of two hats, one winter and one summer, of the old bus driver style. The AHP hat badge was affixed to the front above the bill of the cap. You had to wear it when you were out of the car or there was trouble coming your way! Traffic on US 66 was heavy and travelled very close to where we conducted our traffic stops and I think the truckers delighted in seeing if the wind generated by their trucks would catch our hats and they would go sailing down the road or across the desert like a Frisbee. The hats had a metal spring steel band inside that made the hat rims keep their shape, but it also aided them in rolling down the road! The Smokey Bear hats that we got a few years later weren't much better in that regard and were difficult to wear in the car or getting in and out of the car, but once I got used to wearing it, didn't mind it that much. We also had the black Wooly Booger hats like the Mounties wore and, in the winter, they were great, kept your ears warm! Our issued duty jackets didn't keep us as warm as we would have liked, so long underwear was a must in the winter. Footgear consisted of black Wellingtons or black plain toed low-cut shoes. Our badge, name tag, brass buttons and buckles had to be kept shined as well as our leather belts and boots. No fingerprints on the patent leather bill of our bus driver hats. Our weapon had to be clean and free of fingerprints and lint. Our assigned 12 ga. shotgun had to be clean and had to have the yellow seal attached around the pump action, showing that it had not been fired except on the firing range. It was kept in a scabbard either in the trunk or attached to the front of the front seat, loaded with 00 buckshot and one rifled slug.

Equipment in the trunk consisted of a metal box containing flares, first aid kit, blanket measuring tape, other supplies as necessary, but not limited to: bumper jack, 4-way lug wrench and a 3 gallon water bottle, shovel, the two way radio gear, tow strap and spare tire. Many cars were equipped with a gasoline transfer kit under the hood to transfer up to 3 gallons of fuel to the gas tank of a motorist who ran out of gasoline. Push bumpers were mounted to the front of the patrol cars. Motorists were given an envelope to send back money for the gas they received, but most probably did not ever do that! Outside speakers for the radio were mounted under the hood, as was one of the old-style "wind down" sirens. Emergency lighting consisted of a spotlight, roof mounted fixed lights (AKA Mickey Mouse ears) or the later rotary beacons. Early patrol cars prior to about 1957, had a small single roof mounted red flasher light, similar to what the Arizona Highway Department used on their trucks and road graders. An amber light was mounted inside the car on the rear deck behind the rear seat. Later cars had a red and an amber light until the department went to equipping cars with blue lights. Some cars had lights hidden behind the grille or mounted on the push bumpers. Early patrol car markings consisted of the AHP star on both doors and a single AHP star mounted on the trunk lid. After the death of Patrolman Louie Cochran in December 1958, a reflectorized decal with the words Arizona Highway Patrol in the shape of a bat wing was on patrol cars from 1959 until the mid to late 1970s. Patrol cars were normally painted white after the early 1950s until 1969 when patrol cars came in varied colors. 1969 also saw the upgrade to civil defense radios (AM radios) for better resale value, power steering and power disc brakes and floor carpeting. Patrol cars had been equipped with air conditioning for several years beginning in the early 1960s. Each area squad had an unmarked car, depending on color available.

Patrol cars had always been of various makes and models, with Fords being the most prominent, with Oldsmobiles, Dodges, Plymouths and Mercurys, then after 1966, Chevrolets and American Motors Ambassadors. In the early 1960s, a few Studebaker Larks were used in the mountainous areas due to their quick power, and short turning radius. By the late 1960s smaller Plymouth Belvederes, Chevrolet Malibus, Dodge Coronets and AMC Matadors were used in areas of two-lane highways, but they were equipped with more than sufficient horsepower to do the job required. Enforcement equipment consisted of radar and VASCAR units in the vehicles. Early AHP vehicles also had Indian Motorcycles in the fleet, but after the late 1930s, motorcycles were discontinued until 1973, when federal grant money was used to buy Italian Moto Guzzi Eldorado motorcycles. Several officers and a sergeant were sent to the California Highway Patrol Academy to train for motorcycle enforcement activities. Moto Guzzi motorcycles were used until the late 1970s when Kawasaki motorcycles were purchased. In the 21st century, both BMW and Honda motorcycles have been used. Current DPS vehicles include mostly large SUVs built and equipped for patrol use.

WOOL UNIFORMS AND REMOTE DUTY STATION
Don Uhles #2092

When I first hired on the Department, we were still wearing wool Winter/Class A uniforms. My first duty station was in Winslow, AZ. I remember that these uniforms were hot and itchy; I couldn't imagine wearing these uniforms down south.

One of the challenging aspects of these wool uniforms was cleaning, they had to be dry cleaned. Other than the expense of cleaning was finding a reliable cleaner. As a new patrolman I couldn't afford to own but a few uniforms so I needed a cleaner that would provide a quick turn-a-round. Fortunately for me the officers who were already in Winslow directed me to reliable cleaners.

When we transferred from Winslow to Houck, AZ it was a different story. The uniforms were still hot and itchy but now a round trip drive to the dry cleaners was about an 80-mile trip. This meant uniforms had to be cleaned at home. My wife came up with a system of washing and air drying my uniforms in a way that didn't cause them to shrink. Then came the ironing, lots of ironing, with lots of spray starch!

I don't know who was happier when the polyester uniforms were approved, Julie or me!

LOOKING SHARP
Lee Patterson #2733

In 1983, I was assigned to the Highway Patrol Bureau as a Motor Officer and Instructor in Phoenix Metro District Five. Those were the days when AHP officers were issued duty revolvers and six round ammunition holders. It was then a common practice to borrow our wive's clear fingernail polish and coat the hollow point cartridge tips carried in the ammo holders which were attached to our gun belts. This practice precluded the lead tips from rubbing off on our uniform riding breaches and trousers.

We also coated the tips of our badges as well, as the wind created while riding our motors would leave a black residue transfer from the badge on our tan summer uniform shirts. These little tricks kept us looking sharp and professional back in the "wheel gun" days!

GOOD OLE DAYS
Willie Hall #499

I remember summer and winter uniforms had to be dry cleaned. At my first duty station, Chandler you could have a uniform cleaned for a buck.

When stationed in Sunflower we had no telephone. Dispatch would set off a Quick Call that woke up the whole house. Then you had to go out to your unit to check for traffic.

Walt Gregory was my Sgt. while stationed in Payson. I overheard his mom call him Wally. When that info was passed onto the rest of the squad, he became known as Big Wally. One of the guys made him a desk name plate, you guessed it, it was Big Wally.

Part of the squad was en route to Mesa for a shoot. We were driving his car. It seems that a complaint was made to headquarters that Walt was speeding. The Col called him and advised of the complaint. He questioned us about the incident. We told him the rookie officer was driving, He blamed the rest of us.

Those were the good old days always something going on.

I RECALL
Jeff Trapp #2608

Being trained to use the ADOT front loader to load a scoop of cinders from the Stoneman Lake Rd T.I. into the "retired" TCD 4WD pickup to spread for stuck trucker traction during snowstorms.

Allowing the trucks to stay stuck to "naturally" close the highway and prevent more serious wrecks ahead since ADOT told us that only they could close a highway, even when we knew it needed to be done right away. This tactic taught to me by Frank New, HP-164 (RIP)

Gary Zimmerman HP-424 (RIP) befuddling Flagstaff op-com when he switched from D-5 to D-12 by saying "FourTwoFourTwoFourTwo" (translation "HP-424, I am now using the Mingus Mountain tower KGY-242 to talk to you."

Hiding in plain sight in the green swing car along the green fields of Orme Road and I-17.

THINGS I REMEMBER
Jack Grant #1445

Since I came on after the great badge number alignment, I was not part of that. I do remember when we switched to call signs from badge numbers when calling in on the radio. There was a great deal of confusion, especially among us "compound commandos", at the time.

When I came on, several old timers liked to ask whether 1445 was a badge number or the national debt.

I don't remember doing a lot of blood runs, but I did a number of "student transports" ferrying college students home from NAU to Phoenix for spring break or other reasons.

For a time, I supervised the duty office. Those guys spent an inordinate number of hours trying to arrange transport for prisoners all over the state. On one occasion, we transported an individual from the southeastern portion of the state to Kingman for a traffic warrant. We got a call from him after he was released from jail in Kingman, wanting a ride home, as he had no money when he was arrested and no way home. Unfortunately, we had no provisions for that.

On another occasion, I remember being summoned to meet the DPS airplane at Tucson airport to do a prisoner transfer. I thought this must be a really important prisoner if they were sending the aircraft for him. I met Dave Taylor at the airport, and we flew to Kingman to pick up the prisoner. I was surprised when we got to Kingman and they marched out a guy that had obviously spent several days in the drunk tank and suffering from alcohol withdrawal. Dave had me sit in the rear seat with the prisoner, after making me take off my weapon. That was the longest couple of hours I ever spent.

We were probably one of the last agencies in the free world to switch to semi-automatics.

Long wooden batons were always a problem to find a place in the patrol car where you could access the damn thing, without it being in the way and where a violator couldn't get to it and beat you to death.

The wool uniforms always smelled like wet dog when they got wet. When they introduced the polyester wash and wear uniforms, they neglected to develop a wash and wear shoulder patch, so the patches deteriorated fairly quickly. That was ok, since the uniforms looked like crap after a few months.

Rambler patrol cars: Arguably, the worst car ever made.

When I joined the department, transportation was still at the compound. Not long after, we moved it and the old District 5 to the "Pepsi Plant", a building that had been condemned by DOT in preparation for the extension of I-10 to intersect with I-17. This was temporary until a new site could be found for both. Tempo- rary turned out to be about 10 years. During that time, the state was reluctant to do any repairs to the building, since it was only "temporary". The roof leaked so bad that when it rained, transpor- tation would have to close down and send everyone home.

Due to the inordinate number of rounds accidentally fired within the Holbrook radio room, one lieutenant threatened to in- stall gun lockers and ban the carrying of firearms within the headquarters building. The area was unofficially designated the "radio range".

Charlie Cleveland was the first officer known to be wounded during a squad meeting, when Bill Erkila's .45 Colt accidentally discharged, ricocheted off the floor, and struck Charlie in the leg.

MEMORIES OF MY EARLY DAYS ON THE PATROL
John Kennedy #119

My first duty station in 1959 was Holbrook. I was supposed to go to Sanders but didn't. There were three patrolmen in Holbrook, Jim Snedigar, Carl Back and myself. Our area was from 10 miles east of Winslow to the New Mexico state line. I was sitting at the Sanders Port of Entry one summer day looking south at the thunderstorms down by Show Low, wishing I was there, as it was about 100 degrees at Sanders. An opening came up in Show Low and I got it. We moved to Show Low in the fall of 1960 and rented a little house on the northwest side of town. The house didn't have any insulation, so of course when it turned cold, it got pretty bad. I managed to buy a tin wood stove and chimney pipe and a chain saw at the big store in McNary. We managed to stay warm but had a couple of inches of ice on the inside of the windows. We moved from there to a very small house south of town on the highway to Lakeside, this house was so small I had to hang one of the kid's beds from the ceiling and I had to duck to go through the door. (Note: John was about 6'8" tall).

The first big storm hit and dumped about a foot of snow, so I put snow tires and chains on my patrol car. I remember sliding past the post office on the way to town. I met Patrolman John Consoni and he really ridiculed me about the snow tires and chains. About an hour later he called me and wanted a 45 (meet).

When I got to his location, he was stuck in a snowbank and I had to pull him out. To say the least, I got even with him!

In the wintertime, there was absolutely no traffic after supper time and I would go over to the movie theater in McNary when the movie let out just to see some traffic. One night while cruising around McNary, I saw a light on at the fire station, so I stopped and went in. There were two guys sitting in there and they invited me in to have a cup of coffee. It turned out I had gone to high school with one of them. He was a good friend of mine and that was great.

There was a one cell jail in Pinetop across from the Dew Drop Inn. One night, Consoni called me to 45 him. I met him and as it turned out, he had locked a guy up in the jail 2 days before and forgot about him. If we locked somebody up, we had to take care of them until he went to court. John asked, "What do you think I should do?" I told him to get the guy out, go buy him a steak dinner. He did that and nothing came of it!

Sometimes the Sheriff's Office would bring a prisoner from Holbrook in this jail as a trustee, and he was supposed to keep the place clean. A guy I had put in jail in Holbrook was now a trustee at this jail. Somehow, he got some liquor and got drunk and also got a hand gun and for some reason went across the street to the Dew Drop Inn. He shot the bartender right in the middle of the forehead, with the bullet going in under the skin and over the guy's skull and exited the back of his head.

Another time I got called to the Dew Drop Inn and when I got there some cowboys had cut an Indian's chongo off. That is like a wrapped-up pony tail the Indians would wear on the back of their head. The Indian was still in the fight when I got there. He had kept his money in his chongo and was calmed down when I got that back for him.

We would do blood runs back then and if an outlying hospital needed blood, we would relay it out of Phoenix to the hospital in need. One evening I was having coffee with the local brand inspector, and I got a call on the café's phone that we were relaying blood to the Springerville hospital and told me to head south the pick it up. The brand inspector wanted to ride along, so we headed south about 50-60 miles per hour. We came around a curve in the road and there was a solid herd of elk blocking the road. I put my head down, anticipating the crash. Nothing happened and when I looked up, the road was clear. Neither of us said anything. After a while the inspector asked, "see those elk back there?" I said "Yeah." Miracles happen.

We had an old gal by the name of Dixie Donkersly who lived in the area, and she was double tough. A patrolman had arrested her for DUI, and she had beaten him up pretty good and tore his shirt off in the fight. I really hoped I would never run into her.

THE DEW DROP INN
Paul Palmer #342

After reading John's memories about the Dew Drop Inn, it reminded me about B.C. Irwin. I'll relate it here and maybe someone who was there can fill in the details.

I was up in Show Low on some assignment or other and stopped by B.C. Irwin's house to say hello. While we were sitting in the living room visiting, I noticed on the wall a picture frame that was framing the tattered back pocket of a uniform pants.

I asked B.C. about it, and he said that he was called to the Dew Drop Inn to back up a sheriff's deputy that had responded to a bar fight. The Dew Drop Inn was a pretty rough place. He said he got out of the car and followed the deputy who had a canine with him, inside. They waded into the brawl and the canine got somewhat confused and instead of attacking the bad guys, grabbed B.C. by the butt. His uniform was torn and ruined with blood stains. B.C. said he cut out the back pocket of his pants and framed them as a reminder of that night.

THERE'S A WHAT ON THE HIGHWAY?
Ron Cox #1101

I don't think I told you this one about my first call as a deputy working out of Sanders. I'd gone to high school with a guy named Joe Atkinson. We were close friends during our last two years at Tucson High. His parents owned a store in Tucson named Indian Village Trading Post. When I moved to Sanders in 1968 to work for MVD at the checking station, I found out Joe owned a Trading Post at Allentown between Sanders and Lupton. He was always one to be doing practical jokes.

After two years with MVD, I quit and became a deputy sheriff working out of Sanders. I was stopped at the eastbound port of entry talking with the guy on duty and got a phone call. This was my first day as a deputy. The caller was Joe Atkinson. He very calmly told me to get down there by Allentown right away as there was a Cheetah loose on the westbound lane. My answer was "yeah, right, Joe". I figured it was a practical joke to break in the "new guy". Joe said no, I'm serious, and you need to get down here NOW before it gets away. I told him not to be concerned because Cheetahs cross the highway in that area all the time. Then he got very personal, uttered a few curse words, and said again for me to hurry. That this was NOT a joke!

So, I got in my patrol car, called the deputy in Lupton and told him what was going on. I then had DPS notified as well. I got there, just maybe a half mile west of the Allentown exit, west bound lane. Sure enough, there was a Cheetah. The right of way fence separated the westbound lane from the frontage road. The fence was what we called sheep wire. A Navajo rancher happened by in the frontage road prior to my arrival. His name was Ben Lynch. He had a nylon rope around the cat's neck and it was snugged up against the sheep wire. It also was not happy. There was a truck with 40 cheetahs, all in individual cages, and it was headed for the San Diego Zoo. One cage became unlocked, the cat jumped out on the freeway. It was a bit dazed, and Ben Lynch happened by at the right time. He roped it while it was still dazed, put the rope through the fence, and pulled it up tight. About now, the other deputy, Fred Burk, and DPS officer Don Beckstead arrived. The truck driver was having a fit, and Mr. Lynch was asking for someone to make a decision. The cat was no longer dazed. I mentioned shooting the cheetah and the truck driver was not agreeable with that solution. I had my dispatcher send an animal control officer from Gallup, New Mexico ASAP to our location with a tranquilizer gun. When he arrived, he couldn't believe what he was told was true. He got his book out and didn't have any info as to the amount of tranquilizer to give a cheetah. I speculated that it was roughly the same size as a Great Dane, and all were in agreement. But he didn't have a gun. Only a syringe and needle. The truck driver ok'd the injection. The New Mexico animal control gave it a shot in the rump. And explained that it would NOT completely sedate the animal, only just relax its muscles for a short time. It would be immobilized briefly, but wouldn't be out. The driver got on top of the cage, Mr. Lynch took off the rope, and two deputies, a highway patrolman, and an animal control officer hurriedly lifted the cat up and pushed it in the cage, with the help of the driver. He shut the door, snapped the padlock shut, and the cat came alive. And we all stood there wondering about what had just happened, as the truck with 40 Cheetahs headed to California. Yessir. My first day as a deputy sheriff was interesting. My old friend Joe wasn't joking after all!!

BE CAREFUL WHO YOU BLOW OFF THE ROAD
Tom Clinkenbeard #606

In the early 1970s I was fortunate to be a member of the Tactical Squad, a group of officers who traveled around the state providing relief so districts could send their officers to in-service training as well as adding much needed manpower to special enforcement details. One of those special enforcement projects was always the Parker details during spring and summer holidays when partiers from mostly Southern California inundated the area along the Colorado to let their inhibitions down, drink and generally raise hell.

During one of these details the Squad was sent to Parker for an extended period of time. Normally, our details lasted eight days but this one was scheduled for an extra three or four days. As I recall, we were told on Sunday that we could we could go home the next day. As usual, a number of us, but not all, made arrangements to leave about the same time Monday morning.

Everyone was anxious to get home and we might have been moving on down the road at a pretty good clip. Somewhere between Wenden and Wickenburg I think, we passed, or as it was later described, blew off the road, a car driven by Bill Jacquin, President of the State Senate. Really Bad Timing!

Crap rolls down hill and everyone involved got letters of reprimand. As with any retelling of an incident there is always "the rest of the story". Ron Young, 706, will fill us in on that in a subsequent story.

GUILT BY ASSOCIATION
Ron Young #706

In the early 1970s, I was on assignment with the Tactical Squad in Parker. It had been a long assignment due to back to back details with no return home in between. On Sunday, we were told we could return home on Monday, however in my case, I had court on Monday and couldn't leave Parker with the rest of the squad.

When I returned to Phoenix, I was told about the Senator Bill Jacquin incident and the forthcoming letter of reprimand. I thought to myself being in court in Parker gave me an airtight defense regarding a reprimand.

I told my district commander, Lt. Pemberton, that I was in court in Parker and therefore should not receive a reprimand. Lt. Pemberton said he would tell Col. Mildebrandt that I was in the Parker Justice Court during the Jacquin incident. A couple of days later Lt. Pemberton told me I was still going to get a letter like everyone else. He said Col. Mildebrandt told him I would have been just as guilty as the rest of the squad if I hadn't been in court. I hate to admit it, but the Colonel was probably right. I vaguely remember my return to Phoenix was in the 95 to 100mph range. I also don't remember seeing a letter of reprimand.

PATROLMAN MARTIN KIDNAPPING
Rick Ulrich #182

I don't recall the date the event occurred. I know it was a few months before I went to the patrol academy in 1968, but I am not even sure of the month now.

I was working a day shift in radio. We were down one dispatcher and they sent me a cadet trainee as a replacement. I was monitoring the cadet trainee and he was working the console. We were experiencing a lot of static type noise on the radio. It sounded like a radio technician might be working on a mobile unit. The cadet trainee asked if there was some way we could turn off the channel making the noise. Not this time, since the noise was on the main district channel. I told the cadet trainee that we could try and listen to see if we could identify the voice we could hear. The voice we could hear was not speaking into the microphone. It was like the microphone was being keyed up by accident and just picking up background noise. We turned the console speaker up as loud as it would go and we just listened. It wasn't too long before I heard the person talking say, "I wish you would uncock that gun or point it another direction." With that, I knew we had a real problem. I told the trainee to let me take over the console. At this point, I had a choice to make. I could do a roll call 10-20 check to see who wouldn't answer or I could continue to listen and see if I could identify the voice.

After you have been a dispatcher long enough you can pretty much identify everyone by their voice without hearing their call number. As I continued listening, the person talking said the they were coming to an intersection and a decision needed to be made whether continue straight ahead or to turn left or right. The speaker said if they continued straight ahead they would end up in Gila Bend. If they turned right that road would take them to Phoenix. If they turn left that would take them to Casa Grande. With that information I then knew that the patrol vehicle was headed west and was somewhere between Casa Grande and Phoenix. Since there was no Casa Grande unit on that day, I was fairly certain that the officer involved was HP-85, Jim Martin who was stationed in Coolidge

I called HP-85 on the radio and there was no response, so I was certain that the unit sending the clandestine radio messages was indeed HP-85. I used the radio code for units to switch radio channels to channel two and advised the other units of what was going on. I could never hear what the other person was saying so I didn't know what happened at the intersection.

It wasn't too long before the mike was keyed up again and the person speaking sounded like a driver on a tour bus giving his passengers the royal tour.. The speaker was telling the other person that over there is the stadium where the San Francisco Giants play their spring training games. With that information I knew that the patrol unit had continued straight ahead at the intersection and the car was headed toward Gila Bend on SR-84. After some more time passed, the mike was keyed up again and HP-85 was telling his kidnapper that the cattle feeding operation off to the right was the Red River Land and Cattle Company which is owned by John Wayne. That information was telling me how quickly the patrol car was moving along.

About this time, I get a call from HP-65, Frank Gillette. He advised that he had been working warrants in Tempe and he is in an unmarked car and headed South toward SR-84 if he could be of assistance. I advised him that would be perfect if he could intercept HP-85 somewhere around Stanfield. HP-65 advised that he could observe from a distance until a course of action could be determined.

In just a minute or two, HP-65 advised he was at SR-84 and was turning East. Frank must have been flying to have gotten that far so fast from Tempe. Within about a minute, Frank said that he had just intercepted HP-85 and he believed the subject recognized him as a patrol car. The subject was in the rear seat on the far right side. Frank made a U-turn and was following HP-85 from about a quarter mile back.

Not more than a minute had gone by and HP-65 said that HP-85 was pulling to the side of the road and stopping. Frank said the back seat passenger was emerging from the patrol car and walking off into the desert.

Frank's next radio transmission was advising that HP-85 was not injured and that the two of them would be tracking the suspect into the desert. A couple more minutes passed and HP-65 advised that he and HP-85 had heard a gunshot and they believe the suspect may have taken his own life.

Some more time passed and HP-85 came on the air and advised that the suspect did indeed take his own life and that the Pinal County Sheriff needs to be contacted to have them do the death investigation. Lt. Bill Hanger, the District Six Commander had been notified and he was enroute from the Phoenix Headquarters.

I have to sum this up by saying that this operation was successful as no patrol personnel were injured. Jim Martin did a masterful job of working the radio mike with his leg and keeping us informed of where he was and what was going on. Some might wonder how he was able to key the mike with his leg. It was during this time that the patrol was experimenting with installing a sort of wooden desk between the front seat driver and passenger side of the seat. It was a wooden box with a lid that was used for a desk. The lid opened and items could be stored in the box. The one disadvantage this seat desk created was it covered up the radio controls. Patrolmen took it upon themselves to removed the microphone clip off the radio head and installed it on the desk for easier access to the microphone. It was because of this that Jim Martin was able to dislodge the mike from the desk and wedge it between his knee and the box when he wanted to transmit.

I sent a teletype of the incident to Phoenix and it was distributed to all of the news outlets. It must have been good enough for the news media to create their news stories. I couldn't believe how many out of state news outlets contacted me at the Claypool office in the next day or two to in order to get more information or some clarification.

Another note I should add. Lt. Hanger submitted a request to the department that I should be awarded an official Commendation for that day. That was awarded and I received a letter and plaque that was presented at our academy class graduation party at the T-Bone Steakhouse. That was nice of Lt. Hanger to do that.

IT ONLY TAKES A SECOND
Dick Lewis #176

There it is, an accident on the road.

There are lights flashing and people milling about. The traffic is tied up and there are horns honking. The ambulance leaves and the wrecker tows the car away. After a time the scene is cleared and the people disperse.

The next day the news media adds two more to their dreadful tally. The statistics are climbing. People listen and read. They shake their heads in disbelief and then promptly forget.

When they drive their autos they are being called to by something that is as real as night and day.

The executioner shows his bony cheeks and looks out from beneath his black shroud. He is standing upon a skid marked battered stretch of blood soaked blacktop. There is a crowd gathered about him. They have been thinned out somewhat.
Now the black figure raises a bleached white bony arm.

The crowd shrinks away and cowers, but they can't get away.

They have been captured of their own accord.

The heavy man in front likes to drink. The boy with grease on his hands likes to speed. That one over there is sleepy. None of them are very careful.

Now the death head before them smiles and beckons to the crowd with his fore finger. He has not had enough, he wants more.

A chilling whisper penetrates through the people gathered. "Who is next? Step right up. It only takes a second.

MOTORIST ASSIST
Richard Richardson #188

One of the things the AHP Director Greg O. Hathaway AHP #901 stressed to all uniformed department personnel was the 'Motorist Assist' policy. If a patrolman failed to stop and assist a motorist in distress, there better be a good reason. When a motorist would complain about needing help and observed a patrol car pass by, usually meant a visit to the office of the Superintendent and that was not good for the officer. I really believe that our patrol officers throughout the state were very good at helping stranded motorists, it was one of the things they did automatically.

I was stationed in District #3 and patrolled the Show Low area from 1964 for several years. I had a patrol vehicle that was 'miled' out, meaning time to turn it in. The idea in those days was to remove a vehicle that exceeded 60,000 miles and replace with a new one. This was the way it was done in the early 1960's. That was certainly not like the 'Old Timers' remember back in the early days of the AHP. I drove a 1965 Plymouth at the time and was to pick up a new 1967 Chevrolet at the Phoenix Compound. Sergeant Ray Dahm AHP #708, had some business at the AHP office, so he rode with me to Phoenix, where I would pick up my new vehicle.

I emptied everything from my Plymouth and we headed to Phoenix. I received the new vehicle and we then departed the city, heading back to Show Low. The weather going back was okay until we hit the higher mountains after passing through the Salt River Canyon. The clouds thickened and it was snowing. By the time we were about 15 miles from Show Low, the snow was bad and the road was very slippery. In this kind of weather I would have already placed snow tires on my patrol vehicle. The Chevy didn't have snow tires yet. I would have to obtain used Chevy rims to mount my regular snow tires on the new car. We started going on a fairly steep upgrade. Dahm said later that I did a great job of driving in getting us to Show Low. That uphill drive was something else. I had enough speed to make the hill. Had I stopped, I would have been stuck with a lot of motorists that were already stopped. I drove past quite a few stalled vehicles. I wish that I could have stopped to help them, but all we could do is look at them. I had the feeling that someone would be complaining about a patrol car passing stalled vehicles and we could be knee deep in carpet, in front of AHP #901. That would not be good!

I immediately radioed the dispatcher in Holbrook about the bad road location and requested that the AHD (Arizona Highway Department) be notified and send a sand delivery truck to that specific hill. We observed an AHD truck just leaving Show Low as we neared the city. We knew that help was on the way for those stranded people. I never heard about complaints concerning that matter.

As soon as I arrived at my residence, I loaded the patrol vehicle with all the necessary equipment. I then headed to a garage where I knew I could find used Chevy rims and had my snow tires mounted and then placed on the new car. I was ready for regular patrol duty.

PURSUIT LIGHTS
Frank Glenn #468

When I was working in Williams, I was having a hard time catching speeders so sitting at home one afternoon I came up with an idea. I went to the auto store and bought two yellow clearance lights, some wire and two C clamps along with an alligator clamp. The procedure was to leave all of that stuff in the trunk and just as it got dark, I would fill up with gas so I didn't have to go into town until quitting time. We had those big gumball lights in those days so I would clamp the wired-up clearance lights under those lights and run the wire through the window and when I needed to turn them on the alligator clamp was used on a bare spot on the spot light. I left them off until my suspected speeder went by and after they were out of sight, I would turn the clearance lights on and pursue them. Seems like I could run up on them and not spook them. After pacing them, no vascar or radar, in those days, I'd turn off the clearance lights and let them run for a bit then stop them. All was well for quite a time but one night the Lt called me and he was breaking up quite a bit so I figured he was a ways off. He wanted a meet at a café in Ashfork.

Along about this time I was parked at a wide spot on the two-lane road west of Williams and along came a pickup and a car started passing him which was fine but I never heard the car let up on the gas. Figuring I would catch my speeder on the freeway about 4 miles up the road I turned on those lights and was barreling along and when I topped Ashfork Hill there sits my speeder on the parking shoulder. Knowing the Lt would be along soon I got off at Welsh road madly undoing all my lights and such. When Les McMann, the Lt. called and wanted to know if that was me over there, I said yes. He said I will see you at the Nomad restaurant. As we were walking in he said those lights do look pretty good. That was all that was ever said so I considered that license to keep using them. With that set up I looked just like a ¾ ton truck. I never knew how he found this out.

VIBRATING LIGHT BAR
Bob Singer #2693

My first patrol car was a 1978 Chevy Caprice with the two gumball lights on the light bar. The first thing I noticed was there was not a metal box in the truck to carry all of my forms and flares in. I checked around the Flagstaff 103 and there just wasn't any so I had to come up with an idea of my own. Somewhere, I found a wooden drawer from a clothes dresser so I put that in the trunk and organized my forms in tabbed file holders.

One thing that really bugged me about my car was the square piece of metal that was in the center of the light bar between the two lights. Since I was a licensed pilot and knew that piece of metal sticking up was nothing but a wind drag and obviously wouldn't let the car get to it's best speed, I took the two metal screws holding it onto the light bar out and took it off. The next shift, I checked on and drove out of the state yard. At about 50mph, I heard this vibrating sound start. The faster I went, the louder it got, like when I used to put balloons against the spokes of my bicycle. What I determined was that the light bar would start to vibrate above 50 mph and that the purpose of that piece of flat metal was to put pressure on the bar to keep it from doing that. I went right back to the state yard and put the plate back on.

Note: Following the passing of retiree John Desanti, the following stories were posted.

JOHN DESANTI SHOOTING
Barry Allen #632

I've known John for a long time, his older brother Paul (Phoenix Fire Dept) and I were in the same class at Carl Hayden High School. John was in my squad on the MCSO when he was shot. We had just cleared a fight at the Tanita labor camp at 43 Ave and Peoria, about midnight and we're going to meet up around 2 or 3am for coffee. We worked adjoining beats so we would meet often with other squad members. He went west on Peoria and I went east to my beat area. Around 2 or 3 am, dispatch started doing welfare checks on us in a rather hurried manner and then command officers started checking on the air. John was the only unit not answering. John had gone west on Peoria and had stopped at the railroad tracks at Grand Avenue, when a guy stepped from the bushes and approached John on the blind side. The guy had kidnapped a Globe officer earlier in the evening, and had locked the officer in his car. He was armed and told John to drive west, which he did. When they approached Wickenburg, a police car had a violator stopped and the suspect dropped down to the floor and told John to keep driving. John told me later that his intent was to crash into the bridge abutment on the passenger side of the vehicle. By the time they got to Aguila John had decided to pull in front of a semi, again, so that the passenger's side of the car would take the hit. As John did that the suspect started shooting John, I think five times in the lower abdomen, and the car slid to a halt in front of some cabins. John was seriously injured and was losing consciousness, but he had the presence of mind to retrieve his shotgun. It was interesting to note that all of our shotguns were mounted in a lock in front of the dashboard of our vehicles, except for John's car, which had the shotgun mounted on the prisoner screen behind the driver and passenger's head. The suspect never noticed it. A lady of ample girth came out of the cabins to see what was going on, and the suspect grabbed her around the neck coming back toward John who was now slumped next to the driver's side of his vehicle. John summoned what strength he had and pointed the shotgun at the suspect ordering him to release the woman. The woman had the strength to twist away from the suspect and as she did so his arm and shoulder area was exposed and John fired the shotgun striking the suspect in his left shoulder area, the impact of the round tearing away a good portion of his arm and shoulder and neutralizing him. John started throwing road flares in front of vehicles on the highway but nobody stopped initially. Finally a truck driver stopped, walked over to John to assist him and took John's shotgun, walked over to the suspect who was also laying on the ground, stuck the shotgun under the suspect's chin, and as John

stated, told the suspect, if that cop dies, you're a dead M.....F.....
John was now passing in and out of consciousness and told the truck driver not to kill the suspect.

When citizens called the SO, they called Yuma County SO, since Aguila was then in Yuma County. All of their officers were accounted for so they started calling around to other counties and it was finally determined John was an MCSO officer. That's when dispatch started a serious welfare check on all of us. The truck driver who assisted John was never located to receive a reward, even though a determined effort was made through nationwide truck stops, trucker magazines, and periodicals of the time.

John was taken to Maryvale hospital, and treated for his injuries and where he was hospitalized for some time. During his stay at the hospital, his room was at the end of a long hallway that had an exit door at the end. One evening an unknown male subject, stopped by John's open room and pointed his finger in a weapon like fashion at John, then walked out of the hospital through the hallway door. John was moved to a different room, and for a couple of weeks our squad, and other officers, took turns in John's old room, waiting for the unknown male subject to return and act on his threat. Fortunately for him he did not return. The nursing staff were well aware we were in that room in the dark, and they knew to stay away.

John was a very brave person, and was an excellent officer. Thank you for this opportunity to produce this information to you and the members.

Memory fades but Johns shooting must have been 1967 or 1968. John was a good guy and always called me "CB".

Myself and Dave Koelsch(#639) came over from the SO when DPS was formed and went straight into narcotics. To get into our class as laterals you had to have five years of investigative experience. Both Dave and I had been detectives, and Dave had prior service with Colorado Springs P D. Many other officers had also served with the MCSO. Ron Young (#706), Bob Schulte(#748), Ron Goodson(#738), and others including John DeSanti.

WE TAKE CARE OF OUR OWN
Lannie VanTassel #1606

I first met John Desanti in the Academy class 25 and recall he had previously worked with MCSO and had been shot multiple times in his legs after being kidnapped and later involved in the shootout with the culprit rather than surrender his weapon. The injuries gave him difficulties while running on the compound during our PT periods. We surrounded him and pulled him along until he gave out. We then stuffed him between cars and picked him up on the next pass. We thought we were hiding this from the counselors but I honestly believe they knew of this and ignored it as we were a team and took care of our own.

THE MISSING SHOTGUN
Jim Chilcoat #137

In the late 1960's Cochise County really began to boom. With the increased activity at Fort Huachuca new homes began to spring up along with new businesses and of course traffic increased on the highways.

In Phoenix at Highway Patrol headquarters it had been noted that the increase in traffic alone was causing an increase in the accidents, and traffic volume dictated that to maintain the safety of the residents of the area it would be necessary to increase manpower in the Sierra Vista area, as this was the hub for all the activity.

In March 1968, the Highway Patrol decided to make a fifth area in Cochise County and put an area supervisor in Sierra Vista and assign him six fine patrolmen to concentrate their efforts in the area of the Fort.

The area spread out about twenty miles in each direction on the highways that were in and around Sierra Vista. This area would include SR90, the primary highway into and out of Sierra Vista, and highway 92 which was a backroad south towards the border ending up at the traffic circle in the Warren section of

Bisbee. It could be noted that the Warren Traffic Circle was at that time the only traffic circle on the state or federal highway system in Arizona. US80 would be included in the eastern part of the area as it traversed through the old western frontier town of Tombstone, a tourist draw that is known across the entire 50 states. Last but not least was a portion of SR82 that came up from the southwest across the area to US80 north of Tombstone.

On this wonderful spring day two of the Arizona Highway Patrol's finest where on duty. The two young men were new to the department, but dedicated and ready to make their mark in the agency and prove their worth to the taxpayers of our great state. They were men that any police agency in Arizona would have been proud to call an employee. They were well manicured and nattily dressed in their highway patrol uniforms. Since the department had not gone to the summer uniform they were dressed in full uniform which included a Sam Brown belt and a black tie. They were issued the finest equipment of any police agency in Arizona. The cars were less that two years old , well equipped and maintained by the officers who retained them twenty four hours a day. Call-outs were common and you had to have your vehicle as ready to go as you were. The vehicles contained the latest communications and safety equipment as well as supplies that might be needed for first aid or to prepare a report. In addition to a side arm the officers were also each issued a twelve gauge pump Remington shotgun. A scabbard was provided under the front of the front seat where the officer could open his door and exit the vehicle and if needed, he could reach down and bring out the loaded weapon ready for any type of emergency that may confront him, night or day.

On this particular day, a local young damsel was returning to her home off SR82 just east of the highway 82-90 junction. She was headed west and was turning into a dirt drive with a small downhill angle, when for some unknown reason she lost control of her vehicle, at a very low speed, and ended up off the dirt side road and next to a young mesquite tree.

The first officer on the scene promptly took charge and determined that the young lady was fine. She was dressed in a pair of short shorts and a rather low top blouse, taking advantage of the lovely spring weather at that time of day.

The second officer who decided to drive over and see if the first officer needed any assistance parked his vehicle directly behind the investigating officer's which was parked eastbound on the wrong side of the road, but off the pavement that made up SR82.

As he departed his vehicle in this non-emergency call, he left the vehicle running and the driver's door wide open. This exposed his shotgun to the world and became an open invitation to anyone to change a simple non-injury accident into a spectacle that could have had grave consequences.

Luckily, the area supervisor was on duty and not knowing that the original officer at the scene was being assisted by the other on duty officer, proceeded to the accident scene to see if any assistance might be needed (which by the way, left the entire area without any enforcement capabilities what so ever). As the supervisor pulled up behind the second officer's vehicle, he noted that both officers were very busy assisting the young lady in the short shorts and low cut blouse. Again, it might be noted that the young lady had no injuries, was not complaining of any injuries, nor did her vehicle seem to be any worse for the mishap.

Nevertheless both officers were deeply engrossed in assisting said damsel.

At this point, the area supervisor exited his vehicle, being careful to close the door so as not to expose the shotgun that he also carried under the front seat to any wandering eye of the public at large. Walking up to the afore mentioned open door of the second patrol vehicle, the area supervisor reached in and pulled out the shotgun, waiting for the owner of the weapon to come immediately to his vehicle and explain the negligent manner in which he had left his vehicle and its equipment. Surprisingly neither officer even bothered to look up and away from the young lady. The supervisor then took the weapon, put it in the back seat of his vehicle, backed up and drove west past the incident and the two officers without ever being acknowledged.

Upon returning to his vehicle the officer failed to note the loss of his weapon. Soon thereafter, the supervisor asked the

Nogales radio operator to call the officer and advise him that the armory at headquarters needed the serial number from his 12 gauge Remington shotgun. The next radio dispatch was from the officer to his immediate supervisor, inquiring as to his location at that time. Upon being advised, he asked if he could immediately meet with the supervisor to discuss a most important situation that had just come up.

And that was another spring day in Old Cochise County, among the beauty and harmony of a lovely day which was being enjoyed by many people at that time I think it should be noted that both officers had a very successful career with the Arizona Highway Patrol and later the Department of Public Safety.

137 Area Supervisor

THE GUN BELONGS TO WHO?
Bob Singer #2693

When I was assigned to the Intoxilyzer Unit from 1984-1986, I had to go up to the Prescott 103 to make a modification to the old Intoxilyzer 4011 one Saturday. After I finished, I went to the Denny's before starting my drive back to Phoenix. I had my uniform on and just after sitting down at my table, a waitress came up and told me that there was a gun on the back of the toilet in the men's bathroom. I got up to go check it out and sure enough, on the back of the toilet bowl in one of the stalls was a S&W model 36 five shot revolver. I picked it up and looked it over and found that it had a DPS serial number stamped on it. That next Monday, I went to the armory in the basement of the old Phoenix 103 and told Ed Teague what I had found and gave him the pistol. Ed said it was one of ours and looked up the serial number to see who it was assigned to. It turns out it was assigned to one of our majors who shall remain anonymous. Ed told me with a big twinkle in his eye that I had to give it to him. At this time, Norm Jones and I did not have a sergeant or even a lieutenant over us in the Intoxilyzer Unit. We reported directly to Colonel Thompson, the Highway Patrol Bureau Chief. I took the pistol to Colonel

Thompson's office in the old compound complex, told him the story and gave the pistol to him. He just chuckled, took the pistol and said he would take care of it.

NO SAFETY
Dick Lewis #176

A funny contact over a stop sign happened to me one day. I wrote this lady a citation for not stopping at a stop sign. After she had signed the ticket she asked how long you have to wait at the stop sign before starting out again.

I informed her she must come to a complete stop, check the road both ways and then pull out in safety. She took the gear shift stick on the steering column, pushed it all the way to the top them pulled it all the way to the bottom and said, "But officer I don't think there is a safety on this car." She was serious!

THE NEW NARCS
Colin Peabody #468

Gary Godbold (#401), Rick Ayars (#457) and Danny Tolmachoff(#491) came from MCSO to AHP in February, 1967 and January, 1968 respectively.

I counted at least 50 other officers who came over from the other agencies and went straight into either Narcotics or Liquor and some went to AHP later. Many of those officers served as Cadet Class counselors prior to going into uniform or admin duties. Many served as the base group of instructors in the Training Division. All were true assets to the new DPS.

It was an adjustment period for those of us Highway Patrolmen to find a scruffy bunch of people we didn't recognize now inhabiting our offices and getting to know the different side of law enforcement than our regular highway patrol duties allowed. We were often tasked to provide additional support and back up duties for them. We learned a lot from them, and it was even fun!

My first encounter with the "narcs" came one evening in August of 69, when I was patrolling US 66 west of Winslow and met a "one eye", a beat looking 1964 Chevy station wagon. I got it stopped about 15 miles west of Winslow and 45 miles east of Flagstaff in the middle of no freakin' place and these two long haired guys jump out of the car, the driver holding up a badge yelling "We're with you!" My friends, Smith, Wesson and their 6 little sisters found their way into my right hand as I stopped in my tracks. "I don't see any tan uniform, so you're not with me!" Well, as it turned out, the two long hairs were Tom Hammarstrom and Ron Maskell, who we got to know very well over the years and Tom and his wife Marilyn are two very good friends with my wife and I. They were enroute to work a bar in Winslow and I let them know they wouldn't have much success in that bar due to their light complexions. Which turned out to be true!

SALT RIVER CANYON SHOOTING
Dick Lewis #176

I was asked to submit a story about the shooting I was involved in down in the Salt River Canyon in 1968. Here is the entire report.

April 16, 1968

James J Hegarty, Superintendent

Attention: Colonel T.R. Cochran, Deputy Superintendent
Colonel L.H. Robertson, Deputy Superintendent
Major J.F. Mulcair, Inspector
Major R.E. Broan, Zone Commander
Lieutenant W.O. Dollar, District Commander

I was working in the Salt River Canyon on U.S. 60 east of Globe. I had just talked to Miami Radio at milepost 288, the time 1215. This is a location that I am able to receive and transmit when working in this area.

I started east back into the canyon. When I was at mile-post 289 I could see an area of the road east of me at about milepost 290. I observed a westbound vehicle on this stretch of road. Just after it came into view it swerved across the center line and traveled completely on the wrong side of the road for a short distance. It was traveling upgrade at about 45 miles an hour, which is the speed limit in that area.

I pulled over onto a pull out on the north side of the road and watched the vehicle come up the hill. As it drew near, I turned around and got into a position to pursue it. As the vehicle passed by me I was headed west. I turned on my top lights and honked my horn and pulled in behind the vehicle all about the same time. I could see there were four occupants in the vehicle. Some cloth-ing was hanging in the left rear window. The vehicle was a 1959 Oldsmobile four door with front and rear Texas 1968 registration DWW 290. There were two young men seated in the front and two passengers in the back.

The driver stopped the vehicle in the middle of the road and I stopped behind it. I was motioning them to pull up to a pull out about fifty feet from where we were stopped.

The driver put the vehicle in reverse and backed into a position to the left and abreast of where I was stopped. This all happened before I could get out of my vehicle to ask him to pull his vehicle ahead and off the road. As the vehicle was alongside my left, the driver asked if I had wanted him to stop. I advised him that I did and instructed him to park in the pull out. He com-plied with my instructions.

I got out of my vehicle at the same time as the violator. He walked back toward my vehicle and I met him halfway. I asked him for his operators license. He stated that he didn't have one as he had lost his wallet and when he got it back his drivers license was gone. I asked him for some identification and he pro-duced a draft card in the name of Charles Eddie Park, date of birth 11-13-44. He didn't know his current address and had to ask Dar-rel Green, who was seated on the left side in the rear seat of the Oldsmobile. The address was in Fort Worth, Texas. The explana-tion was that the address was Green's and that Park had been staying with him. I asked Charles Park for the registration or some sort of identification on the vehicle. He stated that he was a hitch-hiker and was only driving. The fellow seated on the right front was the owner. Park remained standing at the right front fender of my vehicle as I went up to the right rear door of the Oldsmobile. I asked the man seated in the passengers seat for identification and the registration to the vehicle. He identified himself as Marvin Dale Hatch by means of a student identification from Kansas State Teacher's College. The card had his picture on it. He stated that he didn't have the license receipts as Texas didn't require that it be carried in the vehicle, and that the papers were in a safe deposit box back home. He showed me a miniature laminated copy of a diploma from the Kansas State Teacher's College. It stated that Marvin Dale Hatch had received a Bachelor of Science Degree in education. The man stated that he was enroute to California to make arrangements for his first teaching job to begin this fall. He didn't like traveling alone so he had picked up two hitchhikers just outside of Fort Worth.

On the basis of his picture on the identification, the diploma and the logical explanation, I accepted his story.

I returned to where "Park" was standing and proceeded to write two tickets in the name of Charles Eddie Park. One for no operators license and the other for driving left of center. I handed the tickets to him to sign and he signed the name of "Jimmy Dodds" and then tried to scratch over it. I took the clip board away from him, made him place his hands on top of the car and searched him for weapons. During this time I advised him of his rights and why he was being arrested. I handcuffed him and strapped him into the passengers seat on the right front of my patrol vehicle.

During this time the three passengers remained seated in their vehicle.

I went back to the vehicle and asked the man who had identified himself as "Marvin Hatch" to open the trunk because I wanted to see what was inside it. He willfully complied. When the trunk was open I asked him to identify his belongings. I could see a suit case, a bowling ball bag, various articles of dirty clothes and a hair dryer in a white plastic case. He stated that everything in the trunk was his except the hair dryer and that belonged to his wife. I accepted the explanation and had him close the trunk lid. He walked back to the right side of his vehicle. I recognized the passenger seated in the right rear as an American Indian. I walked over and asked him his name. He stated it was Chester Cooley and that he was hitch hiking to San Carlos, Arizona. He stated that he had just been picked up. I accepted his story. The man known as "Marvin Hatch" remained standing on the right side of the vehicle. At one time previous when I was working with "Parks", I noticed Hatch take a picture of the scenery with a small camera.

I walked around to the left side of the vehicle and asked the man known as "Green" to get out.

At this time I believed that "Parks" and "Green" were hitch hikers. I believed the story of "Hatch".

It was my intention to take "Parks" and "Green" back to Globe in my vehicle. I had "Green" put his hands on top of my car and placed him in a search position. I advised him that at this time he "Green" was not under arrest, that I was going to search him for weapons only as he was going to ride to town with me. As I searched him I found three wallets in his pockets, each with a different identification. I was asking questions and "Green" had a sudden lapse of memory. He acted stupid.

At the time I was searching "Green" and discovering the wallets, "Hatch" had moved around to the rear of his car and was leaning on the trunk. He asked me if I wanted him to follow me to town and that he was sorry for all of this that had happened.

I had "Green" stand in front of my vehicle where I could watch him. I removed my coat which was hanging in the left rear of my vehicle and put it on. I threw the hanger over the bank. I put a notebook that was in my rear seat in my trunk. The rear seat was clear now. "Hatch" asked my permission to go up to his vehicle and get a cigarette. I could see no reason why he shouldn't and said yes. I had "Green" walk up to the front of the Oldsmobile and stand so I could watch him. I was going up to the right side of the vehicle where "Hatch" was seated in the passenger seat. The door was open and he was seated with his feet on the ground. The Indian was still sitting in the right rear with the door closed.

As I was about at the right rear fender of the Oldsmobile "Hatch" pointed a pistol at me. He was holding it in his right hand

and he was still seated. He said, "Alright, put your hands up" in a moderate tone of voice. I knew that "Green" was standing in front of the Oldsmobile at this time. I said "Uh, okay." I walked a couple of steps forward and turned to face him. I raised both of my hands to midway between my belt and shoulders. "Hatch" started standing up, still pointing the pistol at my chest. He had his left hand on the door. As he was standing up he said, "I mean it, put your hands up." When he was fully erect he waved his left arm with a "come on" motion to "Green" and said, "Get his gun Darrell". At this time "Park" was getting out of my car and the Indian was opening the rear door. I stepped back two steps, drew my pistol and shot at "Hatch" two times. At this time I was about twenty feet from him. He dropped the pistol about four feet from him and grabbed onto the open door. The next instant the Indian was out of the Oldsmobile and reaching for the pistol that "Hatch" had dropped to the ground, then his hand was on it. I shot at him two times. He fell to the ground, then got up and said, "What did you shoot me for, I was trying to help you." He then stood there. "Hatch" was still hanging onto the door. I could see that he was bleeding bad. He said, "Help me Darrell, I'm hit, I'm dying!" Green" was shouting something but I didn't know what it was. He didn't move when I looked at him. "Parks" was standing by the open right front door of my vehicle, transfixed.

This occurred probably in a space of about three seconds. I shouted at "Green" and "Parks" to stay where they were. They didn't move. I was still covering the entire scene when a westbound car went by. It slowed and the passenger looked back as it passed. I shouted and with my left arm motioned for them to come back. They came running.

The two men who came to my assistance were later identified as Ralph L. Larson of Topeka, Kansas and Norman S Norburg of Topeka, Kansas. Mr. Larson knocked "Green" to the ground and searched his pockets as he was sitting on his back. I threw "Hatch's" pistol to Mr. Norburg and instructed him to cover "Green". I went to my car and got my second pair of handcuffs.

At this time I had "Hatch" and the Indian and "Park" all on the ground on the right side of the Oldsmobile. I went back over to "Green" and helped Mr. Larson handcuff him. Then I went back over to my car and got my First Aid Kit and my shotgun. I gave the shotgun to Mr. Norburg to cover me as I worked on "Hatch" and the Indian.

"Hatch" was bleeding profusely from the right thigh. I took out my pocket knife and cut away his trousers. I could see that the femoral artery had been cut by the bullet and the only way to check the bleeding was by direct pressure. He had lost a lot of blood and was in a deep state of shock. I knew that he would probably die from the loss of blood if I didn't get him to the doctor right away.

A Highway Department pickup came by and I instructed one of the occupants to try to contact Miami Radio with the radio in my vehicle. He was unable to "get out".

Mr. Larson was using some of his clean underclothing as a compress on "Hatch". I got in my car and went back to milepost 288, my "hot spot" and advised the dispatcher of this incident. I advised him of my intentions. I left a maintenance unit at the "hot spot" to maintain communications with Miami and went back to the scene.

A Deputy U.S. Marshall had arrived and put extra hand-cuffs on "Hatch". I, with the assistance of several persons loaded "Hatch" onto my blanket and put him on the rear seat of my patrol vehicle. Mr. Larson was put into the right front to steady "Hatch".

I placed the shotgun in the hands of a Highway Department employee, Mr. Campos, whom I know. I instructed the Marshall to allow no one to touch anything.

I made the Indian as comfortable as I could. His right arm was broken near the shoulder, but he had stopped bleeding. The bullet puncture was in an impossible location to bandage.

After being reasonably sure the scene of the incident was secure, I started toward Globe with the seriously wounded "Hatch". I remember my last instructions to a Highway Department employee was to turn the handcuffed "Green" and "Park" so that they weren't lying with their heads downhill.

As I came back into range of Miami Radio I called for a second ambulance to be dispatched to pick up the Indian. My intention was to meet the first ambulance and send "Hatch" with it. I met Walker's ambulance, Patrolman Healy, Lieutenant Dollar and Sergeant Snedigar at milepost 270. The injured man was put into the ambulance and Patrolman Healy was sent along to guard him.

Deputy Sheriff Ted Lewis was dispatched to assist and arrived at the time the rest of the assistance did. We all returned to the scene to find it just as I had left it.

Sergeant Chewning took pictures of the scene. Sergeant Snedigar rode back to Globe with the Indian in the ambulance.

Lieutenant Dollar and Ted Lewis investigated the scene of the incident.

Ellsworth Motors was dispatched to store the vehicle. "Park" and "Green" were transported to the S.O. in Globe.

Park was booked for 28-411 and 28-721A

Green was booked for assault with a deadly weapon

Park was actually Jimmy Eugene Dodds of Valliant, Oklahoma

Green was actually Darrell Edward Green of Forth Worth, Texas

Hatch was actually James David Steele of Forth Worth, Texas

The Indian was Chester Cooley Jr of San Carlos, Arizona

28 February 1969

To: Patrolman Richard A Lewis Subject: Valor

Award

On April 16, 1968 Patrolman Richard A. Lewis was in the process of issuing a citation to a traffic violator in the area of the Salt River Canyon east of Globe, Arizona. While in the process of issuing this citation, it became necessary for Patrolman Lewis to use deadly force in the protection of his life after having an occupant of the vehicle cover him with a loaded revolver.

After realizing that his assailant was attempting to take his life, Patrolman Lewis drew his service revolver firing twice and thus disabling the man. Immediately following this attempt on his life, another passenger of the car attempted to retrieve the weapon which had been dropped to the ground. Patrolman Lewis reacted immediately by again using his service revolver to disable the man.

The reactions of Patrolman Lewis under stress and danger are a tribute to his courage and abilities. Patrolman Lewis is hereby commended for his courage, along with his sound, efficient, non-assuming manner in securing the situation looking to the welfare of the wounded and carrying out the duties in the manner prescribed by the Arizona Highway Patrol.

You are hereby awarded the Arizona Highway Patrol Valor Award.

James J. Hegarty, Superintendent Arizona Highway Patrol

LIFE SAVING AWARD
Loma Jenkins - wife of Bud Jenkins #159

In November 1968 Patrolman Don Hill was on duty on the Navajo Reservation when he struck a horse on US164 just west of Tuba City. The impact was so great, the roof of the car was pushed down and back striking Don in the face. He suffered severe life threatening head injuries and the doctors said that he would probably lose an eye which he later did.

Bud arrived on the scene and provided first aid at the scene and then rode with him to the hospital keeping him alive until the doctors could preform surgery.

Here is the Life Saving Award Bud received:

To: Sergeant W.R. Jenkins, Jr Subject: Life Saving Award

1. On the 1st of November 1968 Patrolman Don Hill sustained near fatal injuries from the result of a motor vehicle accident.

2. Sergeant Jenkins arrived at the scene of the acci- dent and was instrumental in removing Patrolman Hill from the wrecked vehicle. It became apparent to Sergeant Jenkins that patrolman Hill would expire without immediate help to his breathing.

3. Sergeant Jenkins accompanied Patrolman Hill from the moment he arrived at the scene until a tracheotomy operation could be performed, thus keeping him alive by holding him in a semi-upright position and holding Patrol- man Hill's shattered mouth and nose to assist his breathing.

4. You are commended for your prompt and decisive action which resulted in the saving of a human life. For this action you are awarded the Arizona Highway Patrol Life Saving Award.

James J. Hegarty, Director Department of Public Safety

AN AMAZING AND HEROIC RESCUE
Pilot Tom Armstrong #1575
Paramedic Clarence Forbey #286
Sky 12 pilot Jerry Foster
Survivor Gail Mosher

Associated Press Roosevelt
A raft pilot and a high school girl apparently were swept to their deaths when four rafts drifted over a diversion dam and were battered in a backwash of the Salt River near Roosevelt Lake, according to Gila County sheriff deputies.

The above article appeared in April 1979. The following story is told by those involved.

April 13-15 1979
On the 13th, my roommate Lisa Noha and I along with 9 other U of A students who had signed up for a 3 day rafting trip

down the Salt River, met to begin our trip It was a clear beautiful day and we were divided into four small rafts and one large raft that carried our supplies and food. I was a little scared of the water so Lisa and I were allowed to go on the large raft that had several guides in it.

We began our journey and after the first couple of hours the river became more and more choppy. As the day progressed the water grew more and more violent and it became difficult not to tip the raft over.

We made camp that night and it was apparent that the guides felt that we were in serious trouble. They felt the mountains were too narrow to allow a helicopter rescue and the mountains were too high for any of us to climb out. It was decided that we would continue down the river the next day. The second day had some good moments when the river was fairly calm but then we would get in a section that took all of our energy not to capsize. A raft with a photographer who came along to document the trip aboard. At one of the more intense rapids, his raft capsized and he lost all of his expensive equipment. We were able to fish him out of the frigid water and caught his raft and turned it back over.

We all were becoming more and more frightened. One student invited her sister along and they were becoming very terrified and asked to move into the large raft, so Lisa and I tried spots with them.

On the small rafts it was so much more frightening and we had to work very hard not to tip the raft over and fall into the frigid water.

We completed our second day with only one boat capsizing but we were thankful no one was hurt. The guides were feeling much more confident that the worst of the rapids were behind us. We all began to relax, especially when we were told we would only be rafting half a day and then reach our final destination. We were all excited, feeling like the danger was behind us.

The next day we rafted until around noon. The guides told us that 3 or 4 guides were going for the cars and would be back in a few hours. The lead guide told us we needed to float across to the other side of the river and we would be picked up there.

Lisa and I jumped into the small raft that had only one life jacket. We didn't bother to grab another jacket or even put any life jacket on to float to the other side of the river.

We started out and then we looked ahead we could see one of the rafts tip over and disappear. Then we noticed a straight line of water. The guide was signaling and yelling for everyone to get to the shore. Our raft was right in the middle of the river and we could feel the current already grabbing us and sucking us into the dam. In shock and disbelief one side of our raft went straight down the side of the dam. Then the real nightmare started!

The water was rushing over the dam and made such a loud noise it was almost deafening. We were totally in shock trying to figure what had just happened. Water was pouring into our raft and suddenly our raft started to rise up against the dam wall making us throw our bodies on the opposite side of the raft to keep from tipping over. We then noticed we had other rafts on each side of us. They too were fighting against the waves trying to keep their rafts upright.

I remember hearing the screaming from the girl who had brought her sister on the trip. She was screaming her name and frantically looking for her sister. Lisa and I started yelling her name and looking into the water in hopes of finding her. But she was gone. Another girl in another raft started yelling that we were all going to die!

Her screams made one of the guides run to the river's edge and yell that he was going to swim out to help us. Lisa and I pleaded and screamed for him not to attempt to reach us. But he was determined and started to swim in our direction. He swam about half way from the shore and the diversion dam when he suddenly started bobbing up and down and then he simply disappeared.

During all of this, Lisa and I had realized we only had one life jacket between us, so we both put an arm in the sleeve of the life jacket and tied the strap around each of our arms to hopefully not lose it when the boat was being bombarded with ice cold brutal waves and to also keep us close together.

I am still not sure to this day how long we were fighting for our lives when I looked up and discovered multiple police cars on each side of the river along with bystanders looking on. There were kayakers in the water a safe distance from the churning water and waves that we continuously were fighting again.

When we saw a helicopter fly over us, Lisa and I were so relieved! Now someone can lower a ladder or something and get us out of this nightmare. But that didn't happen.

The helicopter kept flying around us but just continued to circle us. When I would occasionally look up I noticed some of the rafts had been pulled to safety. Our raft seemed to be the furthest away from the shore on the other side. My hope was slowly decreasing and then, with a large wave, Lisa slipped right into the water, pulling the life jacket off my arm, but remaining with me due to the rope being tied to my arm. With Lisa suddenly gone, I could feel myself going into shock.

A kayaker was close enough that I could hear shouting.

He threw a rope to me that I was able to grab ahold of and was praying he could just pull the raft and me out of this churning water, but of course that would be impossible. The current was not letting go and the rope fell out of my hands. The kayaker threw the rope again which I grabbed again and he was yelling for me to hold the rope and jump into the water. After witnessing our guide drown in front of me and assuming both Lisa and the other person who we couldn't find were also drowned, there was no way I was going to jump voluntarily into the water.

Suddenly I was shaking uncontrollably and was so exhausted I felt like I couldn't go on. I remember coming to peace with my upcoming death which was just a matter of time I thought, I had lost my father 11 months before and for some reason, I thought it was the exact day of my father's death, so I felt like this was meant to be, I laid my head on the side of the raft and wrapped the small rope that was around the raft to each wrist thinking this would hold me while I rested. I laid my head down. Then all went black.

Gail

Clarence Forbey and I were on call at Air Rescue and were called for a rescue on the upper Salt River. Some students and their guide had gone over a diversion in their rafts. There were several drownings reported and the boats were now trapped against the base of the dam with no way to reach the remaining students.

As we flew over Saguaro Lake we saw Sky 12 sitting at the aid station helipad. We were flying Ranger 27, a Bell Long Ranger. Due to our size we figured we may need Jerry Foster's help with his smaller helicopter. We called Jerry on the radio and he agreed to help with the rescue.

When we reached the scene we saw the swollen river flowing over the dam. The fast current over the dam had created a trough at the base and from there a large wave rose flowing downstream. The two boats were trapped in this trough and held against the dam. One boat held one girl and the other boat had several. They were all struggling to stay in their boats. There were kayakers at the scene but they couldn't get past the waves.

We landed and Clarence and Jerry Foster decided to do the rescue in Sky 12. It was smaller and stronger. Ranger 27 just wasn't powerful enough to accomplish the task. I was to get in the air and guide Sky 12 to the scene.

I took a position upstream of the dam, facing into the wind and alone in the aircraft. I was struggling to keep the engine cool. Jerry with Clarence standing on the skid hovered downwind past the wave to reach the girls. The wave rose so high that they couldn't get into the trough to reach the girls. The boats were beating against the dam and the girls were getting weaker. Jerry tried again. This time the girl that was in a boat solo released her grip and slid out of the boat. My heart sank. I told Jerry we lost her. A few seconds later I saw something pop up downstream behind Sky 12. This girl was the only one not wearing a life jacket but she did have length of rope tied to her with a lifejacket tied to that. The object was the lifejacket. The girl was still underwater. I directed Jerry downstream over the lifejacket.

Clarence crouched on the skid giving Jerry hand signals to try to reach the girl. Clarence lay prone on the skid with his left arm crooked around the cross tube. Jerry dipped down into the water and Clarence grabbed the girl by the wrist. Jerry then lifted up until the girl was completely out of the water. I was telling Jerry to hurry to the shore. I didn't think Clarence would be able to hold that dead weight very long. As they reached the shallow water near the shore, Clarence released the girl. I am still amazed that Clarence could hold the weight of that girl so long with only one hand.

I landed on shore and rigged the helicopter for the medic. Clarence performed CPR on the young girl and she quickly came around. Clarence and I loaded the young girl into Ranger 27 and flew her to the hospital for evaluation.

Being there and watching, it is still hard to believe. Clarence and Jerry will always be my heroes.

Tom

On this April day, which coincided with spring break for many schools, a group of students from the University of Arizona had come up to Phoenix for a boating trip sponsored by the Student Union Activities Board and a couple of sporting businesses. A group of girls would be navigating rubber boats down the normally calm Salt River. But the recent floodwaters filled the lake, causing excess water to spill over the 15 foot diversion dam into the river. When the underpowered boats went over the dam they were caught in a trough at its base and couldn't move forward. Boats and people were all being tossed about.

Two DPS officers had taken the call for help and were headed to the river in Ranger 27, the department's Long Ranger.

When they contacted me, I agreed to head up to the diversion dam. I had a rope with me that I thought would belong enough to reach the victims. When I flew over the trough, I saw two boats trapped there; one with a single female and the other with three or four people. The fuller boat seemed fairly stable, but the one with the lone female was being thrashed about violently. I landed on the shore near Ranger 27 to discuss the plan for their rescue.

Both helicopters took off and for the rescue and with Clarence Forbey on the skids of my helicopter and with Tom Armstrong's guidance from Ranger 27, I lowered the machine as close to the water as I dared. When my skids touched the water I had only about 30 inches clearance between the water and the belly of the aircraft. But I managed to get low enough to allow Forbey to reach the girl.

When I realized Clarence had her, I lifted up from the water and approached the shore. I saw that I couldn't land at the particular spot however, and began to back away, gliding about 12 feet above the shore.

Clarence dropped the girl into the water. There were plenty of spectators, other boaters, tubers and swimmers who had watched this all play out. Several got to the girl and carried her to shore.

I found another place to land and shut down. Clarence ran to the girl and began CPR while one of the bystanders was attempting mouth to mouth resuscitation. The person, while well-intentioned, wasn't well trained in the procedure, so I took over and we got her breathing again.

The girls who had been in the other boat were all wearing life jackets, but were still caught in the trough. The kayakers persuaded them to jump from their boat, which they did. Then the kayakers guided the floating girls to shore where they were all deemed got be in good shape, just exhausted.

It was indeed a joint effort. Without Tom Armstrong guiding me to where I needed to be and without Clarence Forbey bravely hanging on to the skid and reaching into the water to grab and hold on to the girl, she most likely would not have survived.

Jerry

I recall getting a call from the Gila County Sheriffs Office about the need for help of several college students on the Salt River. They had apparently floated from the US60 bridge crossing of the Salt River downstream toward Roosevelt lake area. It was a U of A sponsored trip with U of A supervision. The problem location was an old diversion dam several miles from Roosevelt Lake.

Pilot Tom Armstrong and I headed in that direction and as we passed Saguaro Lake we noticed that the Channel 12 helicopter flown by Jerry Foster was sitting on the pad at the lake.

We radioed Jerry over a mutually known frequency and told him what we were headed for and asked if he would consider helping, as he had always been anxious to assist with any type of rescue or law enforcement type mission.

The aircraft we were flying was a Bell Long Ranger, water injected, and the power of the aircraft was very low for doing hovering or multiple people type rescues.

While enroute we talked to Jerry via radio. He informed me that he had a rope inside his aircraft and that it would be long enough to reach the girls at the diversion dam if I wanted to use his aircraft for the rescue.

The diversion dam was running full bank to bank flow with heavy flood waters. The dam was about 15 feet tall and when the water came over the dam it fell into a trough. As the small unpowered water craft that the students were using came over the dam they were caught in the trough and could not go downstream and were being beaten badly against the dam and the boat was being tossed about.

There were two boats in the trough when we arrived at the scene, one with a single female person and the second with either 3 or 4 persons on board. The boat with several persons seemed fairly stable and the single person boat was being thrashed about violently.

For us to use the Bell helicopter it would have meant for us to land, remove the doors and remove all equipment before we could initiate the start of the rescue. Jerry offered the use of his helicopter, and it was ready, so I decided to give using his helicopter with the rope a try. It was hoped that the girl in the boat could grab the rope, we would lift her to shore and then return to do the same for the others in the second boat.

As we hovered over the water at the dam, the main rotor of Jerry's aircraft was about two feet from the elevated side of the dam and the rope was too short to reach the girl below. We backed out from the dam as the rotor wash was throwing the girls boat around more violently than it had been.

I climbed out onto the skid of Jerry's aircraft so as to have a greater reach of the rope. I was now sitting on the skid holding on with my crossed legs and one hand.

As we approached the dam for the second try at a rescue with the rope, the girl in the boat was thrashed about so violently from the rotor wash that she fell from the boat into the water. The only clothing she had on was a bikini bathing suit.

As I sat on the skid of the helicopter I had no radio communications with either Tom in Ranger 27 or with Jerry in his aircraft. I was attempting to give Jerry hand signals but I could not determine if he was reading or if he could do what I wanted done as the female started floating, face down, down stream in the flood waters.

By some sort of luck Jerry got low enough to the water that I could nearly reach the girl. Jerry's skid gear was a high gear leaving about 30 inches from the water when the skids touch the water.

Eventually Jerry put the skids into the water. At this point from my past teachings of helicopter control, this was not only dangerous, but could very easily put an end to both the helicopter and the people attached to it. As the helicopter sank further into the water, the girl came within reach. I managed to grab her one arm and pull her towards me, trying to get her onto the skid.

Before I could make any type of hand signal, Jerry lifted the helicopter from the water. I now had the girl with one arm, holding her mostly with one hand and hoping to hold myself to the skid with my legs. We approached the south shore about 30 feet into the air and Jerry could see that he could not set down at this particular spot and started to back away from the shore line while about 12 feet from the water edge. I could not continue to hold the weight any longer and dropped the girl about 10 feet to the shore. There were many onlookers and other boaters at the shore that grabbed her and got her to the bank so she could be attended to.

We landed and while Jerry was shutting down his machine, I started CPR with chest compressions. A person on shore attempted doing mouth to mouth breathing for the girl but was not well trained in the procedure. In a couple of minutes, Jerry was by my side and he initiated mouth to mouth with my 5 and 2 CPR. After a few minutes the girl started breathing. The initial beginning (as always) was with a coughing up of water and stomach contents. This was into Jerry's face and mouth but he never missed a beat. He spit out the vomit and continued his mouth to mouth until the girl was conscious and becoming alert.

After the CPR, an IV was started, some drugs the periodical requires, the patient was ready for transport. The DPS helicopter landed and the equipment was readied for transport and the patient was taken to Good Samaritan Hospital in Phoenix.

It was learned after the rescue that all the while I was on the skid without any way of communicating, Tom Armstrong Flying Ranger 27 was telling Jerry via radio what I was seeing, what I was signaling and where to turn so as to get me in position for grabbing the floating body.

The rescue was a fantastic piece of joint effort on the part of the Sky 12 helicopter and pilot and the outstanding abilities of both pilots to use small limited power helicopters to perform a rescue that would seem impossible without the use of a boat and ground crew.

Tom and Jerry were given awards by the DPS Director. I received the first DPS award for valor as a result. The experience of working with two extremely talented pilots that risked not only their equipment but their own lives to save another person was a solemn and sincere honor to be associated with them.

Clarence

After all went black the next thing I remember is waking up in a helicopter heading to the hospital. I began yelling for Lisa and to my surprise her hand came down from the cot above me. She was injured but she was alive. What a relief!

We arrived at the hospital and were rushed off for evaluations. Having been pulled along the bottom of the river, my toenails were all pulled off. My back had numerous bruises and cuts from the rocks and the top of the knuckles on my hand were also bloodied. I had rope burns on each wrist from where I had twisted the raft's rope around my wrists in an attempt to stay in the raft. The biggest concern at that time was that my kidneys had been so beat up from the river that I may have damaged and destroyed both kidneys and would need surgery. I was very lucky that after a day or two in Intensive Care, my kidneys began to work on their own and I was able to be released from the hospital to recover.

The physical wounds recovered much sooner that the emotional wounds. I was very thankful and happy to be alive but truly struggled with survivor's guilt for many years afterward.

Once time had passed I began to realize the sacrifices that people had made and much later realizing how individuals risked their very lives to rescue me, a college student whom they didn't even know. I have realized so many times all the blessings I have received because of their heroism. I was able to graduate from college, get married and have children of my own. So many blessing that just continue on everyday. Tom Armstrong, Clarence Forbey and Jerry Foster will forever be my heroes and part of my family.

Gail

AUTO STATUS AND OTHER MEMORIES
Colin Peabody #481

In my early days with the AHP in 1968 and for a couple of years later, cop communication stuff was done differently. Every 30 minutes, dispatchers had to clear the radio towers they were working, by verbally identifying the station, like KOH-861 Holbrook or KDF-539 Holbrook. So every 30 minutes you would expect to hear that over the radio, oftentimes a sweet sounding female voice, but most often somebody like Paul Palmer, Dennis Keeton or Paul Short. Sometime in 1970, DPS instituted a Morse Code identifier that came over the radio so the dispatchers didn't have to remember to do that every 30 minutes. The dispatchers would also give out a Hot List several times a day on vehicles wanted for some offense, stolen or wanted in another crime.

If you wanted to get a driver's license or registration check out of California, a dispatcher would often call a CHP dispatcher close to the state line to get that information as it was sometimes quicker than going through Phoenix. If you wanted a check on a car as being stolen out of California, a special procedure called Auto-Status was used. You called your dispatcher, requested an Auto Status and the dispatcher would then get on the phone to Phoenix where a dispatcher who had the ability to call the California Highway Patrol and request a stolen check. You then waited until the CHP could handle the request and call the AHP dispatcher back. Then the AHP dispatcher would call the requesting officer with the response. Sometimes this could take 10 minutes, sometimes an hour, depending on how busy the dispatchers on both ends were or some other reason for the delay. I will leave that to your imagination!

One day I have a 60 Chevy stopped about 15 miles west of Winslow and I knew this car was stolen, the young driver had no registration in the car, and no key in the ignition. In those days, Chevy ignition switches didn't always need a key, depending on how worn the lock was. The kid had a short haircut and only a driver's license and no luggage in the car. So anyway, I am waiting for a return on my Auto Status request and trying to keep the "suspect" engaged in peaceful conversation until I get the results of my request. I had my outside speaker on, loud, so I could hear it over the trucks and other traffic, when all of a sudden the station identifier went off. It startled my "suspect" and he said "What the hell was that?" I told him that just let me know that the car was stolen. He confessed right then and there to stealing the car in Oakland the day before and that he was a NAVY AWOL. I cuffed him, advised him of his rights and as I was placing him in the front seat of the patrol car, my return from Auto Status came back, "10-38Frank, 10-40" which is dispatcher speak for "Don't let the suspect hear this, you have a felony stolen vehicle out of California". My response to radio was " 10-4, 10-15 (suspect) in custody, send me a 926(tow truck)." It had only taken about 30 minutes to confirm what I knew 29 minutes before!

SEXY VOICE
Paul Palmer #342

The Auto Status phone line in Phoenix communications was usually answered by Gracie Bertch. I thought the world of Gracie. She was a very nice friendly person who just happened to be very good looking and had the sexiest phone voice you ever heard. All the male dispatchers in the outlaying stations always like to call Auto Status for a 10-29 just to hear Gracie's voice. We were always glad to hear a patrolman ask for a 10-29.

If it was a slow day and no 10-29 requests were coming in, we would occasionally call Auto Status with a license plate that we had made up just so we could hear Gracie's voice. I don't know what we would have done if we had gotten a hit.

WRONG NUMBER
T.K. Waddell #803

Embarrassing antics of two radio dispatch personnel at Phoenix radio.

In early 1971 a comedy act was routinely played on commercial radio. "AJAX LIQUOR STORE" (by Hudson and Landry) a drunk calling the store to see if they deliver and to place an order. This routine was a favorite of two DPS radio/teletype personnel, John Gantt (718) and myself.

I was working the day shift on District 6 radio. The District 6 radio console was located in a small (closet) formerly used as the DPS Morse Code station KOB34. This "closet" had a window which adjoined the Lieutenants office. Sergeant George Falter was using the office to hold a briefing for the swing shift dispatchers. John Gantt was in that briefing, along with other dispatch personnel. Gantt was sitting across from Falters desk looking into the window seeing me making a call on the telephone.

Gantt seeing me making a call on the telephone, made an

assumption when the telephone on Falter's desk rang during the briefing. Gantt, thinking it was me making the call, answered the phone, "AJAX LIQUOR STORE". A moment of silence then, WHO IS THIS? Gantt immediately hung up the phone. Falter then asked Gantt," Who was that?" Gantt said "I don't know, but I bet he will call back! The phone immediately rang again. This time Falter answered. The caller was Lt. Gregg Goodson the Yuma DC. Goodson wanted to know who just answered the phone. Falter explained to Goodson that it was Gantt, and that he thought it was a pranked call from T.K. Waddell. Falter was able to calm Goodson down, and answer Goodson's initial questions. After Goodson's call, Falter counseled Gantt on the proper way to answer a DPS telephone call.

I was unaware of Goodson's phone call but was also counseled by Falter, immediately after shift change.

John Gantt and I still laugh about this when we hear " AJAX LIQUOR STORE"
Moral of this story, don't answer the phone!

THE FOUR DIGIT BADGE NUMBER
Bob Mitchell #2197

Ollie Bond was a dispatcher in Kingman who could strike fear into a new rookie. She could sound rough but she certainly took care of "her patrolmen".

The story goes that a new patrolman with a four digit badge number went into the Kingman office and asked Ollie why she wouldn't answer him on the radio.

Her reply? "I'm not answering any 4 digit badge number radio calls until he comes in here and introduces himself to me."

I'LL GO BUT IT WILL TAKE A WHILE
Jay Atwater #1434

I believe it was in 1974 that the Holbrook dispatch center was closed. Dispatching was transferred to Phoenix dispatch. During this time I was working a swing shift on I-40 in the Chambers area. Phoenix dispatch advised me of a bad injury accident halfway down the Salt River Canyon. I advised Phoenix dispatch I was enroute but it would probably be sometime tomorrow morning before I could arrive. After a short pause, Phoenix dispatch advised me to stand by. A short time later I was advised to disregard.

THE BIG SCARE
Don Barcello #515

The story I am about to tell you took place in about 5 seconds but seemed a heck of a lot longer.

It was in February 1973 and a perfect day to be riding a bike. I was patrolling northbound on SR87 on my Moto Guzzi . I was enjoying the ride and had just passed the Saguaro Lake turn off when a I heard a horrific ear splitting noise. All kinds of thoughts went through my mind. Is my bike getting ready to explode? Is this what you hear just before your Moto Guzzi begins a high speed wobble? All kinds of things were going through my mind as my heart rate doubled.

For whatever reason, I glanced up and about 500 feet above me are two F-16s. It looked like I could reach up and touch them. As they blasted past me, both pilots looked down at me and gave me a thumbs up. If their plan that day was to scare an Arizona Highway Patrol motor officer, the plan worked.

Like me, they are probably still telling people this story to this day. I would like to hear their version.

IN ALL MY GLORY
C.B. Fletcher #923

Around 1972 we were out at the rack track west of Phoenix which later became known as PIR. It was February and it was cold! We were doing motor cycle training. Gene Babcock, Randy VonMeter, Emmit Wilhelm, and Greg Green rounded out the group of instructors. Due to the location we had an RV and a pickup with a camper so we could stay at the track. This allowed us more time to get ready for the next day after each days training. It eliminated the need to drive back and forth to our homes.

One evening after supper I headed to the shower facilities in the infield. After my shower, I stepped out to get dressed and all of my clothes were gone. Only my tennis shoes remained.

Gene Babcock had brought a huge spot light and as I stepped out of the shower area completely nude, except for tennis shoes Gene hit me with this light. I ran naked, trying to zig and zag in an attempt to get out of the bright light.

I got behind the guardrail where we had our bikes parked and jumped on my bike, still completely nude and began to drive around the track with Gene following me with the spotlight keeping me constantly lit.

I crossed the start-finish line at 45 mph completely nude standing up on my bike in all my glory. Well, maybe not full glory. Remember it was February and it was cold!

As far as I know, I am the only motor officer to ride his police motor cycle butt naked.

And that's how I got the nickname "Breezy Rider"!

PUSH-PULL CESSNA MAYDAY
Colin Peabody #481

I was working days out of Winslow and was covering both I-40 east and west of Winslow when radio advised me of a plane having mechanical trouble and needed to land on I-40 east of Winslow. I headed that way and got there just in time to see a Cessna landing on the westbound lanes without interfering with vehicular traffic.

I was able to get behind the plane and when it stopped, the pilot got out. I had never seen a plane like it before, it had a high wing over the fuselage, twin tail booms, with what looked like a wing attached to them and between those booms was a propeller engine, but the front of the plane had another prop engine up there. The pilot told me it was referred to as a Push-Pull Cessna, the front prop pulled the plane and the back prop was a pusher. The problem today was the back prop had sheared a pin or something and the pilot couldn't feather the prop, causing him to be unable to maintain airspeed and altitude, necessitating him to have to land a few miles short of the Winslow Airport.

We pushed the plane off into a wide flat spot in the median and traffic then moved on.

We called the Winslow airport and had a mechanic bring out what the pilot needed to make the repair. The mechanic showed up, made a temporary repair and together we pushed and pulled the Cessna back up on the pavement, the pilot fire it up and I blocked traffic while he took off for the Winslow airport.

I learned that Model 336 and 337 Push-Pull Cessnas required human power to push and pull them without engine power. They were valuable forward observing aircraft in Vietnam during that war. I learned that Arizona Highway Patrolmen also doubled as Air Traffic Controllers!

ANOTHER ROUTINE FLIGHT
John Underwood #419

Back in the Spring of 1974 I was assigned to fly the Citabria out of Tucson surveilling roads that were not being actively patrolled. I had Tucson Patrolman with me, I don't recall his name, but as I recall he was probably 6'2", and probably weighed in at 230. So he had to be squeezed into the Citabria, which he did. We taxied out of our hangar area and took off flying westbound. Pretty quickly Tucson radio assigned us to a possible rollover on the Sasabe highway, so with the highway in sight we descended to about 1,500' above the road and headed South toward Sasabe.

After 10 to 15 minutes sure enough we located a rolled over Porsche 911 with no one around. With the wind out of the north I gave us a right hand downwind and landed on the dirt road heading north just short of the Porsche, which was situated just short of a downward hill. We got out and found blood in the drivers area, but no ID or vehicle paperwork. We gathered what information we could and got ready to depart.

Now to get airborne, again off this dirt highway... the patrolman and I turned the Citabria around, got in, fired up, and taxied southbound on the road with me thinking I must give us enough takeoff room or we will go over the hill that was on the north side of the Porsche. That would not be a fun time...!

So at a point I figured we were safe, I turned the bird around and we departed with that little 150HP Lycoming giving us all it had... I got the tail wheel up pretty quickly, so there we were roaring along on the two main wheels passing the Porsche, and then comes the hill... The little bird just didn't have the speed to fly, so over the hill we go... Sure helped the airspeed increase in a hurry!, so I eased back on the stick gently and we started to become airborne, but sure enough we bounced lightly off the dirt with our tail wheel, and we bid the road good bye. Just another routine flight.

CI OBSERVERS
Jim Heflin #1983

About the time the 55 Air Surveillance program started picking up we got a lot more requests from CI, Narcotics and the guys in the Air Smuggling division to do a lot more surveillance which was great for me, but I quickly learned there was a lot of difference between CI and the Highway 55 program just by the nature of it. It could literally go on for 4-5 days. Sometimes we would drop it and then pick it back up. The key to the success was often your observer. I know some of them did not want to do it, but the ones that complained the most seemed to be the best at it.

Of course Randy Oden and Bob Hopper did not like it but they were good at it. Mike Stevens and Ron Cox were my standbys.

So the surveillance with CI was definitely a little different than the surveillance in the Highway Patrol We had some long hours and long nights. As we all know Mike Stevens was, how would you say, mischievous. But he had a pretty good knowledge of the Citabria. I would let him fly the airplane at times. The Citabria had set of control in the backseat, so sometimes Mike would start messing with me and turn the carburetor heat on which would cause a reduction in power and I couldn't figure out why we were losing altitude and things like that just to keep us going thru a long surveillance. I remember one night we had been on this surveillance for about 2-3 days and finally the bust went down in Casa Grande and we got some good weight and a few vehicles. Mike had been my observer the whole time. So it was about 3 in the morning with a beautiful Arizona desert night and we were on our way back to Phoenix over Chandler and I looked back and Mike was sound to sleep. So I thought to myself I am going to pay you back for all the messing you've done to me, so I pushed the nose and got some airspeed and begin a slow barrel roll and about that time Mike woke up and was looking down at Phoenix. There were a few seconds where I thought that maybe this was not a good idea because he came unglued and maybe rightfully so. He said he thought we were going to crash. I said no just a slow roll to wake you up before we land. When we landed he couldn't get out the aircraft fast enough and headed to the bathroom, not sure what that was about. But after that he did not mess with me.

I was assigned to work with Ron Cox on the Air marijuana suppression program. Ron was the best there was in finding these fields. We would pack a lunch, take off and fly all day depending on the light. We looked up and down every river and canyon in Northern Arizona or the eastern part. He just had the knack for finding the grows. They would go in with the search warrant and think maybe 50 plants and end up finding 100's.

I think the biggest was the one out by the Palo Verde Plant. Ron has pictures of that. The shortest one I remember was when we headed up, and thinking it would be a 8-9 hour stretch,

Ron said head toward Tucson and go up about 5000 feet so we could get out of the traffic pattern, then he said head back left over the end of the airport. Evidently Charlie Serino had a tip there was a grow on the edge of the I-10 over toward the Tempe River. Charlie confirmed, so we headed back to the airport. They served a warrant and it was a good bust.

Depending on the wind, it was a good day in the Citabria when I could keep up with the cars on the highway. If was really gusty I would watch the semi go faster then we were. So there were many more memories but will save them for later.

SKY KING TO THE RESCUE
Colin Peabody #481

In our previous book, we recorded a story about Everett Bowman, a former World Champion Rodeo cowboy turned rancher-turned Arizona Highway Patrolman, who had quite a reputation for getting his job done with whatever means he had available. One of those stories told of him chasing a speeder that he couldn't catch with his patrol car, but he was near his ranch so he got his airplane out and tracked the speeder, got in front of him a good distance, landed and stopped the speeder, then wrote him up before flying back to his ranch and resuming his patrol work in his car.

I was reminded of an incident involving Patrolman Ron DeLong#466 and a low and slow flying, high wing Cessna that buzzed him west of Winslow on US66. The pilot buzzed Ron several times while Ron was dealing with a violator and came very close to crashing the plane. Ron took chase and called it in to Flagstaff radio describing the plane and even its N number, the equivalent of a car's license plate. He was close enough at times he was able to give a description of the pilot. As the plane got closer to the forested area near Flagstaff, the pilot gained altitude and Ron couldn't follow him but had chased the plane for nearly 60 miles! Fortunately the pilot called the Flagstaff airport for clearance to land, which occurred. Flagstaff officers met the plane and arrested the pilot for being under the influence of alcohol. The

FAA took the guys pilots license based on the radio traffic Ron had with the Flag Patrol dispatcher, and they charged him with a federal offense that amounted to reckless flying.

Ron was hoping he might have to appear in a hearing that could have been held In California where the pilot and plane were based. But, that didn't happen, much to Ron's dismay. We teased him for quite a while calling him Sky King!

A FREE DINNER
Rich Richardson #188

I remember a story that Dick Raymond used to tell in the academy about Harley Thompson. Maybe you heard the story, as best that I remember:

Raymond said that he and Thompson were in Seligman back in early patrol days. That old 1949 Ford in one of your pictures you sent to me may have been similar to what they were driving in those days. Anyway Raymond was driving thru Seligman and observed a patrol vehicle parked at a café. He believed that it was Thompson. A sneaky idea hit Raymond, why not drive past the café real fast. The café was on a twisted portion of old US 66. The speed resulted in squealing the tires and drew the attention of Thompson. Apparently Thompson didn't know it was a patrol car making the noise. As the story goes, Thompson ran out to his car quickly and went in pursuit of the speeding car. What Thompson didn't know was the speeder had turned off the street onto a side road. Thompson headed west to catch up with the speeder and never located the suspect car. In the mean time Raymond parked his car near the café and entered. He observed the food on the counter that belonged to Thompson and commenced to eat the food. When Thompson returned empty-handed to the café, he saw Raymond seated at the counter. Raymond asked where Thompson had gone, leaving a nearly full plat of food. Apparently Thompson didn't put two and two together and thought that the speeder got away and didn't know it was Raymond pulling the prank. Some time later Thompson did find out it was Raymond all the time. I suppose Thompson had to finally admit that

Raymond got the best at that time. I could just see Thompson's facial expression once he found out what happened that day in Seligman.

During my time with the patrol, I served in Yuma, Seligman, Flagstaff, Holbrook and Show Low, all during the first 12 years in uniform. I transferred to Narcotics Unit in Phoenix for a year, and then to Intelligence Unit for another 4 years. I then transferred to my final duty station in Tucson, working Intelligence Unit. After retiring during 1982 in Tucson (Criminal Intelligence Unit), I became a DPS Reserve officer #9791 from 1982-1985 in Tucson. During the last 6 months before leaving the reserves, I did work for the AZ Dept. of Motor Vehicles as an Inspector in Tucson.

KIDS SAY THE DARNDEST THINGS
Tom Ticer #490

In the early 70's I patrolled Hwy 60 near Bell Road and out Wickenburg way. One afternoon the Sheriff's Dept. was investigating a cattle truck rollover on Bell Road near Highway 60. Several yearlings were killed and the ones that survived were trotting all over the country side. And they were NOT happy! I was outside my patrol vehicle rerouting traffic away from the accident scene, which was about one mile away.

Back then the Highway Patrol's cover was not the Smoky Bear Hat. Our head cover was what we called a Gas Station Hat. I was standing in front of my Patrol Vehicle when one of the 200 pound yearlings' approached me and stopped about 15 feet away. I took off my hat, waived it at the yearling and yelled at it. It charged me and hit me in the knees, throwing me head first into my push bumper. I woke up a short time later as unknown persons in the area got me to my feet. The yearling was gone and I had a bloody uniform from three cuts on my head. After awhile my Sgt. arrived and took me to Boswell Hospital where they sewed me up. I was driven home wearing a white gauze turban, compliments of Boswell Hospital.

My wife was grocery shopping at the time, using the family car which was a 1972 International Travel-All. We had four children, so we needed a large vehicle to hold lots of groceries. I told my children not to tell Mom what happened to me. I would tell her myself when she came into the house. The Travel-All soon entered the driveway and before she could get out of the vehicle my 9 year old, Bill, hit the door running, and yelled to my wife "Mom, Mom, guess what happened to Dad!". She looked around and didn't see my patrol car and naturally panicked.. Bill finished his exciting explanation by telling her that "Dad got gored by a bull!!"

You older folks remember the old TV program hosted by Art Linkletter called "Kids Say The Darndest Things." Well, this was a typical example of that program. We still laugh about it 50 years later.

GRANDPA
Dick Lewis #176

While working as a patrolman during the famous Fiesta De Los Vaqueros in Tucson, Arizona, my attention was called to a small three year old boy. The child was dressed in a cowboy outfit, complete with cap pistols and a large hat. He was crying and very frightened and I learned that he was lost from his grandpa.

I began comforting the young cowboy by saying, "Don't cry, come with me and we will find your grandpa." Inquiring further into the matter I asked, "What is your grandpa's name?"

A very impatient expression came across the lad's face and I could see that he was quite annoyed at my ignorance, as he replied disgustedly; "Grandpa!"

Needless to say, we were both found by grandpa shortly afterwards.

YA DONE GOOD - KINDA
Colin Peabody #481

In February 1970, I was working evening shift west of Winslow when I wound up with a day off without pay and a letter of commendation both on the same shift.

I was having my code 7 at home when I got a call from our dispatcher, so I responded to an Officer Needs Help call from one of our guys at a trading post on St. Rt. 87 just south of the Reservation line 15 miles north of Winslow. I made the turn at the Minnetonka Trading Post onto St. Rt.87 off US 66, got in some gravel, fishtailed off the road and hit a right of way fence post, putting a dent in the left rear fender of my car. I was also stuck in the soft sand of the shoulder. Fortunately, John Thompson, the local rancher who owned the ranch where Bob Varner's killer committed suicide 18 years later, pulled me out using his Ford pickup and a chain and I headed north. Turned out the officer didn't need help, but while up there, I got a call assigning me to what turned out to be a 5 time fatal right there at the west end of the Minnetonka Trading Post parking lot at the 87 and 66 junction. That accident resulted in the deaths of a woman in an Oldsmobile from Prescott, her two young daughters and two young Navajo boys in a 55 Chevy from Winslow.

I spent a lot of hours getting the report done correctly and within the time frame we had for completing fatal accident reports. Due to the number of lives lost, Major Raymond was sent up to Winslow to oversee the reconstruction investigation I was doing and was pleased with the work I had done on it.

So, nearly one year later, my accident report got me a letter of commendation from Major Raymond but the damage to my vehicle got me a day off without pay from Major Milldebrandt six months before I got that letter of commendation!

GOOD NEWS/BAD NEWS
Gregg Girard #1151

This is another story about one of my missions where I had to stand tall in front of my sergeant, "Doc" Holloway #291.

One day out at Air Rescue at Falcon Field in Mesa, the crew was eagerly awaiting the next call. I was the duty officer/paramedic. My pilot was Joe Whisenhunt #2612. Joe is a great guy. He spend a good deal of time teaching me how to fly the helicopter, or should I say, beat the air into submission.

The first call came in shortly after the preflight duties in the morning. It came from the Tempe police department, via the DPS dispatcher.

There was a robbery by two perpetrators at the Howard Johnson's restaurant across from the Arizona State University campus. The two suspects were exiting out the front door after the robbery as two Tempe police officers were coming in the westside entrance. As soon as the employees of the restaurant and the customers saw the police officers, there was a lot of yelling and pointing. The police officers immediately turned and ran back out to their vehicle in the parking lot. The suspects peeled out of the parking lot and headed west on Mill Avenue. The police cruiser was in hot pursuit. When Mill Avenue makes turn to the right and heads north a short distance away, the driver lost control and hit either a pole or a tree, I forget which. At any rate, which was now zero, they were stopped in their tracks. The driver was trapped but the passenger suspect fled on foot. One officer stayed with the driver to secure a weapon and to wait for the fire department for extrication. The other officer called for backup and commenced a foot pursuit of the other suspect who was now out of sight but heading for the downtown Tempe area. This is about the time we got the call, ran to the helicopter and cranked it up. (Just an expression).

While enroute we received word that a lot of pedestrians were pointing toward where the suspect was running. The last report was that he was seen running up "A" mountain at the northwest area of the university. It took us only about 10 minutes to reach "A" mountain and we started a concentric search beginning at the base and the working our way up. The description we had was a Black male, white T-shirt, blue jeans and tennis shoes. About halfway up the mountain I saw a small cave like opening with two blue jean legs sticking out. I told Joe, "Will you look at that?" He replied, "I can get him out of there." I advised the dispatcher that we had a suspect spotted and were trying to get him out of an outcropping of rock. This must have left the dispatcher scratching her head. Joe tilted the aircraft and the rotor wash blew rocks, dirt, sand and junk into and under the little cave he was in. That kind of made the suspect a little upset and he came out, looked at us and held his hands out as if to ask, what is going on? I reached for my weapon, but uh-oh had left it back at base. I unzipped Joe's flight suit and reached in to secure his weapon from his shoulder holster. I opened my window and pointed it at the suspect. He immediately realized I was serious and he raised his hand. At that time a Tempe officer ran up behind and tackled him. We hovered away from the scene and after the suspect was handcuffed, the officer showed us a weapon and pointed to the back waistband of the suspect indicating where the suspect had it. Feeling good about ourselves, we headed back to base.

After landing and refueling the aircraft we went inside. Joe immediately went into the sergeant's office and began to tell him about our exciting mission. He got to the point where I unzipped his flight suit and removed his weapon. Rapidly the sergeant excitedly said, "STOP! GIRARD GET IN HERE". Sheepishly I had to admit that I had left my weapon and shoulder holster back here at base.

About a week later Joe and I were called into the supervisor's office. Sergeant Holloway handed Joe a Letter of Commendation for his exceptional flying skill during the capture of an armed robbery suspect. I also received a Letter of Commendation for the same mission...however...the sarge also handed me a Letter of Instruction to never go out on a mission again and leave my weapon.

Imagine that! A Letter of Commendation and a Letter of Instruction for the same mission. An "Atta Boy" and an "Oh Darn" (or words to the same effect) for the same thing.

THE PARKING TICKET
Dick Lewis #176

A traffic ticket is regarded as harassment by the receivers most of the time. Some are hard to sell and some are not. A parking ticket is the hardest, not to mention a stop sign. To issue a parking ticket you want to fill it out quickly, stick it under the wiper on the windshield and get out of there before the owner arrives.

THE LITTERBUG
Tom Ticer #490

Back in the early 70's I worked Highway 60 from Peoria to Wickenberg. It was a 2 lane road that was the main Highway for LA/Phoenix traffic. The I-10 freeway out of LA stopped at about Quartzsite. I did not have Radar or Vascar at this time. You had to pace vehicles to write your speed citation. This was done by cracking your driver side window so you could hear the vehicle going in the opposite direction. The louder the vehicle was, the faster it was going. You allowed the vehicle to go for awhile, then you turned, and overtook it in about a mile and paced it.

One of my paces this day was a Greyhound bus. It was going about 8 to 10 MPH over and I prepared to stop it for a warning. The speed limit back then was 55 MPH. Before I turned on my lights the bus made a left turn onto Bell Road and stopped for the railroad tracks as it was required to do. As it again got underway, a Styrofoam coffee cup was thrown out a window onto the roadway. The stop was made and I explained to the driver that I was going to give him a warning for his speed violation. I also told him he should relate to his passengers to not litter our road with coffee cups. He really got my attention when he stated "I am empty. I don't have any passengers". He was cited for littering and after he picked up the coffee cup, he was allowed to continue.

THE FRITO BANDITO
Tim Hughes #793

While stationed in Salome, I was working a night shift on US 60 west of Salome. I stopped a truck for either a warning or repair order. As I talked to the driver of the truck, he thanked me for not citing him. Turns out, this was a Fritos truck. I told him it would be awful to cite the Frito Bandito as they produced great chips. He immediately offered me a case of Fritos and I explained that we could not accept any gratuities.

After he signed the contact, he asked me if there was an obstruction on the road that was a hazard, would I need to remove it to keep the highway safe. I told him that yes I would need to remove the hazard. He left going east and I went west. A short time later, I was headed east and lo and behold, there was a case of Frito's on the road that could have been considered a hazard, so I removed it and took it to the Desert Gem trailer Park where the other HP families enjoyed the unexpected treat. I was never able to make the case of littering by the Frito Bandito!!

THE WATERMELON
Paul Palmer #342

When I heard about the passing of Joe Hernandez this week it hit me kinda hard. Joe was a friend and a special kind of guy. Always a smile on his face and a ready joke. I never saw Joe in a bad mood.

Major Walt Sheets was in charge of transportation when it was located on the compound where supply is today. One day when Joe was eating his lunch, he had a slice of watermelon. He had the idea to plant a watermelon seed in the area just outside of the transportation offices. There was a small bare spot between the sidewalk and the building. Major Sheets came by as Joe was planting the seed and asked Joe what he was doing. Joe told him that he was planting a watermelon and the Major laughed and told him that one could not possible be grown there.

Joe watered the area every day and soon a small plant began to grow. As it grew bigger Joe told the Major, "I told you I was going to grow a watermelon." The major was still skeptical. Finally a very small melon appeared and Joe called the major out to look at it. I'll be damned he said.

The small melon never grew much bigger that a plum but Joe had an idea. He went to the store and bought the smallest watermelon he could find and placed it on top of the plant. Joe would hide and watch the major each morning as the major came to work. He would always look down at the watermelon plant before he went into his office.

Each week Joe would buy a larger melon and replace the one he had put on the plant the week before. It wasn't long before the melon was so big it outgrew the small patch of dirt and covered part of the sidewalk.

Each week he would hide and watch the major walk by, look at the melon and shake his head.

Finally Joe got tired of the game and told the major that he was going to have a watermelon bust the next day. He put the melon on ice overnight and at lunchtime the following day, he called the major in to join everyone and eat the melon. The major said, "That is the best watermelon I ever ate". The major couldn't understand why Joe was laughing. Joe never told the major the truth and the guys in the shop kept Joe's secret.
Joe was special.

FIRE! FIRE! FIRE!
T.K. Waddell #803
Larry Jensen #819

The OLD Phoenix Communications "radio/teletype/road and weather" room, was located on the South side of DPS Headquarters, 2010 W. Encanto Blvd. The large Communications room contained two radio rooms, a large teletype room with NLETS computers and Road and Weather telephone area. This large room had a pubic entrance on Encanto and a back door exiting to the compound parking lot. It was routinely used by visiting officers and radio personnel . Radio personnel parked their vehicles in the main parking area, along with other employees working at headquarters.

At the time of this story, Larry Jensen and myself were working the swing shift in teletype. Lt. Ron Hoffman was the day shift Lieutenant. He was upset that the rear door, locked from the inside, required a loud knock on the door to enter from the parking lot. It was routinely used by visiting officers, staff personnel and radio personnel causing excessive noise in the main room and his office.

This exit was also used to access the snack wagon aka "roach coach" during breaks. The driver would relocate his truck around the parking area for anyone who wanted a snack during midday breaks or daytime or evening lunch hours. This was a convenience to all, since we had no break rooms or designated lunch areas.

Lt. Hoffman attempted to stop this ingress/egress through the back door by taping a paper sign on the inside of the door stating "EXIT DURING FIRE ONLY"

WELL, this was a big problem for us in radio. Not to be impeded, Jensen had an idea. It was lunch time and the snack wagon would not wait long for us if there was nobody waiting at that particular stop. Soooo, Jensen had an idea, and whipped out his cigarette lighter setting the paper notice on fire, while quietly telling me FIRE, FIRE. We extinguished the flame and exited the door heading to the snack wagon.

Although complying with the notice posted on the door, Hoffman had our butts in his office the next day,

threatening time off for the scam. Well we didn't get time off, but did get a letter and a PPR entry.

This fire notice did not reappear after our escapade.

MY WIFE WAS NOT IMPRESSED
Steve Genler #1064

There are times when our adventures in Highway Patrolin' involve a patient, understanding wife – even if they don't see the humor of the event. That was the case in 1974 when I was in pursuit of a stolen car west of Picacho Peak on I-10.

My new Mercury was capable of 140 mph and I could turn on, and catch up with, <u>any</u> evil do'er who ventured into my patrol area (of course stopping at that speed was quite a show with the smoke from the brakes *billowing* behind as my Mercury rolled past any violator who had dutifully pulled over when I "lit 'em up")

That certainly wasn't the case on the day in question as this dude accelerated when I hit the lights and after a few minutes with lights <u>and</u> siren, it was obviously a pursuit. I called it in, the stolen car was verified, and we exited at high speed onto SR84 heading for Eloy; which interestingly enough, was where I lived! Eloy being what you might laughingly call an urban area, I backed way off and the "pursuit" slowed to 45mph on SR84 through town.

Now this being a fine spring morning, my wife and little daughter were headed west to Casa Grande on SR84 near Estrella Road when, as my wife Margie tells it, "a car went rocketing past; the guy behind the wheel steering with his left hand, arm on the driver side door and relaxing with his right arm resting on top of the passenger seat" (she admitted to thinking of this guy in terms not *suitable for mixed company* and was irritated 'cause there's <u>never</u> a cop around when you need 'em). About then our daughter began yelling Daddy! Daddy! Daddy! Margie looked over, and there I was, lights blazing, engine howling, exhaust smoke pouring out behind the big Mercury, eyes locked on target as the poster boy for truth, justice and the American way roared past in pursuit of the evil do'er while clutching the steering wheel with both hands in a white knuckle *death grip*.

About that time, Tom Hawley, who was responding to the call, was coming east on SR84 when the suspect apparently spotted him and hung a quick two wheel left onto Sunland Gin Road; Tom picked up the pursuit. I, of course, applied my brakes to slow down and make the turn with the usual result; smoke billowing from the back as the brakes burned, steam shooting from the over-heated engine and the Mercury continuing down the road for a quarter mile until I could finally get it stopped and turned around. My wife drove by like this was just a normal day in Eloy while my daughter waved and called out through the open window Daddy! Daddy! Daddy! The engine then died from overheating and all I could do was park by the side of the road pretending I was there in case the stolen car doubled back as I listen to the pursuit on the radio!

At least justice was served when the guy was captured later after abandoning the stolen car and hiding under the seat in an outhouse near Arizona City.

A WIFE'S MEMORIES
Lynn Diehl - Wife of Jerry Diehl #201

Jerry began his career with the highway patrol November 1, 1962 as a CW operator. He worked as a CW operator for many years until computers came about and he became a dispatcher. Jerry was one of the dispatchers that went to the abbreviated high-way patrol school in 1968. I don't really remember when he went out on the road but I do remember the first day that he went by himself he had the dayshift which began at 6 o'clock and it was very dark because we had no power. He got in his patrol car and took off and an hour later he came back home because he had forgotten his gun. He had gotten dressed by kerosene lantern and it wasn't easy finding everything he needed to get dressed. This wasn't the only time he forgot his gun. One day while he was writing a ticket, the violator asked why he wasn't carrying a gun. Without missing a bit, Jerry replied, "Its optional" Another time as he was finishing up writing a ticket, again with an empty hol-ster, Dave Mattingly drove up. Hey Jerry he said, "I wish I was as big as you are and be able to stand alongside the highway with-out a gun." He really enjoyed working on the road and when they had the opportunity of getting a Kevlar vest we borrowed money and got him the best because it wasn't paid for by the patrol. He had to supply his own firearm as well.

When Jerry joined the patrol his badge number was 516. After he went through a patrol school his badge number changed to 449 and then when they did the re-organization he ended up with badge number 201. After going to the academy he came back to Flagstaff and became a dispatcher. He worked at that position for a while but wasn't really happy. He wanted to go on the road. He was trained by a couple of the guys in Flagstaff who called him their ten year rookie. I can't remember the year but he helped in the production of the movie Gumball Rally. His job was to drive the producers and directors around as they plotted the turns in the clover links and what roads would be the best to shoot the movie. The movie was released in 1976 so I think the filming was in early 1976.

Jerry was also given a brand new 1973 Mercury patrol car. He got to choose the color, and picked copper, and all the gadgets that they could put on it. When he finally reached the top mileage his dad bought it at auction and it stayed in the family for quite a few years. It was later purchased and the owner loaned the car to the museum for display for a short time.

Jerry was either the first or one of the first to have a CB radio in his Patrol car. The truck drivers gave him the nickname of "The Hawk" as they said he would swoop down and get them.

THE GRIM REAPER
Dick Lewis #176

There is a bad one in the canyon reported by a trucker. I advise the dispatcher and go screaming through the night. My thoughts are racing, don't let them die. Maybe I can get there in time. Arrangements are made for the ambulance and wrecker. Hold up on the coroner, I request. I'm still hoping.

Upon my arrival at the scene a face in the crowd calls to me, "Over here officer, I think this lady is hurt". There, crouched in the debris sits a woman. There is blood on her dress. She holds a blanket wrapped baby close to her bosom, and whimpers with

tears streaming down her motherly cheeks. The mother in uninjured. The infant is dead.

The crowd can sense this and is quiet. Everyone is heart-
broken.

As I stand with the baby in my arms, the mother is led,
stunned, through the crowd to a car in the background. She pleads
to our Almighty Lord, and cries unashamed.

I choke back my tears and council my emotions. I
couldn't have made it in time. There is an investigation to do.

On through the night, and every night afterward, the grim
reaper rides down this ribbon of asphalt. He swings his scythe and
grins eternally.

HAUNTING MEMORIES
Bill Rogers #3578

I am not scared of death. I'm scared of how I'm going to
die, whether it be painful, vicious or violent. I don't consider myself overly brave our heroic. I don't like pain. But I have a belief
in my Good that grants me his peace so that I don't have to fear
death. It was not always so.

I have been to many more fatal collisions that I care to
think about. The death of an adult can create their own haunting
memories. The death of a child can create painful irresolvable
blisters in someone's memory bank. God's mercy and grace can
seem a long way off during a death, especially loved ones.

Remembering the first DPS fatal collision I investigated,
I hear the painful wails of a mother. Her seventeen year old son
was ejected before the vehicle rolled over and crushed him. To
try to ease her pain I assured her that his death was instantaneous,
even though I wasn't sure. My white lie helped.

I was haunted by an incident I had years ago. While stationed in Apache Junction I responded to a five time fatal
collision that had caught fire to everything, including bodies. The
vehicle at fault was a depressed middle-aged man that was intoxicated. He decided to commit suicide by driving into oncoming
traffic. His target that late night contained a son and his wife, with

his mom and a friend. The son had picked up his mother at the airport for a visit during the holidays. A friend accompanied the mother during her trip.

The suicide bomb struck the innocent vehicle and they both burst into flames. I can only hope their demise was quick. After the traffic was controlled, the fire department doused the fire. I relaxed as a cool breeze blew. I was the supervisor at the scene and was assisting the young officer on his first fatal investigation.

It was now time to assist the medical examiner's office with the gruesome job of removing the charred bodies from the wreckage. We experienced the horrendous sights, smells and sounds during the terrible but necessary task. At some point, gallows humor entered into the picture.

This was not out of disrespect, but protection. My own protection against the horror of the whole ordeal. An emergency worker develops a sick sense of humor. Some people never do, they don't last. Mine was well-honed as I used it often. Most of the public doesn't understand this, so you must be careful who's within earshot.

I have always treated the dead with respect and honor as I would want my loved ones to be treated. I did my best to complete the best investigation possible. Drunk or impaired drivers are responsible for most of them. I hate their actions by forgive the person.

J.J.
Dick Lewis #176

This is a story of an acquaintance of mine. It is not an easy story to tell as I only knew this person for five minutes. He never knew me.

When I arrived at the scene, the car was on its top in a sand wash. A crumpled pile of twisted steel. There were personal belongings strewn all about.

Beside the car lying on a pillow and covered with coats was a small baby. He was bruised on the whole left side of his body. There was a cut on the left side of his head. He would move his right arm when I touched it. His right eyelid would open and he would look, but not see, then go back to sleep. He was alive when we put him on the stretcher.

His father was there urging us to please hurry. Then he would say, "Oh I think he is dead. Oh J.J. He don't look good does he?" I had the father taken away and instructed the man who was helping to keep him occupied.

There was only 150 feet to go to the waiting ambulance. Four of us big men carried this small boy very tenderly but swiftly up the incline to the ambulance. There wasn't a second to waste. He had been lying there for over an hour.

We placed him in the ambulance so gently and secured the stretcher for the rush trip to the hospital. I leaned over J.J. to see if he was comfortable.

His grandmother who was to ride in the ambulance with him and look after him was sitting in the front seat. She was crying. She said through her tears, "He is dead isn't he?" It wasn't a question. It wasn't a statement. It was a plea.

I could only shake my head no, and instruct the driver to get him to the hospital in a hurry.
This was the last time I saw J.J. for several hours.

The next time I saw him I took pictures of him. They weren't happy, smiling pictures. These were the pictures of the official nature.

So, you see, this is not a happy story. It's the story of a person I only knew for the last five minutes of his life.

He never spoke. He couldn't have if he had been able. You see, he had never learned how to talk yet. J.J. was only seven months old.

A KINDER, GENTLER SERGEANT
Tim Hughes #793

I was called out to investigate a single 963 on SR 87 near Blue Ridge on top of the Mogollon Rim. I was stationed in Payson and Dick Lewis #176 was my Sergeant. When I got to the scene which was about 55 miles north of Payson, there were several folks there and indeed there was 1 fatality. I called for an ambulance and wrecker and everyone left the scene leaving me alone at the scene. Now to paint a picture, it was pitch dark, there was no traffic, and there I was with a deceased person at the wreck. Now anyone who has been in that position knows how lonely that is and kind of eerie. We had very poor radio reception at the location so I was very alone. After a while, I finally saw a car coming north, the first in quite a while.

As the car approached, I realized it was a semi marked DPS vehicle and who stepped out but Dick Lewis. I was shocked because since we had poor communications, I never heard him check on. I was never so glad to see a friendly face and asked Dick what he was doing up there in the middle of the night. Dick looked at me and said "I thought you might be lonely up here". Now that was amazing to me as I had always been told what a gruff down to business guy Dick was. I learned that night what a feeling and concerned person Dick is and I was so grateful that he showed up.

MY FIRST FATAL
Vern Andrews #264

I was working the evening shift east of Holbrook on I-40 when I got dispatched to an accident on US666 (now US191). It was reported as an injury accident.

When I arrived, I saw that it was a one vehicle roll over. A husband and wife had come upon the accident and were assisting the injured. The wife was tending to two small children and the father. The husband was kneeling by the side of the car tending to an injured woman.

The woman had been partially ejected and suffered severe head injuries that I knew she could not survive.

I called for an ambulance and a wrecker and began my investigation while the good samaritans tended to the accident victims.

The ambulance arrived and transported the woman to the hospital in Holbrook. After my work at the scene, I transported the husband and children to Holbrook.

I had been advised by radio that the woman arrived at the Holbrook hospital DOA. I knew I had been spared the unpleasant task of informing the husband that his wife had died, but just knowing that this family's life had just been shattered made the drive to Holbrook seem a lot longer.

As I drove toward Holbrook, I would look in the rear view mirror and see the husband and children. I will never forget the looks on their faces. I thought, how does a father tell his small children that their mother is dead?

I investigated other fatalities, but this one stuck with me.

SOME THINGS NEVER CHANGE
Jim Phillips #36

There was a time when first aid training was just as important as accident investigation or traffic law training in our academies.

When I came on in the early 50's I was stationed in Gila Bend. My patrol area was from Gila Bend south to the Mexican border, north to 51st Avenue in Phoenix, west to the Yuma County line and east to Stanfield. There were times when you were called out and you came home only to change your uniform and head out again. Overtime? No such thing.

When you were assigned to an accident, you never knew what you would find, no matter what the information you were given. You would roll up on a car that was totally destroyed and there would be minor injuries and then you would roll up on a car that had only minor damage and it would be a fatality.

The cars had no real safety features. No seat belts, no collapsible steering wheel, no air bag, no crush zones and on and on. It was more like a steel cage. And of course, in a rollover the occupants would fly around inside the interior of the car being literally beaten to death, or thrown from the vehicle only to be crushed as the vehicle rolled over them. In a head on crash, occupants would be thrown through the windshield or impaled on the steering wheel.

When we arrived on the scene, our first aid training meant the life or death of the injured. We had no helicopters or paramedics with advanced life saving equipment. We carried a first aid kit which had the basic supplies. Most officers, at their own expense added extra supplies. We had basic supplies to treat whatever we were faced with. We carried small splints to stabilize broken bones and traction splints to treat broken femurs. It was up to us to treat whatever injuries we were faced with or if we were lucky someone with medical training would stop and assist.

Today, the first aid training is more advanced and helicopters with paramedics are available, with some exceptions of course, depending on where the officer is stationed. The cars are better designed with safety features built into the vehicle.

But today, no matter how well trained and equipped the officers are, people still foolishly find ways to kill themselves and others in traffic accidents.
Some things never change.

THE BIG SNOW
John Kennedy #119

When we first moved to Cordes Jct in 1961 we usually had two or three snow storms a winter. Usually enough to make the roads slick and cause a lot of accidents. I remember one day investigating a fatal in the northbound lane, and another in the southbound. Usually the snow went away in a day or two. Then in 1967, about a week before Christmas it started snowing, and snowing. When it finally quit we had four feet of snow on the level. We live about a half mile off the highway on a dirt road. While it was still snowing I tried to drive to our house. I got about a hundred yards in and my car got up on top of the snow and I thought I had broke the drive line, the wheels just spun but no traction. I was in pretty good shape back then, but by the time I got to the house I was plum give out. Everything in that area came to a compete stop for a day or two. Ted Cypert and Dan Leonard lived in the state yard. I made it out to Ted's house and used his vehicle while he was off. One day I got the state blade man to hook onto my car, all we managed to do was pull the bumper off it. I stuck it in the snow and went on. We were about out of propane so I asked a propane truck driver if he would try and get into our place. He said if I would get the states caterpillar tractor and follow him in and out and he'd do it. I had to hook onto him once on the way out. We had a milk cow at our place at that time so we kept everyone in the state yard in milk. About a week or so after the storm quit I was told to go to the top of Copper Canyon (that's the top of the hill before you go down to Camp Verde) and set up a road block, I guess to turn people around. I was sitting on the trunk of my vehicle, wearing a pair of Levi's, my uniform shirt, and a pair of irrigating boots. Not a single vehicle showed up. Finally after I'd been there for some time, I could see a vehicle coming. I thought wow, I'm going to get to talk with someone. The vehicle pulled to a stop and out stepped director Hegarty. I thought oh ———, I think I bought the farm. We had a very nice visit, he complemented me on my uniform. It wasn't too long after that we were issued coveralls.

THE BIG SNOW Of 1967 FROM MY POINT OF VIEW!
Peg Kennedy, wife of John Kennedy #119

(The Kennedys were stationed at Cordes Junction along with Ted and Bobby Cypert and were living in a small house near the state yard. Peg is from a pioneer Arizona family. Peg still lives in that same house. John passed away in December 2019 at the age of 87. He managed to ride his horse and do a little bit of roping on his 87th birthday. He wrote his memories for the Coalition books in the months before he passed away. In rural Arizona even into the 1960's, Arizona was still in the wild, wild west.)

While the patrolmen were busy, we gals had a few things to think about too. Not only did we have a milk cow (guess who was the milker?) but horses, chickens and calves to feed and take care of. Our daughter Lynn was 12 and the two boys were about 9 and 6. They were all used to doing chores, keeping the wood box full, and helping with the animals. Pop (John) was over on the freeway one morning, hitting his siren a little and had his lights on. I slogged through the snow and caught a horse and hopped on bareback (I was much younger then!) and rode him out to the two-lane road. He said, "Tell the kids no school until next year!" The horses pretty much had pretty free rein to roam as they could go over by the state fence by the highway yard. We rode them over there and took their bridles off so they could roam.

One of the guys was able to get to the barn and milk the cow so we had milk for all of us. At that point we moved in with Ted and Bobby. There were no phones then and when our daughter was in the 7th grade, we got an 8-party phone line. Up until then, we had to go to the Junction, turned off the highway and followed the power line to the 3rd pole, which had a pay phone attached to it so we could call out.

Meanwhile, Bobby and I were trying to take care of the kids, feed the guys whenever they came in at all times of the day and night, warm up the coffee, as there were no restaurants at the Junction then, and then try to keep the whole tribe ready for just about anything. The state houses were not very big and Bobby and Ted had 2 girls, so it was tricky getting around on the floor.

COURTEOUS VIGILANCE
Paul Palmer #342

I remember well the snow storm that John Kennedy talked about. I was dispatching in Holbrook at the time.

There were so many different scenarios going on at the same time, it was hard to keep track of everything.

Lt Don Naval was on his way from Phoenix to Holbrook and made it to about 12 miles south of Holbrook on SR77 when the snow became so deep he could go no further. Several other cars were also stranded at that location and a snow cat took food and coffee to the people stranded there. Patrolman Jim Wilson was also stranded on SR77. The snowplows that DOT had in Holbrook were unable to reach them. Springerville DOT had just purchased a snowblower snow plow and it was sent to clear the road so the stranded people could reach Holbrook.

Early in the storm, radio technician Ralph Munday was out at the radio site at Roberts Ranch near Sanders. KGJ767 was not working and Ralph had gone out to make repairs. After making repairs Ralph found that it had snowed so much while he was working that it was now impossible for him to drive out. It took several hours for equipment to get to him and get him back to Sanders.

A large group of cars was stranded north of Holbrook on SR77. Once again the department's snowcat took coffee and food to the people stranded. The snowcat actually drive over top of the right of way fence which was buried under the snow. Someone saw a road grader parked off the highway and fired it up and plowed a road up to the stranded people. They were then able to follow the grader into Holbrook.

I-40 was completely closed down across the state due to the deep snow. Motels in Holbrook were full and they were charging people to sleep on cots or in sleeping bags in the lobby. The stores were running low on food. Tire chains if you could find them went from $15.00 to $50.00.

Patrolmen from around the state were sent up north to assist. Patrolman Bill Algeri who was stationed in Yuma told me that he had been sitting beside the highway and it was snowing so hard, it was a total whiteout. He said the snow was swirling in every direction and that he got vertigo and didn't know which side was up. He told me that was the most frightened he had ever been.

The city's snowplow cleared the main street by plowing the snow so that there was a pile of snow between the east and westbound lanes with cutouts in the snow for entry into businesses. Snow was also plowed into empty parking lots. After getting tired of hearing, "Whatcha gonna do with all this snow?" He would tell people that he was going to plow it all into a parking lot and burn it. You have to have a sense of humor!

The patrol office was on the east end of Holbrook right on US66 and a roadblock was set up directly across from the patrol office. As John mentioned, a uniform comprised of what would keep you warm, usually Levi's and a uniform shirt and any kind of warm jacket you could find. I wish I had taken photos of some of the combinations the guys wore. Across the highway from the patrol office was a truck stop and the Mesa Cafe.

The large parking lot was packed with stranded motorists and semi trucks were lined up for what seemed forever. There was one semi loaded with fresh flowers and a hearse with a body headed for a funeral. People were upset and angry about being stranded. One day I walked over to the roadblock with Capt. Don Naval to shoot the breeze with the patrolmen manning the roadblock. We were standing around talking when this belligerent truck driver was loudly cussing the Highway Patrol and state of Arizona as a whole. He then began saying that the Arizona Highways Magazine didn't say anything about Arizona not being able to keep roads open etc. Capt. Naval walked over to him and talked to him in a very quiet voice and then turned around and walked back over the patrol office. The truck driver became very quiet and then came over to us and said, "I believe your captain just told me to shove that Arizona Highways Magazine up my $^%$" Nothing more was heard from the guy. COURTEOUS VIGILANCE!

After the storm eased up and the streets became passable, I was able to take the snow chains off my car, but the driveway up to my apartment was still deep in snow. There was a driveway from the street to the alley in front of the apartments with just enough room to park your car in front of your apartment. Neither the city nor the apartment manager would clear the driveway. I talked to Carlton Hill who had a Jeep wagon and he came over and used his Jeep to push snow enough so that I could now park in front of my apartment.

Holbrook received 3 1/2 feet of snow and everyone who experienced this storm event complained and said how bad it was. Being from Gila Bend, I thought it was kind of neat.

SNOWED IN
Rich Richardson #188

The National Weather Service reported that the December 1967 snow storm was Arizona's most notable snow storm of the 20th Century.

The record snow storms of December 1967, reminds me of a story that might interest a few readers. I was stationed in District 3, Holbrook and assigned to the Show Low area along with several other patrolmen. Ray Dahm was my sergeant at the time. The National Weather Service issued a snow storm warning on December 7 indicating a standard snow storm was expected to hit Arizona's high country during the second week of December. What the weather service didn't know was there would be more than one storm and they would create more snow than expected. The Mogollon Rim Country had one of its worst series of storms ever recorded.

My residence was located at the state yard at Honda (Indian Pine), 18 miles south of Show Low.

I was on regular patrol duty during Monday, December 11, 1967. The 18 miles of state highway between Show Low and Honda (Indian Pine) were dry and traffic was light. I made 8 contacts during that shift. The next day Sergeant Dahm and I travelled to Phoenix in my assigned patrol vehicle and switched to my new issued patrol car. The weather was cloudy and the roads were dry. Later that afternoon, we headed back to the White Mountains. In the higher pine treed forested regions we encountered hazardous snow driving conditions, with about 6" falling at the time. This was the start of many days of snow that would reach high snow levels in the White Mountains. What we didn't know at the time was how much snow would fall over the next 8 days. We later discovered there were actually two different major the storms.

I patrolled on Wednesday December 13th and recorded another 6" of snow falling. Thursday and Friday were my assigned days off. Other officers were on duty at the time. I did record snow fall at my residence (Honda) on Thursday at 10", then on Friday another 14". On Saturday December 16th, the roads were cleared enough so I could get back on the highway. I didn't make any traffic stops due to the dangerous road and weather conditions. I did investigate a Code 962 (Injury crash) during a 15" snow fall on this day. I can recall driving for two hours before I saw a car on the road. Traffic was at a near standstill.

Saturday, I went outside my residence to discover that my patrol car was mostly covered with drifting snow. The snow drift depth was believed to be a total of 39 inches of wet snow. The Highway Department had ceased to work the highways and my patrol car was snowed in. I notified Holbrook dispatch about the situation and would return to regular patrol duty once my vehicle had a clear path to the main highway. Sunday 6" of snow fell, then Monday another 10" fell. My patrol vehicle was now completely covered with snow.

The highway department had called for help in blading the highways that were closed. This included every road in my area. What I learned soon was that help had arrived. The loggers working timber high in the mountains brought their heavy caterpillar tractors with 16 foot wide blades to aid in clearing the highways during Sunday and Monday. I later heard that a caterpillar did run over a Volkswagen beetle that was parked at the U S Post Office building in Lakeside. According to another patrol officer, the heavy equipment driver said that he didn't see the little snow covered car until after running over it. There was no occupant in the damaged vehicle.

By Tuesday afternoon my patrol car had a clear path to patrol the highway. I patrolled the roads as best I could under extremely dangerous conditions. I made no traffic stops that could endanger the public. An additional 10" of snow fell during my shift. Traffic was very, very light during these bad road conditions. Wednesday I patrolled the same as the day before. There was an additional 2" of snow and one minor traffic crash to investigate. A motorist's car struck a highway department snow plow.

The snow levels varied in the area, depending on the snow fall on the terrain mentioned, above sea level elevation.. Show Low is about 6345', Pinetop 6909', Honda 7175', and Flagstaff 6909'. A total of about 85" of wet snow fell in Flagstaff and Pinetop over the period of two major snow storms. The wet snow of these two storms resulted in many roofs collapsing. In Pinetop, a large grocery store (Wilbur's Market) collapsed. At my residence at Honda, I was on top my roof twice, and shoveled about 4' off the roof and then another 3' from the roof a couple days later. If I hadn't have done that, my roof would have collapsed like so many other roofs did in the mountains. This was an experience that I will never forget. Other patrol personnel in the Mogollon Rim storm region will also attest to such an experience as, "I never want to see something like that again!"

The remainder of the month, I investigated 6 traffic crashes (all weather related) and stopped very few vehicles because of continued hazardous road conditions.

THE BIG 67 SNOW
Alex Carrillo #313

The big snow of 1967 started around the 16th of December and I was on a day off. I was living in an apartment that was accessed from the alley behind the Desert Inn on US66. It was early evening and I had parked my Camp trailer next to the staircase to my apartment and next to that was my 1965 Plymouth patrol vehicle. There was a window in the stair case that allowed me to see the roof of the camper so I was able to use a push broom and keep the weight off the roof of the camper.

At about 5 am, I received a call from Holbrook Radio and was told there were reports of multiple accidents east of Holbrook. They let me know they had an ADOT snowplow enroute to clear the alley so I could get my vehicle out. I got into uniform and went down to warm up my vehicle and was surprised by the snow heap it was under. There was at least 4 feet of snow on top and the level in the alley was a good 3 plus feet. I got a shovel and started to dig my way in. The snow plow arrived and he plowed the alley and came back to pull my car out. I had removed enough snow to reach the left side of the car and I was able to hook a chain onto the frame. The car was yanked out enough for me to get in and steer. After some time, I was able to get out of the alley and head east.

Those who know the Holbrook Area know there is a fairly steep incline you have to climb to go east. Being from Tucson and having limited experience on snow and ice, I felt pretty lucky that my fifth run got me over the top with no damage, especially since I had a couple of spins that left me headed back into town

I got just east of the Holbrook office and was to meet the ADOT snowplow driver. I followed the snowplow east and soon picked up a driver that had run off the road. A tow truck had not been able to get to him. There was no way to make a u-turn as the snow level was about 4 ft in the medium. The snow plow driver advised me we would go to SR 77 and head back to Holbrook. By the time we got to SR77, we had pushed three vehicles off the road and picked up four more passengers and had two vehicles following us.

We got to the office and I was advised that Mr. Slade from Western States Telephone had a 4-wheel drive Chevrolet Suburban I could use. I picked up the Suburban and went to the ADOT radio shop where they temporarily installed a radio and a light bar. I then headed east and pushed numerous vehicles off the road and picked up the stranded passengers. We had been notified that I-40 had been closed in New Mexico and the conditions were such that no one would be headed east for some time. When the suburban was full, I made a U-turn in the east bound lane and took the passengers to Holbrook. At about 9pm I made it to the Sun Valley Exit and was able to get back to Holbrook. I left the suburban and got my patrol vehicle and headed home. I was thoroughly drenched

and wasn't sure how I would dry out my boots. Luckily, Felix Alcorn had brought over a pair of waterproof boots and with a little toe stuffing I was able to make them work.

The next day we were assigned 12 hour shifts on the road-block just east of the office and I got the 6am to 6pm shift. We were told to wear what kept us warm. I wore long johns, two pairs of Levi's, a uniform shirt a Patrol short jacket, an issued winter cap with fur ear warmers and a Heavy Army over coat. There were a lot of truckers very upset that we had closed the road and threatened to run the road block. There were also truckers who asked if there was a food bank as the eggs, vegetables or fruit they were hauling would not be any good if they froze. All their food was donated to various churches and civic organization.

There were many generous and caring residents of Holbrook who helped stranded motorists and provided them shelter for the week we were a closed down. There were also many who took advantage of the stranded and were charging $10.00 for a sleeping bag space.

During this time there were reports of stranded motorist on SR 77 and the snowcat was used to try and assist those motorists. I believe that Patrolman Pete Perkins was one patrolman who went in the snow cat. All communications was lost for about two or three days, they were able to assist a number of motorists.

One day we were surprised by Patrolman Emory Collins who was stationed at the Painted Desert. He had borrowed a 4-wheel drive grader and had come to Holbrook to get supplies.

Lt Naval had been enroute from Phoenix to Holbrook and had traveled from Payson to Snowflake and then north towards Holbrook. He ran into Patrolman Jim Wilson who was with a group of motorists that had been stopped by a heavy snow drift, quite a few feet high. The Highway Department had purchased a new snow blower for the Show Low area and was sent to assist. It got there and promptly broke down. The snow cat was then sent out to bring in some of the stranded motorist. Over the radio was heard a sergeant who advised Holbrook radio to contact the snow-cat and make sure Lt Naval was on the first trip back. An angry Lt Naval quickly replied that he would be on the last trip as there were women and children to be evacuated first. On of the first things Lt Naval did upon his return was to invite the sergeant into his office. We can only guess as to the meeting, but I would be willing to bet it involved a big chewing out.

Eventually the highway was to be reopened and I was assigned to check out the road conditions west to Winslow. I headed west at daybreak and found the road was very icy and there were many areas with black ice. I was traveling quite slowly arriving in Winslow at about 4pm. My return trip took a little less time as the highway crews were out plowing and putting down cinders.

SNOW, SNOW AND MORE SNOW
J.R. Ham #142

Greenlee County is narrow, with the upper two-thirds being mostly high mountains and forest. The lower one-third holds the towns of Duncan, Clifton, and Morenci, a mining town owned and operated by Phelps Dodge Copper Corporation, at the time. U.S. Highway 70 runs east and west through Duncan. Arizona Highway 75 goes north out of Duncan to the 3-Way Junction. Arizona Highway 78 goes from the 3-Way to the New Mexico state line. U.S. Highway 666 (now 191) goes north and south meeting 75 and 78 at the 3-Way and continuing through Clifton to the north county line. Most of the population and vehicle traffic is in the bottom one-third of the county.

On December 21, 1967 the general forecast was for the possibility of snow. I got out of bed and checked for snow, but there was none. When I got out of the shower and checked again, it had started snowing hard. There were 2-3 inches already on the ground. While my wife, Parthenia, prepared my breakfast, I was able to get snow tires on my vehicle. By the time I finished breakfast and checked on the air at 6:00 a.m., 3-5 inches had fallen. Little did I know what was coming!

Locally, Arizona Department of Transportation (ADOT) had two or three snowplows, Greenlee County had two, and Clifton had none. Phelps Dodge (PD) Mine had four snowplows to keep the roads and streets open in Old Morenci, Stargo, and Plantsite. PD began plowing those streets at 7:00 a.m. The ADOT equipment and the county plows started working about 8:00 a.m. All of the snowplows were working hard, but could not keep up.

Heavy, thick snow was coming down fast. That first day, I didn't get home until 8:00 p.m.

ADOT had been notified of the expected big snow. They called the Stray Horse Highway Camp and told them to evacuate to Clifton and to pick up everyone and their equipment at Grey's Peak Highway Camp on the way. Lastly, they told them to bring the snowblower down. That decision saved us lots of time when the snow finally stopped.

The next few days, I went to work as the snow continued to fall. The third day, the roof of Clifton's JCPenney store caved in from the weight of the snow. Also on the third day, I lost all communication with the Globe dispatchers. All I had was my Sheriff's radio. Our phones could only communicate within Greenlee County.

By the fourth or fifth day of continuous snow, highways everywhere were becoming blocked. US 70 from Safford to Duncan was closed because the Safford area AzDOT did not have more than two plows. US 666 (now 191) was blocked from Safford to Clifton. State Highway 78 was blocked going toward New Mexico. US 666 was blocked from Clifton to Alpine with 10 to 15 feet of snow. US 666 from Clifton to the 3-Way intersection, and from the 3-Way to Duncan was being plowed by AzDOT. The highway from Clifton to Duncan was open or closed from time to time depending on how hard it was snowing. Because many of the PD mine workers lived outside of the Morenci/Clifton area, the local workers were doing double and triple shifts until the mine shut down on Christmas Day.

On one run south to check the highway, going up Smelter Hill out of Clifton, I saw six cars coming down the hill. There was only one lane open, so I pulled off into the snowbank to let them go by. Of course, when I tried to pull onto the road, I was stuck. After 20 minutes of digging, I was on my way again.

The snow stopped falling on December 26th. Sheriff Forest Wilkerson was very worried about the ranchers in the Blue River Area. He called me on the radio and asked me to go by the PD headquarters to ask them to clear the snow off the Morenci High School football field. I found out later that he had managed to get three military helicopters from Phoenix that were willing to come up for a Search and Rescue effort in the high country of Northern Greenlee County. The helicopters were being ferried to the coast to be shipped to Vietnam. There was aircraft fuel available because the mining company had been using a helicopter to transport a survey crew to the Reservation for a new power line to the Black River Pump Station. Fuel was also available at the Safford Airport. The following day, they arrived. The pilots were great and had a ball flying the area. They flew up to a cabin where a 70 year old cowboy worked. While the helicopter hovered above the ground, Sheriff Wilkerson dropped out of the chopper and disappeared into the snow, all 6' 4" of him. He broke out of the snow onto the path that the ranch hand had cleared to the corrals. The cowboy was ok, but the Sheriff told him he was being evacuated by helicopter. They gave the horses extra feed, climbed up on a building to board the chopper, and flew to Morenci where the cowboy was put up in the motel. For three days, they made many trips, but didn't find anyone else in need of help. On the fourth day, the Sheriff released them to continue on to their original destination. The night before they returned to Phoenix, Sheriff Wilkerson, four deputies, and I treated the six pilots to a steak dinner at the Morenci Motel.

I investigated no accidents during the storm, but the Highway Department and I pulled many cars out of the snowbanks. Fortunately for the community, the PD Mercantile was well stocked because of Christmas. My neighbors on Cedar Street would call the store with orders for groceries and supplies. On my way home, I picked up these orders, signed the charge tickets, and delivered them when I got home.

As the snowfall slowed, all the snowplows continued working to clear the roads. Highway foreman McQuin and I decided to see how far south we could drive on 666. We left the 3-Way junction and had to turn around at the top El Puente Hill after only 2 miles. The foreman decided he would see about getting the snowblower operating. I took an hour break from patrolling to clear the 3 feet of snow off my roof. Sgt. Bill Chewning and Patrolman Red Hull borrowed the Radio Technician's 4-wheel-drive vehicle to try to get from Safford to Duncan on Highway 70. They told me they had to break through 15 ft. snowdrifts.

Gradually, the roads in Morenci and Stargo were cleared. Greenlee County continued to clear the county roads. Federal and State highways were slowly opened. The Highway Department had to battle 15-18 ft. of icy snow from the Mogollon Rim to Alpine. US 666, to Alpine was finally opened in the middle of February, 1968.

I ALMOST MISSED MY WEDDING
Ric Miller #744

I was a student at Northern Arizona University in Flagstaff and working at Flag. PD during the BIG Snow. It was early December 1967 when the snow started in Flag. I was working a graveyard shift as a dispatcher. I remember it was about 2430 hrs. when I noticed it had starting to snow. We monitored the street department by radio and they immediately started plowing. By dawn they were falling behind and could not continue to plow residential streets. Within hours they were plowing only the main streets from Santa Fe Rd. to the hospital in downtown and 4th Ave. in East Flag. The roads leading out of and into Flag began closing and traffic began backing up. At this time, I-40 had not bypassed Flagstaff, and Route 66 was the only highway through town. The PD officers had to notify drivers in the road blocks to shut off motors due excessive exhaust. During the first day the PD arranged with a 4WD club to assist with patrols and response to emergency calls. The 4WD had CB radios and could maintain contact with the station.

ADOT was overwhelmed and could not keep up with highways and was barely able to keep Santa Fe Rd. plowed. The only access to Flag was by railroad. Supplies were loaded on flat cars in Ash Fork and bought in on the rails.

Schools in town closed and businesses tried to stay open. The problem was there was no way to get around. A lot of able bodied guys made a lot of money shoveling snow off roofs and driveways NAU closed classes, but said classes would reopen the next day. This continued every day for several days. Finally, there was a break in the storm and ADOT announced they had opened one lane on I-17 south. Within minutes the NAU campus was deserted. NAU decided to start the holiday break early, probably because there was no one left to attend class. It began to snow again and things continued to get worse. My car was in the dorm parking lot covered in snow. I could see about 6" of the radio antenna. There was no way I was going to be able to get out. Classes reopened in early January, 1968 for the end of the fall semester. There was supposed to be final exams and then a semester break, but they cancelled the break to make up for the long holiday vacation. Final exams were rescheduled for the last week of January, the same time my wedding was scheduled. That caused more problems for me. My wedding was scheduled for the 28th of January with a rehearsal the 27th. My last exam was late on the 27th. I made it to Phoenix just in time. We have been married for 54 years.

By the end of the storm, 103 inches of snow had fallen.

SNOWBOUND
Lyn Diehl - Wife of Jerry Diehl #201

During the big snow in 1967 in Flagstaff, Jerry got off work and we lived on the US naval observatory road and he was barely able to make it up the hill and into our driveway. He was sick as a dog and went right to bed. I called the doctor the next morning and he diagnosed Jerry with pneumonia and told me what I could do because we couldn't get him out and couldn't get an ambulance in so I just kept giving him fluids and giving him aspirin to reduce the temperature. The doctor called us twice a day and finally after about five days he was able to get up and move around a little bit by himself.

I was listening to the radio and they said that the roof on the Red Cross building had collapsed and as I was looking down the hallway of the trailer I realize the hallway walls were bowing in towards each other so I got the ladder and shoveled off the roof. It looked like about four or 5 feet of snow off the top of the trailer. I didn't know 10 x 50' was so long but it sure seemed like it. When I got back in the house though the walls were now straight so I felt that we were OK for a while. After 10 days of being snowed in the Patrol sent in a snow cat and they brought it to the office. We got a patrol car and we picked up the paycheck at the post office and went shopping for groceries because at that point we were down to bread and jelly. Believe me every year after that by September I had a fully stocked freezer and fully stocked pantry. Two days later the state sent in a D8 cat, front loader and dump trucks to dig out the road. Because we had to haul our own water I was melting snow to flush the toilet, wash clothes in the kitchen sink and used it for anything else that we didn't eat or drink.

SOCKS
Jim Gentner #287

I was stationed in Flagstaff during the big storm in 1967. The thoughts that come to mind were that the officers did not have adequate cold weather coats. With Flagstaff being isolated and working a minimum of 12 hour shifts out in the elements the District Lieutenant gave all of us permission to wear whatever we had that could keep us warm. I wore my old Air Force winter parka, kept the hood up and the snow from going down my neck. I was working SR79, now I-17, when the brass from Phoenix came up after the roads were finally open. They were surprised to see my Air Force coat with my uniform. "They later agreed it was OK".

Due to the constant traffic tie-ups on I-17 in the winter, there was no place to take a coffee or lunch break south of Flagstaff. Fortunately a fellow officer in Flagstaff was also a member of the National Guard and gave me a case of C Rations which I kept in the trunk of the patrol car. During the many weekend snow storm traffic jams which took into the wee hours of the morning to clear up due to the number of abandoned vehicles left on the highway from people running out of gas while in the tragic jam and hitching a ride with others when the road was cleared. These all took time with paperwork required making tow truck requests and the requisite inventory reports. A can of C Rations placed on the manifold of my idling patrol car would warm up in 14 minutes. Seemed like a life saver at the time.

During the snow storm it was snowing so hard that the highway department closed all the roads, putting all of their snow plows on I-17 to try and get the Christmas holiday traffic south and out of the snow country. This was unsuccessful and I was sent to make one final pass south on I-17 to make sure there were no stranded motorists then the road would be closed. I had to go as far south as Stoneman Lake Interchange before I could turn around and try and return to Flagstaff. It was snowing so hard that it became a whiteout. The roads had not been plowed because it was now closed. I had to drive at 40 mph to be able to move the snow and keep traction. All I could see was a light gray outline of the tree line on both sides of the road. Staying in the middle, I made progress until I reached Munds Park where the surrounding area opened up without the close trees. I was now in a total white-out and ended up driving into the median with the patrol car sinking into the snow. All I could see was about one inch of light at the top of the driver's side window. I had to turn the patrol car off to avoid asphyxiation. I called the situation in to dispatch and giving my estimated location I waited for help. It became very cold by the time a snow plow found me but due to the accumulation of snow the one snow could not pull my patrol car out. A second plow arrived and hooked to the first plow and they were able to pull me out. I then continued the adventure getting back to Flagstaff where I-17 was then closed.

With US66 and SR79 (I-17) closed, all of the Christmas holiday traffic was isolated in Flagstaff. Hotels were full so the National Guard Armory and the school gyms were used to house the stranded motorists.

I bought a pair of electric socks to keep warm during the time spent standing on the snow pack directing traffic and digging motorists out of snow banks. The electric socks used "D" cell batteries, the same as used in the issued flashlights. As an expendable supply item I kept warm in the winter but had to deal with "socks" as my new nickname.

WHATEVER IT TAKES
Doug Kluender #363

During the Big Storm of '67 I was finally on my own and working U.S. 60 out of Globe. When the storm hit the Highway Department would close the road around 1600 hours when the black ice started forming. They closed the road from the Show Low end at the same time. Our standing orders were to drive the road and meet the Show Low officer to make sure one was stranded.

One particularly stormy afternoon I started north around 1600 hours? About 20 miles out town I began encountering vehicles stuck in the snow. I was able to help some of them get moving and had to call tow trucks for others. The Highway Department crews were spreading cinders on the uphill sections to help keep traffic moving.

After meeting the Show Low officer at the Flying V maintenance yard I started back toward Globe. I encountered a Highway Department truck at Timber Camp and learned that their cinder spreader had broken down. He had a full load of cinders but no way to get them where needed. Together we continued south and found a few cars having trouble gaining traction. Semi's were stopped on the road at steepest grades.

I parked my patrol car and stashed my weapon in the trunk. Armed with a shovel I climbed up into the bed of the Highway Department truck. We systematically got in front of the Semi's and shoveled cinders under their wheels to get them moving. I lost track of the number of trucks and cars we rescued this way. It took several hours but we cleared the roadway with nobody stranded that night.

I retrieved my patrol car and headed home for 10-7. The Highway Department repaired the cinder spreader before my next shift and I was able to retire the shovel.

A FRIEND NEEDS HELP
Colin Peabody #481

One cold snowy winter night I picked up radio traffic about Ben Smith #661 who was working way out east of Holbrook , nearly to the NM State Line. Ben apparently had attempted to cross the snowy median of I-40 and gotten stuck. He called for a tow truck to come and pull him out. This wasn't something you wanted to do as the State of Arizona was reluctant to pay towing fees on one of their vehicles. The other officers in my squad heard about this and just said that is a No-No and that they would never call in on that unless there was no other way out.

Well, as luck would have it a couple of nights later, about 8:30 or so, I found myself working in the snow and I crossed the median a few miles west of Winslow where I had safely crossed a couple of times earlier that evening and yes, I got my patrol car stuck in the snowy median. With the event involving Ben Smith still fresh in my mind and not wanting to be a laughing stock among my fellow squad members, I was perplexed. What can I do to get out of this situation? Then the idea hit me like a bolt of lightning.

"481 Flagstaff "…"Go ahead 481" "Can you call 231(Ptlm George McGuire) at his 10-42 and advise him a friend of his is stuck in the snow off the highway and needs him to bring his 4WD Dodge Power Wagon and a chain out to milepost 247 and pull him out, please?" "10-4, 481" "Flagstaff, 481, we are 10-98 with 231, he will be out in a few minutes." "10-4 Flagstaff, thanks."

About 25 minutes later, George shows up in that beast Power Wagon and I get out of my warm patrol car to greet him. He is a bundled up and looking around and says, "So where is this friend of mine who needs to be pulled out of the snow?" "Uhh, that would be me George." "You mean to tell me you called me out of my nice warm house at nearly my bedtime, to come out here and pull your dumb butt out of the median? Why didn't you call a damn tow truck?" "Well, I didn't want you to laugh at me and ridicule me like you did when you heard Ben got stuck in the snow a couple of nights ago." Further conversation became un-printable, but George did pull me out of the median with the Power Wagon and went back home to his nice warm bed. Maybe I was getting back at him for all the times we had to dig that damn Power Wagon out of the gooey, black mud when we went fishing at Long Lake or Kinnikinick down on the rim. We are still very good friends over 50 years later, honest!

WHO IS STUCK IN THE MEDIAN?
Dennis McNulty #1959

In 1984 while still in Winslow, I transferred into CVSS for truck enforcement & Haz Mat. At that time we all drove Chevy Suburbans. One night Flag opcom called me at home to tell me that #231(George McGuire) wanted to call me out and to 45 him east of North Park drive on I-40. It had rained hard all day and I guess George forgot that wet caliche clay was a trap waiting to happen. As soon as I cleared on the radio, George got me car to car and said I needed to pull him out of the median where he was frame deep in the mud. Took a little while but I was able to drag him out. He definitely needed a car wash from that one. He asked me to kinda keep it all on the down low. I think he didn't want Bob Varner yucking it up on him.

CATTLE GUARD THIEVES
Frank Glenn #468

This one is on me, my first year working so I was wet behind the ears. While stationed in Williams I was working west of Ashfork, the road at that point was divided but not a freeway with controlled access. There was an old road south of that road that had been abandoned and a bridge. I had not been on that road because it had no access. There was an interchange with on and off ramps that went nowhere about four miles west of Ashfork. Just before dark I was parked on the eastbound on ramp eating my dinner in the dark. A while later I saw a pickup enter through the fence where they were building a cattle guard. Pretty soon I heard clinking and thought, what is going on, so I aimed my spot light where I thought the noise was coming from. I was outside my car when I powered up the spotlight and there were two guys frozen like a deer being spotlighted. In just a few seconds they took off down the old road. I smoked off the off ramp and missed the hole in the fence, got turned around and was running about 90 MPH so when I came to the bridge, I could not see the road and thought it had been washed out then thought this is really going to hurt. Well, the road had just sunk down about a few inches is why I didn't see it. Quite a ride crossing the bridge! The truck had stopped a short distance after crossing the bridge, so there stood my two culprits outside the truck. I determined they were stealing the parts of the cattle guard so I told them to follow me and took them to the jail in Ashfork. It was at this time I could see they were drunk. I cannot arrest the driver due to the fact I had told him to drive so I just fixed them up with a room in the cross-bar hotel. Nothing happened to them as the foreman just fired them and that was the end of that.

SUPERINTENDENT HATHAWAY
Richard Richardson #188

The first time I met Superintendent Greg O. Hathaway #901, was when he greeted our cadet Class #3 on opening day at the Training Academy in Phoenix, February 15, 1962. I didn't know anything about him at the time, but heard a lot about him in the weeks to come and eventually over the years while he was the head of the AHP. He had a very stern look about him, with those piercing eyes. He definitely was the man in charge and everyone knew it.

The second time I met him was about halfway through the 16-week training program. One afternoon the class was on a break. I happened to be walking alone down the main hallway of the training building that leads to several offices. I was familiar with the office of Jean Ruskas AHP ID # 181 (next door to the classroom). She was one of the people that helped the instructors with paperwork concerning the classes we cadets attended. We called her 'Mama Bear'. She knew that and didn't mind. A nicer lady, well there wasn't anyone like her.

The hallway was dimly lit and I noticed some plaques hanging on the wall. They were plaques honoring the first two official graduating classes of the new men that were part of the 73 cadets making up the three classes 1961-1962. As I mentioned earlier, my class was the third. Eventually our plaque and more plaques would be hanging on the same wall in the years to come.

I really wasn't paying attention around me, but someone quietly walked up behind me. You know when you sense something behind you and you realized that you aren't alone. I turned and it was Greg Hathaway. I had already heard a few stories in class about him and that he wasn't one to fool around. He was feared by many of the old timers working with the patrol. One of the things was mentioned about him, was an officer didn't want to get into trouble and be standing knee deep in the carpet in his office.

I was almost speechless, but when he spoke, I smiled and wasn't sure if I should salute or shake his hand. He reached out and then I did shake his hand. I relaxed. He wasn't such a tiger that I heard about. We chatted for several minutes. He was interested in how I was doing in class and what I thought of the instructors. I was honest and told him that all of the instructors are very professional and our class was learning a great deal of information. I didn't feel intimidated during our conversation. I believe that he wanted to hear a cadet speak freely and know my thoughts. I realized it was time to head back to the classroom and said goodbye.

I knew one thing for sure and that is I wouldn't want to get on the bad side of him.

SUPT. HATHAWAY ACCEPTING KEYS TO 1960
STUDEBAKER LARK PATROL CAR

AHP 59 OLDSMOBILE, CHP 59 DODGE PATROL CARS AT
ACCIDENT NEAR AZ/CAL BORDER

RETIRED OFFICER JOHN KENNEDY PINNING THE USBP
BADGE ON HIS GRANDSON ORAN KENNEDY

DICK LEWIS SHOOTING IN SALT
RIVER CANYON 1968

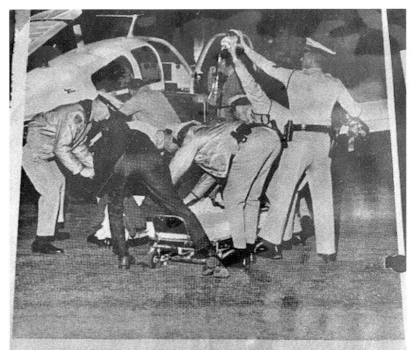

Patrolman Injured

AIR AMBULANCE -- Arizona Highway Patrolmen aid in transfering patrolman Donald F. Hill to an airplane for a flight to Phoenix. Hill was injured Saturday night when his car struck a horse on U.S. 164 seven miles west of Tuba City. The patrolman suffered severe head injuries and is listed in fair condition this morning at Barrow's Institute at St. Joseph's Hospital. Hill's injuries were believed to be severe enough to cause the loss of an eye, but the highway patrol reports doctors believe they can save the eye although it will be sometime before the results of treatment will be known. Hill, 33, was on patrol duty in the Tuba City area when the accident occured. Navajo Police took Hill to the Tuba City hospital for treatment after the accident from where he was transferred to the Flagstaff Community Hospital before being flown to Phoenix.

(SUNfoto)

DON HILL RESCUE AND AIR AMBULANCE AFTER HIS
ACCIDENT NEAR TUBA CITY 1968

SALT RIVER RESCUE RANGER 27 PILOTED BY DPS
OFFICER TOM ARMSTRONG APPEARS IN BACK-
GROUND CLARENCE FORBEY ON THE SKIDS OF SKY 12
PILOTED BY JERRY FOSTER IN 1979

PATROLMAN MIKE STEPHENS IN HIS 66 CHEVY IN THE
SNOW DEC. 1967

BOB VARNER MEMORIAL WITH OFFICERS HE WORKED
WITH

FIRST DPS SWAT TEAM- TYSON MANHUNT 1978

STATE PRISON RIOT 1973

1931 MODEL A FORD PATROL CAR, AHP/AMES
HELICOPTER/HORSE ABOUT 1970

1940s SALOME BILLBOARD "THAT'LL
BE $100"

ARIZONA RANGERS IN MORENCI DURING COPPER STRIKE
1903

DPS OFFICERS IN AJO COPPER STRIKE 1983

PTLMN BOB VARNER GETS A RAMBLER TO REPLACE
HIS 72 MERCURY

PAUL PALMER WITH JIM PHILLIPS' FAMOUS FORD
THUNDERBIRD

JIM PHILLIPS WITH GOVERNOR PAUL FANNIN AND
CADILLAC WITH AZ # 1 PLATE

MEXICAN BORDER LIAISON GROUP
AZDPS/CHP/MEXICAN FEDERAL POLICE

AIR FORCE ONE AND DPS MOTORS SECURITY DETAIL
ABOUT 1995

DPS FIRST HOSTAGE NEGOTIATION UNIT LATE 1970s

DPS PIG BOWL FOOTBALL TEAM 1979

Merry Christmas and a Safe New Year

Arizona Highway Patrol

1958 AHP CHRISTMAS CARD WITH 1958 FORD PATROL CAR

NATIONAL AWARD WINNING PSA WITH DPS AND USMC
AIR STATION YUMA

FIRST HONORARY DPS OFFICER AND MAKE-A-WISH
CHILD, CHRIS GRECIUS WITH RON COX AND TOMMY
AUSTIN

LOUIE COCHRAN MEMORIAL CROSS, 1ST LINE OF DUTY
DEATH FOR AHP 1958

A MORNING WAKE UP
Colin Peabody #481

When I was stationed in Winslow, I was living alone in a two bedroom house and had a young, single patrolman renting a room from me. Being single, he had a few friends of the female type. As the weather got colder up north, this patrolman had trouble getting his car started in the mornings. He would stomp the gas pedal several times in an effort to get the car started, but wound up flooding the engine with gas and she wouldn't start. I would go out, give it a couple of minutes and then gently hold the gas pedal down to close the choke and she would fire right up. After several mornings of this, I decided to leave him a note in his patrol car from his patrol car. Not being a complete idiot, he finally caught on.

"Dear Dudley Dummass, "

"I don't think you know how to turn me on in the morning."

"I'm not just one of your other girls, you know. Just a light touch all the way down there is enough. You know where I mean.....my Go!!! Pedal."

"That other nice patrolman has that "special touch."
"Sigh!"

"I get very tired of you playing with those other girls every night and all I get are the leftovers in the morning.
Love and Leftovers, C-527".

I KNOW YOU
Dick Lewis #176

I was working 5 to 2 between Globe-Miami. The mine shift had changed and most of the workers had gone home.

The weather was good and it was a pleasant night. We had our windows down and I was enjoying the night air.

An older Lincoln passed by going east from Copper Hills at the tracks. It had a busted tail light and was showing very white to the rear. There was no speed involved and I jumped on this terrible violation very gently going east at about the Justa West Café.

I leisurely got out of my car and talking to myself out loud said "Have I stopped this car before?" As I walked up to the driver I repeated the question, "Have I stopped you before?

He said very gruffly, "No, you haven't stopped me before. I know you patrolmen, and none of you are worth a damn except for old Bill Lewis!" I replied, "You mean Dick Lewis?" He said, "Yes, that's him." I said, "That's me." He replied, "Oh, hi Dick. I didn't recognize you there in the dark." His mouth had dropped open wide enough to bang on the window sill.

The truth is, I didn't know the guy. I had never seen him before.

So after that, anytime I went for coffee and he was in the cafe, I couldn't pay for anything!

I THOUGHT YOU LOOKED FAMILIAR
Ric Miller #744

I was working I-40 out by the Petrified Forest, east of Holbrook in the early 1970s when I saw dark colored vehicle east bound hitting the high spots of the highway. After about a 20 mile chase to catch up to it and get a pace at 90+MPH, I finally got it stopped by Navajo station. The driver came back to right side of my patrol car and I introduced my self and informed him my intentions to issue a citation. The driver then explained that he was on his way to Oklahoma for his mother's funeral. I sympathized with him about his loss and completed the contact.

A couple of weeks later I was again working in the same area when I observed a familiar looking dark colored vehicle west bound, again at high rate of speed. I crossed the median and chased it down. I recognized the driver as the man in the earlier incident. Again, I introduced myself and informed him I was going to issue a citation. He commenced to again explain he was on his way to California for his mother's funeral. I looked up at him and asked, "How many mothers do you have? That's what you told me when I stopped you a couple weeks ago when you were headed to Oklahoma!" He paused a second and said, "I thought you looked familiar." He signed the ticket and when on his way.

I'M NO STRANGER TO THESE PARTS
Dick Lewis #176

I will tell you this story without mentioning any names. It's still funny! This is an example of sending a boy back to his hometown to work.

I was working east of Globe on US70 out around the airport at Cutter. It was summer and everything was slow and laid back. The car windows were down and it was peaceful and easy. I saw some car lights coming down the grade of the old highway from the Coolidge dam road. That road was not used much anymore so I decided to check it out.

After observing how the vehicle was being operated, safe of course, I stopped it as it headed back towards Globe on US70. It was just before dark.

As I walked up to the driver's side, the driver said, "How come, when me and my wife to out for an evening drive, one of you guys stop me? I replied, "Well sir, that's not your wife. Your wife taught me in the third grade. The lady in the car is an employee of yours. I went through school with her daughter."

The driver became very friendly suddenly and was very apologetic. The lady passenger was really getting a kick out of the encounter.

Anyway, I found out who it was. I didn't inquire about their business. Enough said.

WHERE ARE THE PINES
Steve Gendler #1064

In early 1981 I was promoted to District Commander in northeastern Arizona and assigned to Holbrook. This opportunity literally bubbled over with new adventures and humorous stories, however, for my wonderful wife Margie it didn't start off that way.

At the moment we were living in Mesa and had already relocated three times for career related assignments. Margie had grown up in Mesa, and, except for our Highway Patrol transfers, had not been north of Phoenix other than day trips to Payson or overnights to Prescott, Sedona and Flagstaff. I remember vividly the evening I came home from work and over dinner informed Margie and my daughters that "we were promoted" and would be moving to northern Arizona!!! The little girls were delighted thinking in terms of building snowmen and forts in a winter wonderland and my wife was imagining a cabin in the forest with a swing on the front porch to enjoy the cool summer temperatures.

It wasn't until later in the evening that Margie casually asked me "where in northern Arizona are we going, Prescott, Flagstaff, Sedona"? and I knew immediately I'd better choose my words carefully; this was going to be a challenge to say the least ...."oops I said, did I forget to mention that?   ".we are going to the north eastern part   ever hear of the painted desert, petrified forest, white mountains, Holbrook, Show Low, Hawley Lake?" "Well of course I have "heard" of those places she said, except for Holbrook. "Well that's a coincidence I said, Holbrook is the district headquarters and the patrol is going to actually let us live there: it's right on the banks of the Little Colorado River, let me show you on a map"

We spread the map out on the kitchen table and I showed her my new district. "see, here is Show Low, in my district, the Apache-Sitgreaves National Forest is in the district, oh look, the Petrified Forest just east of Holbrook is in the district and see this, the Coconino National Forest is just west of Winslow which is in the district. Wow, this is going to be great"!!

So far so good, except the next week we had to go to Holbrook and begin my duties while Margie finds a house. After dropping the girls at the in-laws, we started out for Holbrook in the late afternoon. About the time we got up the rim near Heber the sun was setting; "roll down the windows, smell the pine trees" I said, "we are now in my new patrol district" ...."this isn't so bad", she said as we motored happily along SR260 east toward Show Low enjoying the pines, the clean air, and the aroma of the forest. By the time we reached Show Low, it was dark and we stopped for dinner. "Yep, I said "we're only 45 minutes from Holbrook, did I mention it is the county seat so we will have all kinds of county services right there". About a half hour later, as we cruised up SR77 past Snowflake Margie began to notice it was pitch dark outside   I mean nothing, no traffic, no lights from distant farms, no nuthin; the smell of pines had disappeared and the wind was blowing just under hurricane speed. "Trees are probably blocking the view and the breeze is probably blowing the forest aroma away", I explained. Finally, we arrived on the mesa south of the Little Colorado River and there, spread out before us, were the lights of Holbrook. Now, as you know, without some frame of reference to measure against, a batch of lights in a pitch dark night looks pretty spectacular and Holbrook at night was no exception. it looked bigger than the whole Phoenix Metro area at that moment. "This won't be too bad", she said - and this, as they say in the history books, was the "high water mark".

We drove slowly and carefully across the old narrow bridge over the Little Colorado (which of course was a dry riverbed) and turned right onto Hopi, past all the boarded up adobe buildings blowing papers and transients sleeping on the sidewalk, then left at the only stoplight in town, Navajo Blvd, to find a hotel. The wind and dust were brisk and there wasn't a pine tree in sight.

We checked into a second floor room, up the hill, overlooking the town and I got the distinct feeling that something was amiss with my wife.

Comes the dawn. I get up quietly, leave for the district office and arrange for Charlie Cleveland, my administrative officer and longtime resident of Holbrook, to show my wife around town as well as advise her on where to look for a house. As I headed east toward Houck to start getting acquainted with the district, I got a radio call from Charlie asking me to change channels for a message (of course, at the same time every unit in the district naturally tunes in to find out what's going on). I remember the "message", word for word to this day, "1064, I am at the hotel and I see your wife out on the balcony looking south.   I think you have a problem".

(Note) Although Margie "mentions" (quite often) that she still doesn't think it's funny nor appreciate her "introduction" to Holbrook; thanks to Charlie, the patrol, and the town, it turned out to be one of the most enjoyable places I have dragged her and the girls to around the state.

THE MIRAGE
Paul Palmer #342

I can relate to Steve's Holbrook story. Being born and raised in Gila Bend our White Mountain vacations were the highlight of the summer. We would spend a couple of weeks camping at Sheeps Crossing between Greer and Big Lake. It was paradise. The White Mountains are still my favorite part of Arizona.

In March of 1966 I had a meeting with Major Jack Monschein at the patrol headquarters. Having just gotten out of the Navy a little over a month prior, I was looking for a job as a dispatcher. Major Monschein told me he had an opening for a dispatcher in Holbrook but I would have to be there within a week. I would start on April 1st 1966. Was I interested? OH, heck yes! I had never been to Holbrook but I knew it was north of Show Low and I knew Show Low was in the pines. Was I lucky or what! You get on up to Holbrook and we will give you an employment exam later he said. Come on and I'll introduce you to Superintendent Hathaway. Having just gotten out of the Navy I was very rank conscious. To say I was nervous would be an understatement. We walked into the Chief's office and the Major introduced us. Hathaway welcomed me to the patrol and then it was back to Major Monschein's office where he gave me directions and instructions. I was walking on air as I left the headquarters building.

I threw what belongings I had into my old jalopy and headed north. What a pleasant drive, but after I turned north on SR77 from Show Low a change took place. The pines disappeared and the smell of pines was replaced by the odor of the pig farms near Snowflake and the stench from the pulp plant that was located between Holbrook and Heber. I began to have doubts.

I saw Holbrook in the distance and couldn't believe it. It has to be a mirage. Where are the pines. I rolled into town from the south side and it is pretty much as Steve described it. I was dumbfounded to see that the streets in Holbrook weren't paved. Then it dawned on me. That was just the sand blowing across the pavement. The streets are paved. For the most part anyway.

As much of a disappointment of not seeing pines, I must say that my assignment in Holbrook from 1966-1969 has to be some of the best years of my career. What wonderful memories I have. Some of the best people you could ever hope to meet were assigned there. People who are friends to this day. And by the way, I met my future wife in Holbrook.

BARELY GETTING BY
Alex Carrillo #313

When I joined the Highway Patrol, I had been with Servicesoft Soft water company in Tucson for four years and in 1964 earned $16,000 for service and sales. I joined the Highway Patrol at $6240 annually, $520 a month. We were paid twice a month and by the time we paid social security, Highway Patrol retirement and our full cost of hospitalization, I brought home $125 and some change twice a month. The apartment I rented in Holbrook was $125 a month and I had a furniture payment of $30 a month, life ins at $20 a month and car and renter's insurance at $25 a month. This left $50 a month to live on. With a wife and one child, money was very tight. My Landlords, Felix and Ruby Alcorn, were very good friends of the Highway Patrol and did so many things for us that without them I probably would have gone bankrupt. We had a gas clothes dryer with no gas hook up so cloth diapers had to be hung out to dry. When in January, Felix found frozen diapers on the clothesline and asked my wife why we didn't use the dryer. She explained the problem and he had a plumber there within an hour to get the dryer working. He and Ruby asked my wife if she would be willing to answer the phone when they were gone as they were the only ambulance service in the area. She was paid fifty cents an hour. Sometimes for a number of days with one or two calls to answer. In June of 1966, he approached me and asked if I would be willing to drive to the Phoenix airport and deliver deceased that had to be flown to their final destination. He would pay $50 dollars a trip. He knew we could not work other jobs but somehow had gotten it approved by Lt Naval. I made many trips to Phoenix. On one, I asked Carlton Hill if he wanted to ride to Phoenix with me and found out he was pretty squeamish about being in a vehicle with a deceased. I told him not to worry, they were great listeners and didn't talk back. We had a great trip. One trip I blew a tire in the construction zone on 87 when it was being divided and had to place the coffin on the side of the road to get the spare out. I held up traffic for a short time while I changed the tire. By then I was quite experienced in changing tire, as most Highway Patrolmen were in the old days. Felix and Ruby would come and take our daughter so we could get an evening out and after my son was born, take both kids. They became family to us and many other families. When they traveled to the valley, they would bring back cases of fresh oranges and grapefruit and give it to many of us. They also brought back many toys to spoil my kids. They were great people and I have many good memories of them.

SLIP SLIDING AWAY
Bill Rogers #3578

I have had more than a few incidents which I believed that I was going to cash it in. I am not one of those macho men that claims he was never scared. Oh, I have been scared, with a pucker power so high that a gnat would have been denied access. The difference between being scared and being courageous is ability. An ability to act in a positive way to obtain a satisfactory conclusion.

This is what causes a normal soldier to earn the Congressional Medal of Honor. Now I am not saying that I am one of those heroes that earn that Medal. I have been able to act even when scared, knowing that my actions were due to training or reaction. Not a conscious thought anywhere in my mind.

I was assigned by the Highway Patrol to the Globe District. I was driving after a snow storm that had blanketed the area. The highways were covered by splotches of ice. In addition to that black ice patches were waiting for the unprepared. The area was mountainous with numerous curves and changing elevations in the road levels. I was on-call for late, or early incidents, and was dispatched to State Route 177, south of Superior to check for a reported collision.

I have seen plenty of collisions during my career ranging from the comical to the horrific. From the burned crispy critters of a former person, to the murder of a child by a DUI. I have seen vehicles go over the edge of the roadway, twisting, turning, falling, end over end, vaulting, to pain and destruction. I have had several vehicle incidents driving my patrol cars. This supplies a pretty good idea of the damaging velocity involved in a collision. That knowledge was soon to haunt me.

I had just exited the town of Superior headed south on the snow cleared Highway. The snow plows had been out early as it was only about seven o'clock in the morning. There was no traffic in sight. In fact, I did not see any traffic for the next several hours. I never found any collision, disabled motorist, or see any person.

I drove with purpose, not quickly, but carefully. I was not an officer that over drove his abilities, knowing that an officer that does not arrive, is no good, and becomes a liability.

My car was a Ford Crown Victoria, the standard issue for patrol cars for years. I maintained it well, for I depended on it, like a cowboy on his horse. I was driving at a constant speed when it happened. As quick as you blink your eye, no even quicker, my car was in a driver side broad side skid. black ice had rotated my car and I was not any longer in full control. I immediately turned my car's tires into the direction of the skid. This would cause my back end to whip around as soon as the tires caught traction again. This was not my immediate danger.

As luck would have it, all bad. I was on a steep downhill slope with a sharp right-hand curve at the bottom. The curve was protected by a guardrail, which I knew was made for peace of mind. The speed I was traveling at, and increasing, the guardrail would not do anything but damage the car when I busted through it. Past the guardrail was about four feet of vegetation, then a sheer drop of about one hundred feet.

I was actually thinking that I was glad there was a guardrail there. This would allow the officer later looking for me to know where I went off the roadway. I figured after several hours of no radio contact someone would come looking for my where-a-bouts. I didn't figure that I was going to survive this one. I looked out the driver's window watching my end play out. Sitting here now, it amazes me how much I remember thinking about in such a short period of time.

I remembered thinking that I was glad that I believed in God and Heaven. I was glad that I was raised in a loving family. I wondered what my children would remember of me. I spoke to God asking for, and receiving His forgiveness once more. I prepared for the explosion that I was witnessing unable to alter it.

Once again, God touched my Life. I do not know what the turning radius of a Crown Vic is. I do know that the black ice patch I had driven onto, ended. My tires caught traction and the car immediately rotated correcting it's direction of travel. Now instead of being broadside to the guardrail, I was facing it. I snapped the steering wheel to the right. The patrol car responded as the guardrail whipped by just inches from me. If I'd had my window down, I could have touched the guardrail.

THE LONG SLIDE
Frank Glenn #468

When I was in Williams, I usually worked to the west however for some reason I was working Williams east on this day. As they say while I was on routine patrol, I spotted what I suspected was a speeder traveling westbound. I was not familiar with the turn arounds due to not ever working on that side. I finally found one so I cranked up my speed to 115 or so shortly coming up on some traffic, there was a semi and 2-3 cars following him then another car I think a jeep wagoner catching up to that traffic. It fell in line and stayed there for quite a bit so I figured he saw me coming. Well, much to my surprise it suddenly moved into the fast lane and I tromped the brake pedal to the floor and started skidding down the road, soon passing those cars and truck with the wheels locked up. I am still gaining on that jeep and saw there was a guard rail on my left and cars I was passing on my right so no options there. I continued to skid my way along starting to think this is going to hurt soon. I skidded up on that jeep until the license plate disappeared from view then slowly the jeep started separating from me. At which point I let off the break. I later went back and stepped off the length of my skid marks and it came out to 188 feet. If the tires and breaks had not been up to snuff, I might have not been able to tell this story. Was I scared? Not until I had that guy stopped did the shakes start. I will close this out without comment on what I said to that guy, needless to say I was not happy.

FLOODS
Colin Peabody #481

Recently, during the summer of 2021, Arizona has suffered tremendous losses of property and lives due to wildfires and subsequent monsoon rains that followed. Wildfires are not unusual for Arizona nor are our summer monsoons, but when they arrive close together, they spell trouble for all of us.

This week, torrential rain arrived in several areas of our state, and two young children were swept away and died in the flooding that followed. The fire south of Globe/Miami/Superior area earlier in the summer covered thousands of acres of timber and brush and when heavy rains arrived there the last couple of days of July, 2021, heavy flooding occurred in Globe and Miami, but fortunately with no loss of life. I was visiting with Dick Lewis #176 the next morning and he mentioned that he was stationed in Payson in September, 1970, Labor Day week end, when resulting flooding cost the lives of many campers in the Tonto Creek and Tonto Basin areas. He had gone down the Bee Line Highway below Sycamore creek, crossed the bridge and headed back up to Payson, when our dispatchers lost contact with Patrolman Gib Duthie #143, who was working north on the Bee Line out of Mesa. Gib lost his life when his patrol car was washed away when that bridge later collapsed. Dick was thankful the someone upstairs was looking out for him when he was able to traverse that bridge safely.

During this conversation, I was reminded of December, 1978, when heavy rains caused the Agua Fria River to flood, washing out both the north and south bound bridges of I-17 late at night, resulting in the deaths of 9 citizens. Patrolman Chuck Torrie #1945 was working out of Black Canyon City that night and called dispatch to let them know the bridges had been washed out and that DOT was blocking both south I-17 and now the northbound lanes. The old bridge crossing the river downstream in Black Canyon City appeared to be undamaged and was able to be crossed by emergency vehicles only. It was anchored in bedrock on both sides of the river.

I was the only supervisor working District 5 that evening and was riding with Patrolman Jack Urick #704. We immediately headed north in response to Chuck's call for assistance. When we arrived on the southern approach of the southbound lanes, there was a Pontiac sitting there with the front end suspension out from underneath it, a sign that it was the last car to actually make it across as the bridge went into the water. I had never personally seen flood waters of this magnitude before and the sound of the water was horrendous and even as dark as it was, you could see whitecaps on the water's high waves which appeared to be nearly level with the highway pavement.

Shortly after, Lt. Rick Ayars #457, our District Commander arrived and the four of us, Chuck, Jack, Rick and I were standing close to the edge of the pavement talking and assessing the situation. The water was flowing very close to just below where we were standing and appeared to be undercutting the earth below us. I suggested that we better move back away from that area, which we did rapidly! Within a couple of minutes, that entire area where we had been standing went into the water. Had we not moved back, all four of us would have been washed away and no one would have known what happened to 4 Highway Patrolmen. God was definitely watching over us that night!

The water subsided later in the morning after the sun was up and Jack and I spotted the tips of 4 tires sticking up through the mud and silt about 100 yards downstream from us. By then we knew that probably the last car that went in the water was a GMC Sprint/ El Camino type car. Jack and I made our way to where the tires were showing and with shovels, began to dig to see if we could find a body or even a survivor inside the vehicle. We dug for a couple of hours, but were unable to find any sign of a person in the crumpled mess of that car. The driver's body was later found about ½ mile downstream from where his car was located. A Mercury station wagon was also found and in the next couple of days, the bodies of other victims of that disaster were found downstream.

FLOODED JAIL
Paul Palmer #342

The August 2021 monsoon season wreaked havoc on Gila Bend. The canal broke and the south side of Gila Bend was flooded and became a disaster area. My niece had to be rescued from the roof of her home and her home and vehicle were destroyed. After watching news video night after night, I was reminded of a story that Jim Phillips #36 told me. Jim was assigned to Gila Bend in the early 50's.

During one summer monsoon in the early 50's the canal broke and the south side of Gila Bend was flooded. The county jail was located just south of the railroad tracks on old SR85 and on the south side of the canal. When the canal broke, the jail was flooded. MCSO sergeant Tibbets contacted Jim and said they had to get the prisoners out. They got to the jail and waded into the jail and rescued the prisoners. Jim said they were standing waist deep in water and the water was rising when they finally got to them. He said that was the first time he saw a prisoner who was glad to see a police officer.

The old jail building still stands today.

YOU NEVER KNOW
Bob Osborn #1159

In 1975 or 1976 heavy rains had closed SR 87 due to flooding. At MP 220 Sycamore Creek had washed out the road. All of the north bound lane and half of the south bound lane were gone.

The Verde River bridge had suffered destruction of both the north and south approaches at MP 194. At MP 233 the highway cut had caved in leaving approximately

6 ft of dirt and rocks that had closed both lanes. I was assigned to patrol 13 miles of SR 87 with no traffic at all.

The Payson ADOT had to clean out all of the dirt and rocks at MP 233 before they could even get a look at MP 220 and what the Sycamore Creek had done to the roadway.

The 1st or the 2nd day after the closure a helicopter from news station in Phx set down near the DPS compound in Sunflower. They had brought with them some food and other supplies. They asked if I was familiar with the Sunflower area and if I knew were other people might be trapped because of the high water. I told them yes I was and gave them the following list. Area #1. Two mining claims in Pine Mt area north west of Mt Ord.

Area #2. One claim where the two branches of the Sycamore Creek came together. Area #3. There

was an area of private property with a cabin on the south west side of Mt Ord up Kiddy Joe Canyon. Area #4. There was a mining claim in Ram Valley a few miles south east from the Sunflower store, the home of Jess and Virginia . Area #5. The Sunflower Store. Area #6. There were two ranch headquarters , the Circle Bar at MP 218 and the Cross F at MP 223.

The pilot asked if I would accompany them on their flight. I called dispatch and told them what I was going to do. We did flybys at most of the locations as everything looked ok and no one was around.

Also at most locations there was no area to land the helicopter. We did set down at the Micuria mine on Pine Mt. No one there. We also set down at Jess and Virginia mining claim In Ram Valley. They were grateful for the supplies.

The pilot (can't remember his name) asked if there was anything they could do for us. I said yes as I knew that some of the people would need additional supplies. It looked like It would at least a week before the SR 87 was back open.
The pilot also asked about the kids that lived in the area.
I told him that it would be of great help if he could contact

the school in Fountain Hills and get them to package up study guides and homework supplies for each of them. 2 kids from the Circle Bar ranch, 3 kids from the Cross F ranch and 4 kids from the DPS compound. The news station got that done for us. A few days later they flew back up to the DPS compound with additional food supplies and the kids homework supplies.

The next day I delivered food and home work assignments to the two ranches. I borrowed a horse from the Circle Bar ranch and headed off to Jess and Virginia's house with more food supplies. The Sycamore Creek had subsided and I was able to cross it on horse back.

No one went hungry or fell behind in their school work. I had an interesting week.

You never know what is going to happen or what you will be doing when you check 10-8.

A SWIM IN THE DITCH
C.B. Fletcher #923

It was around 1973-74 and Skip Fink and I were working on our motor cycles at fleet which was at that time located at the old Pepsi plant off I-17 south of McDowell. It was during the summer and a monsoon storm was raging. I was dressed in a t-shirt, shorts and tennis shoes.

A bolt of lightning had struck a control panel and all the pumps on the freeway had quit working and the freeway was under 3 to 4 feet of water.

I stopped working on my bike and told Skip, "Take me down to Van Buren." "What for", he asked. "Never mind" I said, "Just take me down to Van Buren."

We jumped in a patrol car and Skip took me down to Van Buren. I got out of the car and crawled down from the frontage road to the freeway. I jumped in the water and swam from Van Buren to McDowell. I hold the distinction of being the only Arizona Highway Patrolman to ever swim I-17.

AHOY THERE!
John Underwood #419

What year was it that I-17 flooded out down around Thomas Rd/Van Buren Street, 1972? Anyway, I was assigned to District 5 evening shift under Sgt Ron Bryan, and Ernie Johnson was the district commander. It had been raining for a couple of days and something happened that allowed the "ditch" to stop-up with many, many feet of water. Around dark we got a dispatch that there was a boat in the water in an area of roadway that had now grown to quite a large in size. I responded along with a couple other guys and I parked on the east side of the freeway, and with our spotlights found the boaters. I got out of the car and started yelling at the two in the boat to come over and get out of the water. My comments were met with a lot of four letter words and one fingered salutes. So now we get serious! I recall someone parked on the west side of the freeway yelled that they were under arrest, and that too brought out the expletives and hand gestures. This droned on for hours!!! Finally (after running out beer) they decided to park the boat on the east side and give up. I was the arresting officer, and we later found out they were two ADOT worker bee's who thought it would be fun to say they went boating from Thomas Rd to Van Buren.

So now I am off to Dist. 5 to write out the arrest report... knowing that Lt Johnson would review the report in the AM. I thought I would test his early morning sense of humor, so I wrote the "real report" for the official report, but the report I left for Ernie was chocked full of nautical terms, e.g. ...told these two sailors arrested for no navigation lights, no current boat registration, failing to come ashore and dock the boat, no boating license, failed to identify the Captain of the vessel, failed to heave-to when commanded to do so,.... I thought that would be enough.... and it was! The next day I was indeed called before the grim faced boss-man to explain an arrest report filled with marine jargon. I was nervous to see how he would take it,... and shortly into my explanation Ernie exploded into laughter saying "I hope you didn't send that on"... No sir!

ONE SIZE FITS ALL
Ric Miller #744

In the early '70s I was working on East I-40 in Lupton, near the New Mexico - Az state line when I arrested a DUI non Indian. I called for a tow truck for the car and began FSTs, etc. The tow truck arrived driven by a local man who worked at the bar the driver had just left. Since the driver was a non-Indian I had to drive the hour and half to St. Johns to the jail for booking. The next day I had to make the trip again to get the offender and take him before the JP in Lupton for arraignment. When we walked into the courtroom , which was next to the bar, the driver started groaning and talking to himself. I asked him what the problem was. He said the guy at the desk was the bar tender that served him, the tow truck driver that towed his car and, now he is the Judge. He said this is like you read about this stuff happening in the South. I assured his he was in Arizona. That was the "old days" out east of Holbrook.

Also, that old Sanders Jail was still there in those days. Charlie Cleveland was my mentor for my first couple of weeks on the road and he pointed it out and said it was no longer in use, but it was a good scare tactic to violators. I used it several times to uncooperative violators.

TALK TO MY SUPERVISOR
Ron Young #706

I started my law enforcement career with the Maricopa County Sheriff's Office and worked out of the Glendale Substation. Working the night shift, the only other law enforcement close by was the Highway Patrol, so we all looked out for each other.

One evening I had just begun my shift when I observed Patrolman Gary Zimmerman had a vehicle stopped on Grand Avenue, Northbound. As I got closer, it looked like the violator was getting a little more animated, so I pulled in close behind Zimmerman's patrol vehicle to serve as a backup if necessary.

As I walked up to them, I heard Zimmerman tell the taxpayer, "You wanted to talk to my supervisor, here he is now." The violator then started telling me what a rude and unprofessional officer Zimmerman was, and he wanted to lodge a formal complaint. To go along with Zimmerman's ruse, I told the violator that we took taxpayer complaints very seriously and he could rest assured that I would deal with Patrolman Zimmerman.

The guy got in his car and drove away, satisfied that he had gotten Patrolman Zimmerman a reprimand. The guy was so intent on getting Zimmerman in trouble that he never snapped to the fact that Zimmerman and I wore different uniforms and our police vehicles had different markings.

That incident offered Zimmerman and I a lot of laughs over the years!

THE BRUTE
Steve Mason #408

I was working a Parker motor assignment and had made a traffic stop that went terribly bad. I had stopped the "Brute". It was later determined that the guy was a body builder and a police hater. He also had a history of assaulting firemen, of all things!

We got down and dirty and I was wrestling him beside the road in the brush. He had me pinned and he was crushing me and I was taking a lot of blows. I felt that he was going to take me and grab my weapon.

I managed to get my weapon and I jabbed it into his gut and told him if he got off, I wouldn't shoot him. He peeled off and ran into the bushes. He was arrested the next day totally without resistance, dry and hungry.

Actually, I was pulling hard on the trigger, but the trigger wouldn't pull though, praise God! He was one of several I was blessed to have not killed in my career.

JUST ANOTHER SHIFT
Dennis McNulty #1859

In the spring of 1983, my Sergeant, Thad Hale #685 came to me with an offer. The District 12 squads were going to have a large all hands party and one officer was needed to cover a shift on SR-89A through Sedona, one of my favorite spots in the state. All expenses paid for a nights stay at a motel in town and full per diem with overtime and would I like to go. You betcha sarge, I'm your guy.

On the appointed day I drive down to Sedona, checked into the hotel and started my shift. I love Oak Creek Canyon and was having a great time patrolling the area. My shift was set to end around 9pm when Flag Opcom radioed me to meet with a Coconino SO deputy for a backup assist for an unruly guest at the Poco Diablo Hotel near the center of Sedona. I met up with the deputy and we go into the motel lobby. The manager met us and took us up to the 2nd floor were a male and female had been "fighting" in their room. Standing out in the hall was a WM subject with a torn shirt and blood on his face. He tells us that he and his girlfriend had just done "a little bit of Coke" and then the girlfriend when nuts and attacked him. He said he ran out of the room in fear for his life and was scared to go back in. Now, in 1983, we had been trained on how to recognize various types of dangerous and narcotic drugs and paraphernalia but the condition and term "cocaine psychosis" was not well known.

The deputy and I opened the room door and went inside. The room was torn up and then we saw the girlfriend. She was crouched up on top of the room dresser. It is hard to describe the wild look on her face but she hissed at us. We both looked at each other and the deputy then started to say "ma'am, step down to the floor" but as he started to speak, this girl leaps off the dresser and launches herself at us with a scream. We catch her midair, all collapse on the bed and the fight is on. She is kicking, scratching, punching and screaming at us and finally, we get her pinned down and hand cuffed. Because she is still fighting, we wrapped her up in the bed spread and carried he downstairs. This girl was totally out of her mind and incoherent. The deputy asked if we could use my car because his was near empty of gas and said he would take the arrest. We chucked her in my prisoner cage and I told Flag Opcom we were in route the jail in Flagstaff and gave the 101 mileage. I later learned the dispatchers were having a good laugh because each time they gave me a Code-20 check, of which there were many, they could hear the prisoner in the background screaming and cursing us all the way to the jail. Just another shift.

MY FIRST TICKET
Tim Hughes #793

As a new and shiny Patrolman assigned to Salome in 1971, I was on my first day alone, convinced that I would be able to rid the world of bad guys. As I cruised US 60 at the Quartzsite underpass, I noticed a motorcycle parked under the overpass on the south side of the road of the eastbound side. I pulled over to see what was going on and saw where the driver of the motorcycle had been cutting on a cactus with a knife. I asked him what he was doing and he told me he was thirsty so he was cutting the cactus to get some relief for his thirst. He provided me his California driver's license and I was pretty sure this was illegal. I called Kingman radio and probably talked to Ollie Bond and explained what I had, After a brief period of time, Ollie called back and gave me a statute number for mutilating cactus. I cited the driver into Judge Hagley in Quartzsite and that was the first citation I ever wrote. I suspect that this is the first time a new Highway Patrolman wrote a ticket to someone for something other than a traffic offense.

KEETON-BECKSTEAD SHOOTINGS
Colin Peabody #481

I was working a 1500 to 2300 shift west of Winslow, and our district boundary was at Milepost 230 on I-40, at Two Guns, AZ. I had checked on and made a pass out to Two Guns and returned to about 5 miles west of Winslow where I set up a VASCAR distance. As I made the turn on to Job Corp overpass at 245, I heard the dispatcher (Rich Erwin) give a 27, 28, 29 return to Ptlm. Jim Keeton who was working east of Holbrook. Rich tried numerous times to call Jim, but got no response. Rich was new to radio and must have switched on all the towers as I heard then Pltm Ben Smith, stationed at Houck, come on the air with Code three traffic that Jim had been shot and was "963". About that time there was garbled radio traffic about Ptlm. Don Beckstead who was a few miles east of the location where Jim was. I heard Ben say he was enroute to Don's location. I also heard Sgt. Bob Harvey was enroute from Holbrook. I headed for Winslow as fast as I could and then heard Ben come on the air that he was with Don, who had been shot and Ben was leaving his car there, and taking Don in Don's car to Gallup. He also advised that Don saw the suspect vehicle, a Pontiac, now heading west on I-40. I got into Winslow, advised our sergeant, Hank Shearer of what I had heard. We made quick calls and George McGuire and Ron DeLong both checked 10-8 headed for Holbrook and east. I was assigned to set up a roadblock at St. Rt. 87 and U.S. 66 just east of Winslow in case the suspect continued westbound or got up on the Reservation and heading south on 87. I got hold of our reserve officer, Dan Sullivan and he and I set up the roadblock as ordered. We manned that post until roughly 2 AM or so, stopping every westbound vehicle that came through on 66 and southbound on 87.

During the course of the night, we monitored radio traffic and knew that Sgt. Harvey had found the driver's license of the suspect, Bertram Greenberg, and that information was given out. The 10-28 information was given out as a Chevrolet stake bed truck registered to Ben Dreher at Two Guns. Ben Dreher was our Justice of the Peace, and we then knew the plate had been stolen and put on Greenberg's car, which Don had described as a Pontiac sedan. The plate had apparently been stolen a couple of hours before I went on duty that day.

Once Greenberg's identity was known, we learned that he was wanted in the rape and murder of a 13 year old girl in Los Angeles and that he was a paroled ex-convict with a conviction for rape and assault in California. We continued monitoring the radio traffic and learned that Greenberg had stopped a newlywed couple by feigning car trouble, had forced the wife to commit a sexual act on him, then shot and killed the husband, and then shot the wife, before stealing their yellow Volkswagen. The wife, although wounded, had been able to go to a home close by and describe what happened. Jim's weapon had been used in all the killings. It was later found empty near the body of the husband and by the Pontiac.

With the arrival of the CI investigators and brass from Phoenix and a relief dispatcher, Paul Short to take Rich Erwin's place, updated new information was broadcast as we did not know which direction the VW was going either. Truckers coming through the roadblock were telling us what the traffic on the CB was and all wished us safety and hopes that the killer would be dealt with severely. We listened on my car radio to KOB radio in Albuquerque and learned that New Mexico State Police and local Deputies in Grants had encountered the yellow VW, followed it and had subsequently shot and killed Greenberg.

We advised our dispatcher of that report and asked if we were able to secure, but were given the order to stay in place. We had not heard any reports on Don's condition, but we did know that George McGuire had been assigned to deliver next of kin to Jim's brother Dennis, who was one of our Holbrook dispatchers who was on a day off. We also learned that Charlie Cleveland had been assigned to secure Jim's car and his body as a crime scene. Charlie never got over that as he and his wife lived next door to Jim and had seen him less than an hour before Jim's death. Ron DeLong arrived and secured the scene where Don had been shot as well.

By Saturday we had learned most of the details that the Department would release and by Sunday, we learned that Don had passed away as well. My shifts on Saturday and Sunday were accomplished as two man units as our collective nerves in District 3 were on edge. On Sunday, I had Navajo County Deputy Bill Wilbanks riding with me from my 10-8 time. We encountered a different situation nearly as soon as we got to MP 250, the Co-conino County line, when we met up with a television satirist named Mort Sahl, whom both Bill and I recognized from his national TV appearances on late night television shows. That is another story for another time.

Memories like these are things we experience and they remain with us forever. We lost two friends on that fateful weekend 50 years ago.

We later learned that Greenberg had been released from prison early by California authorities, had gotten married and then kidnapped, raped and killed a 13 year old girl before fleeing in his wife's Pontiac.

Charlie Cleveland and his wife Mary and Jim and Connie lived next door to each other in Navajo and Mary told me a few months ago, that they had been talking with Jim on their front step less than 45 minutes before he was killed. Charlie passed away in October 2019, in Holbrook. His wife and children live in Holbrook

Ben Smith still survives living in Kingman. George McGuire recently passed away at the age of 89, in Winslow. Bob Varner retired from the AZDPS, went to work for Navajo County Sheriff's Office and was shot and killed in the line of duty New Years weekend, 1988-89 in Winslow. George McGuire, his wife and two of their children are interred in a plot next to Bob Varner, his wife and their youngest daughter in Winslow. Reserve Officer Dan Sullivan completed a full career with the FBI and passed away in Baltimore Maryland 7 years ago. Sgt. Bob Harvey retired from the AZDPS in 1976, and was the JP in Holbrook for many years. He passed away in January, 2014 in Holbrook. Ron Delong passed away in 2015 in Kingman, AZ. Rich Erwin left the patrol after a couple of years and is living in Cleveland, TN. Dispatcher Paul Short retired and passed away about 12 years ago in Phoenix.

Memories like these are things we experience and they remain with us forever. We lost two friends on that fateful weekend 50 years ago.

THE MORT SAHL STORY
Colin Peabody #481

As you may have read, the weekend of February 5-7, 1971 was a tragic few days for the Arizona DPS. In the space of a few minutes, two of our officers had been shot, one fatally and one passed away many hours later. The shooter of both officers was subsequently shot and killed outside Grants NM by State Police and Deputy sheriffs from the Grants area.

The shock of the weekend had all officers nervous and as a result we tried to team up as double man units, something the DPS did not do ordinarily. My shift was to begin at 3 PM, on

Sunday, February 7, so I had Navajo County Deputy Bill Wilbanks riding with me. Both of us were in our mid to late 20s. Bill is a big man, 6-4, well over 250 lbs. As we left Winslow westbound, we just cleared the Winslow city limits at MP 250 on I-40 when we saw a small blue sports car parked across the median with a male subject standing outside it. As we pulled up, both of us recognized the male as TV personality/satirical comedian Mort Sahl. We got out of our car and approached him, calling him by name. He told us he was needing some help as he had crashed his car and there were 5000 Marines with landing nets very close to his location. We looked around us and saw no Marines or landing nets. He kept insisting he had been in an accident with a train, however there was no damage to his new 1971 Saab Sonnet sports car and the ATSF railroad tracks were at least 50 yards away from where we were standing. As we continued to talk with Mr. Sahl, he appeared more confused and disoriented. We couldn't smell any illegal substances about his person, no alcohol odor. We asked him about when he had slept last and he responded a few days earlier when he left New York. He became more confused and disjointed in his conversation so we suggested that he might be ill and maybe should see a doctor, to which he agreed. We mentioned we would take him to the Winslow Hospital to be checked out and he was agreeable to that. We did tell him we couldn't leave his car out there and would have to have it towed but we would get a reputable service to get his car. For safekeeping, we inventoried the contents of the car per policy. We did find a supply of NoDoz tablets in the front seat.

We called for the tow truck and Ames Ford arrived and we instructed the driver to properly secure the car and we gave him his copy of the tow truck request form. We then proceeded to the Winslow Hospital where Mr. Sahl was examined by a local doctor, who found that Mr. Sahl was suffering from a lack of sleep and a possible overdose of medications designed to keep him going. He recommended that Mr. Sahl spend the night at the hospital for observation, but Mr. Sahl insisted that he had to get to Los Angeles. We told him we were not going to let him drive, so he would have to have another way to get to LA. He carried a schedule of airline flights and found one leaving Phoenix later that night for Los Angeles, but he had no way to get to Phoenix as no airlines were currently flying in and out of Winslow. He called a local cab company and hired a driver to take him to Phoenix. That was the last we saw of him that night.

Several months passed and I was in Phoenix for cadet graduation and an awards presentation in April. When I got back to Winslow, my sergeant Hank Shearer told me that a complaint had been filed against me by Mr. Sahl for stealing his property. I was able to provide Sgt. Shearer with my copy of the incident report and the tow truck form listing all of Mr. Sahl's property. Sgt. Shearer went to the tow truck company, the local Ford Agency and went through their records and learned that a man had arrived at the dealership about a week later in February, presented documentation allowing him to take possession of the car and its belongings, so the car was released. End of Story? Not.

Apparently Mr. Sahl had recently made several late night TV show appearances and stated on national tv that an Arizona Highway Patrolman in Winslow, Arizona had stolen all his property after he had a wreck with a train and further stated that thievery was not limited to criminals but included cops as well. One of his statements was to the effect, If you see a Highway Patrolman in Winslow Arizona wearing bell bottom pants and wearing sunglasses, that's the guy. His clothes wouldn't have fit me anyway, as he is much smaller than I was then!

Since all of Mr. Sahl's property had been accounted for when the car was released, I was off the hook, but what happened to the property? As it turned out, the man who picked up the car suffered a fatal heart attack in Scottsdale and the funeral home who handled the body, packaged up all the items in the car and shipped them to this man's family in Texas. DPS investigators were able to then contact the Texas Rangers for assistance and the property belonging to Mr. Sahl was all located and re-inventoried by the Rangers and sent to DPS headquarters in Phoenix, who contacted Mr. Sahl's attorney. It was my understanding that Director Hegarty personally contacted Sahl's attorney directly, informed him of the findings and advised him to let his client,

Mr. Sahl, know that any further statements he might make on national television about Arizona Highway Patrol officers stealing his property , would find him being sued by the State of Arizona Department of Public Safety. Knowing Director Hegarty's legal background as a member of the Arizona Bar, and of his ability to make a point clearly with no misunderstanding on the part of whom he was talking to, I suspect the point was made and Mr. Sahl did refrain from disparaging me and the Highway Patrol.

A couple of months after this occurred, I got a phone call from my Patrol Academy roommate who was stationed in Benson, Arizona, that he had stopped Mr. Sahl for speeding and recognized him. He told Mr. Sahl he was aware of the problems he had caused us and that if he knew what was good for him, he would take the ticket he was being issued and get the hell out of Arizona.

Just a few years ago, I read an article in the paper that said authorities were searching for Mort Sahl as he had left a "health care facility " without permission and local police were looking for him. I couldn't let that pass, I had to call that agency and spoke with the Chief and told him of my experience with Mr. Sahl nearly 40 years earlier, urging caution on behalf of their officers because this man would make up stories to defame his officers and agency. The Chief thanked me and said they had it under control and that Mr. Sahl had been located. Last year, I saw an article that Mr. Sahl had celebrated his 93rd birthday and he is still alive today.

As I write this paragraph on October 27, 2021, the final chapter of the Mort Sahl story has been written. Yesterday, Mort Sahl died of natural causes at his home in Mill Valley, California at the age of 94, some 50 years, 8 months and 3 weeks after our meeting. Case adjudicated by a higher authority!

'66 PROJECT
Richard Richardson #188

During the three months stationed at Yuma, I was one of the officers assigned duty on I-40 during the last two weeks of the infamous summer long 'US 66 Project'. Arizona provided a project to see what happens when selective enforcement is done on a major highway in the state. US 66 was under construction at the time and portions of the famous old highway were becoming the new Interstate Highway, I-40. The construction would take years to complete. The Chicago to LA was noted for a high rate of traffic crashes resulting in fatalities. The idea of placing many patrolmen over nearly 400 mile stretch of the road could prove to be of value in researching the reason for the high rate of deaths.

A Navajo Motel was located at a small community referred to as Navajo, AZ, about 50 miles west of Lupton which is located at the New Mexico State Line. I was assigned to patrol the 50 mile stretch of highway, mostly near Navajo. There were two patrolmen in Lupton that covered that area. The two week period of time that I patrolled came to a quick end after the 12th day of my assignment. I had an incident with the 1959 patrol vehicle I drove. I had gassed the car at the only service station at Navajo. Apparently the gas station attendant didn't close the hood properly and the double latch didn't click correctly. I had remained in the car at the time doing some paperwork. I was on regular patrol about half way between Navajo and Lupton heading eastbound into a head wind. The double latch came loose (not secured properly) released the hood, causing it to open and flying over the top of the vehicle. The hood knocked off the top mounted emergency lights. I could see the hood still flying in the air in my rear view mirror. By the time I stopped and started backing up, another westbound patrolman had witnessed the event and crossed the median to assist me. It was a good thing that traffic was light at the time. We managed to get part of the hood in the trunk and tie down the trunk lid as best we could. I returned to Navajo and met Sergeant Carl Back #724. He advised me to return to Yuma and made sure the hood was secure in the trunk.

I already knew that I was being transferred to Seligman upon the completion of the two-week tour and had my belongings ready for the move. I had an old half-ton pickup already loaded and ready to go. Sergeant Lawwill approved for me to depart ahead of the scheduled transfer time. He said that Flagstaff District would assign me a vehicle once I arrived in Seligman. Sergeant William 'Bill' Hangar #723 met me in Seligman a couple days later. There was a vehicle that belonged to an officer that was no longer with the patrol. I never knew who or the details of his departure. I now had a patrol vehicle with a hood attached. From now on I learned to double check service station attendants closing the hood.

WHO?
Ron Cox #1101

While in CI in Phoenix, I was told one day to stop by OpCom and pick up subpoenas that had been dropped off. I thought it odd since it's the only time I'd heard of subpoenas being left there. I'd been involved with Gamble Dick in some sort of investigation. I went over there and was given an envelope. On the outside was written: AGENTS DICK AND COX.

Everyone at OpCom busted out laughing, as did I.

DUMB COWS
Frank Glenn #468

The wisdom or lack of it by some people. I was called out for a car cow accident on 64 going up to the Grand Canyon one night. The only thing hurt was the cow. The guy was understandably somewhat upset pacing around soon he said " I sure hope the person that owns that cow has insurance". I ask him if he had noticed those signs stating "open range" he said he had seen them. Then I said that means the cows have the right away. Then he about floored me with the comment "what the hell is the matter with those cows don't they know they might get run over if they get out on the road"? Yep, he was from back east but I don't remember what state.

IT'S NOT OVER TILL THE FAT LADY CRIES
Bernie Gazdzik #1930

While stationed in the bubbling metropolis of St. Johns Arizona, I was working a night shift. It hadn't too busy that evening (which never really was that busy to be honest) I had stopped at my mobile home for a dinner break. Why they sent a single guy like myself up there I will never know. But I digress....

Anyway, I received a phone call from Flagstaff Radio of a car cow accident north of town on US 666. No injuries were reported but I proceeded up there as quick as I could. Of course I had to dodge porcupines on this road which received very little traffic and was mostly used by truckers trying to avoid the port of entry at Sanders on I40.

I soon arrived at the scene of a car with a headlight out just south of the Witch Wells junction. As I had been on my own for about a month I felt fully trained to handle the situation.

I drove past the vehicle, turned around and properly parked by vehicle behind the damaged car. I had turned on my overheads and notified radio I was on scene. But then as I looked to open my car door I was immediately faced a rather large lady crying hysterically and asking for help. I had to instruct her to step back so I could get out of the car. Almost pushing her out of the way she kept exclaiming "the poor cow, its hurt, can you help"? She ushered me to the side of the road and pointed down to a cow laying on the ground. I went down to it, shined my flashlight and saw it was a black angus with a brand. I could still hear the lady crying loudly. I knew in my mind what was going to happen but decided not to say anything to her. I went back up on the road and asked the lady for her driver's license and registration. She said she would get it for me but she wasn't the driver. At this point, I SUDDENLY realized that I should check for injuries and who else was in the car. (My training finally kicked in) I then noticed a gentleman leaning against the car smoking a cigarette. I approached him and he kind of laughed and said that he was driving. He also informed me THEIR TWO KIDS (!) in car were not hurt and asleep in the car. I am thinking to myself that ,GEE, I should have done this first....

I went back to my patrol car and advised radio to call the Livestock Inspector and started the paperwork. I stayed in my car trying to avoid this lady and wanting to get it done as quick as I could. In no time I got what I needed and walked back to the driver to explain that I would do a report and they were free to go. I told him the livestock inspector was on his way and I would take care of the cow. However, this man said his wife wanted to see how we would "help" the cow. I explained clearly to the man that they could go and that the cow would be euthanized. They probably didn't want to see that. He said his wife, this large lady, refused to leave until the inspector arrived.

Well sure enough, here comes the inspector in his pickup truck with his little light flashing on the top. He parks behind me and I explain the situation. We then went down to the cow and he asked about the crying lady. I said I tried to get them to leave but SHE refused. I could hear her telling her husband that the inspector was going to "help" the cow. I told the inspector to do what he had to do. He said "ok" and walked to his truck, took a rifle off the gun rack, walked back and then "BOOM", shot the cow in the head.

The lady let out a horrible scream and started crying even louder. The inspector and I just stood there thinking " what did she think we were going to do?" Her husband then took the lady by her arm and gently placed her in his vehicle. I could hear her continue to cry as they drove off into the darkness..

I guess the moral of this story is that when you arrive on the scene of a wreck , check for injuries first , no matter how big and hysterical the crying lady may be.........

I'LL TAKE TWO PLEASE
Heber John Davis #156

When the Department was considering going from the "Bus Driver" hats to the Smokey Bear hats about 50 years ago, Major Dick Raymond came to me and asked me to wear the hat for a couple of months to evaluate it. I agreed to do that. A couple of months went by and Major Raymond met up with me and asked how I liked the hat.

I told him we needed two of them. Major Raymond said, Yeah right, one for summer and one for winter.
"No," I said," one to s**t in and the other to cover it up with."
I am a tall man and I found the hat difficult to deal with in getting in and out of the car with it on or off and trying to put it on while having to meet up with a vehicle driver. I didn't think they could be worn inside the car for anyone over 6 ft. tall.

PATROLMAN BOB VARNER
Colin Peabody #481

Prelude:

On December 31, 1988, retired DPS Officer Bob Varner had been working for the Navajo County Sheriff's Office as a deputy for several months, and he encountered a vehicle at MP 253 on I-40 with a headlight out. In true Highway Patrol form, Bob stopped the car and the passenger, later identified as Douglas Savory, came out shooting with a Mac-10 semi automatic pistol. At least 30 rounds hit Bob's marked unit, with several striking Bob. Responding units got Bob to the Winslow hospital and he was then transferred by DPS Ranger helicopter to Barrows Neurological Center at St. Joseph's Hospital in Phoenix. Bob passed away early on the morning of January 2, 1989.

This story began as a thread on Facebook in January, 2021 32 years after the time of Bob's passing (January 2, 1989), as his daughter Cheryl Varner Jordan posted a memory of him. Several of her friends chimed in and then David Denlinger, who was a DPS patrolman stationed in Winslow at the time of Bob's murder added some comments, which attracted the attention of then DPS Captain Mike Denney who also added comments. Captain Denney was in charge of the DPS Special Operations Unit (SOU) at that time. I was SOU Team 1 supervisor as a sergeant and had been on the department for 21 years. Bob Varner had been my training officer when I was in the Arizona Highway Patrol Academy in early 1968, and we had been on the same squad in Winslow for 6 years until my transfer to the Training Division in November, 1973. Comments between Mike and David also pinged my phone on Facebook and I was able to add my comments. When put together in sequence, they give a fairly accurate accounting of much of what happened with regard to the capture and suicide of the two perpetrators on the night and days following December 31, 1988 through January 2, 1989.

Suzanne Holbert – When I was a baby dispatcher, a long time ago, I did a ride along with Bob. We stopped for dinner with several guys on the squad. A pitcher of soda had been ordered and somewhere during the course of the meal Bob bumped the pitcher and the soda got spilled all over me! I rode the rest of the shift a bit stickier than I started.

About a year later I married a highway patrolman. I had just gotten off work on my Friday, working graveyard shift. We, on the spur of the moment, decided to be married that day, so we asked my husband-to-be's squad to cover calls for the few minutes the ceremony would take. The ceremony was held at the courthouse, officiated by another retired patrolman who was now a justice of the peace.

Bob was shot and killed that night. My husband and the "photographer" patrolman who'd attended our "ceremony" spent the next 16+ hours spending our wedding night together on a roadblock looking for the shooter. I will never forget that night and will also forever miss Bob. 32 years ago he died and 32 years ago I was married.

Frank Shankwitz – Knew Bob well and enjoyed working with him during our Motor Tac Squad assignments in his area. I had only been transferred to the Special Investigations Unit (SIU) a few weeks before his death. Our team was sent to Winslow and I assigned to stay in Phoenix and collect evidence from Bob's body.
Something I will never erase from my memory is the respect and dignity the nurses at the hospital showed during the evidence gathering, so gentle, so caring.

God Bless. (On January 22, 2021, retired Detective Frank Shankwitz passed away from cancer, just days after posting his comments on Facebook.)

Christy N Mike Denney – I remember that so well. I was with SOU and got the call out. I stood on an overpass at Joseph City wearing all the cold weather gear I had and still froze every time a semi went by. I was there several days and got home just in time to go back when one of the cowards who shot "Smokestack" barricaded himself in a rancher's house near Joe City. He killed himself like the coward he was. That was one of the most difficult SWAT calls I ever went on. We all knew Bob. He was bigger than life and losing him just did not seem real.

David Denlinger – I had the ranch house owner with me. Dave Audsley thought he could blow up a six foot thick concrete wall. Remember the pup tent the rancher lived in?

Christy N Mike Denney – I asked Audsley to blow the wall because there was only one door which was an unreasonably dangerous entry portal. McCance would not let us do it. And the walls were made of adobe rather than concrete as I recall. I do remember the tent but it was a good sized one and he had dug a living area in the ground. He lived in the tent because he had been caught in a house fire when he was younger.

<u>David Denlinger</u> – He said his wife's ghost lived in the house too. Crazy (awful) memories. I later got assigned as the li- aison to SIU. They were great. And you have a great memory. One way in and out.

<u>Christy N Mike Denney</u> – I also remember the Navajo SO SWAT team wanted to make the entry but had never done one. So, Sgt. Cooper from Flag PD agreed to lead them in behind the canine from Gila County. (The K9 handler was Danny Alexander who had worked with me at Cochise County). We put a crapload of gas in the house before the entry. Someone threw a flashbang in and then tossed the dog in. The dog came right back out and bit Coop.

<u>Colin Peabody</u> – David, your memories are pretty good. Larry Troutt, Randy Oden and I were at a friends New Years party with our wives when Mike hit my pager. I called him and he told me about Bob. He didn't know Bob had been my OJT Coach 20+ years before. We all met at the hangar just as the King Air arrived with Cathy and Joanie. I promised Cathy we would get the guys. On Sunday morning, Larry Troutt, Audsley and I were the closest to the house and had low crawled up to the water tower and stock tank. I raised my head up and I was looking down the barrel of Savory's AK-47 look- a-like SKS. We made sure it wasn't booby trapped and I handed it back to Audsley. We pumped 3 rounds of gas at the few windows, DOC pumped about a dozen rounds. A few actually got inside. The team the new sheriff put together had zero experience, so we gave them a quickie plan on how to do the entry, equipped them with two flash bangs and urged them to check the tent that old John Thompson who owned the ranch would stay in when he was there. One of the entry guys slit a hole in the tent and stepped inside, falling 4 feet down to the floor of the dug out.

Once they attempted entry to the house, the event with the dog took place. He didn't want any part of the noise or the cloud of gas dust that formed after the flash bang went off. The team went in, saw a body and I ordered them out. Troutt and I entered, verified the body and the LA Gear shoe prints we had followed from Holbrook. The gas was so thick you couldn't see more than a couple of feet. One of the flash bangs did not detonate and it was caught in the crook of Savory's arm. Audsley had to disarm it so Lannie and Lee could go in to process the scene.

There was a small bulldozer close to the ranch house and earlier I offered to use it to knock the house down. In my former life, I had been a heavy equipment operator. I told McCance I would pay John Thompson for tearing the house down, but that got vetoed also.

Once my team secured, I called my wife on Allan Schmidt's car phone to let her know it was over and one of the bad guys was captured and the other dead. Lillian, Don and Carlene Williams and Dennis McNulty had stayed with Cathy and Joanie during the time at the hospital.

Promise to Cathy fulfilled, however sad the circumstances.

David Denlinger – Where did your team start? After the gunfire died down in the riverbed at Geronimo Road, we stayed all night until the manhunt started from the shooting scene. About 20 minutes after the shooting the geese on the property of the judge south of us went nuts. I had Ranger with the FLIR check that area, as well as, I think, the Flag PD SWAT team. I stayed behind at that scene when the tracking teams left. Detective Bill Cloud showed up and asked me which way they went. I pointed west where the teams went. Bill, a tracker, said no, they split up and one went south. I accompanied him as he tracked, no idea what he could see. He actually showed me where the guy had laid down. He showed me a bush that had been disturbed, and the Mac 10 was inside it. That was the driver who was found in Holbrook the morning of the 2nd.

<u>Colin Peabody</u> – Once we arrived in Holbrook we checked trains that had stopped with negative results. We went out to Joe City and met with George (McGuire) on top of the overpass, then we went to the house where the couple was kidnapped and their car stolen. We went down the canal bank and found the car off the side. It was starting to get light and we saw where they had split up. There were several boxes of ammo discarded, probably because they were too heavy to carry a long distance. We took the tracks heading west, identified them as LA Gear shoes. We followed them for nearly 30 miles, with a team from Flag PD alongside with a dog. We were out in open ground with no cover for miles. We were past the Hibbert Road siding and we lost his tracks once he crossed back over the river. They diverted us back to the siding where we checked all the railroad cars on the siding, with negative results. We were then transported back to the SO where Tom Hawley had been running intel stuff for hours to give us a better background on both suspects. We finally got something to eat and then my team was advised to return to Phoenix on the King Air for some strange reason. We returned to Phx, got a couple hours sleep before we were called out to return to Winslow in the King Air. Savory had encountered several deputies, disabling their vehicles and took shots at the Customs Blackhawk with the AK. Once in Winslow, they transported us out to John Thompson's ranch's here we encountered George (McGuire) again on the outer perimeter. He had been going since Friday night with no rest and you know George, he let his displeasure be known. I assured George we were going to take care of the situation. From there we went to the CP and then deployed to what became the inner perimeter. The rest is history.

<u>David Denlinger</u> – When we got a couple of hours sleep, we were called to the sheriff's office in the wee hours of the

2nd. We were informed that Bob had passed away, and that John Thompson had returned to his house late to find he thought somebody was inside. I was with Jack Johnson's team that day since he was not there. We were briefing to enter the house and I had John draw a sketch of the house when a deputy approached the house and the gunfire rang out. It was Michael Godinez who broadcast shots fired at the ranch house. We set up the perimeter, and waited for you. I actually had a guy belly crawl up next to me and say he was a sniper from the Apache County SWAT team. He had an iron sighted Winchester lever action rifle.

Colin Peabody – We had several well-meaning but untrained officers wanting to help, and while we appreciated their offers, it was better to keep the DPS teams who had trained together performing the necessary tasks. Now that time has passed, I did not agree with the change in the entry team, but that decision was made by folks at a higher pay grade than mine and in a " new" political position if you get my drift.

Bob Singer – I remember that night clearly. I got the call in Springerville and myself and Corky Mueller drove code 3 up 180 to about 4 miles South to a bluff in the highway where we could see all the way to Holbrook and set up a roadblock there. A sad night never to be forgotten.

Dee Dee Williams – I'll never forget my mom calling me at just about this time that night. Changed my world forever. I miss you Bob and even though my dad BEGGED you not to tease my mom about that wreck...you always called her crash! Loved you then and always will. Give my mom a big hug for me!

Tony Fajardo – Worked along side Bob for a few years while stationed In Holbrook. Bob was the most professional, Highly respected Patrolman in the area! Not only with the citizens in Winslow and Holbrook but with all the Truckers driving up and down I-40. God Speed Bob Varner

Don Uhles – That night will always be imprinted in my mind. Bob was not only my mentor but a friend and a family member. I was flying on the DPS helicopter that night and flew Bob to Barrows in Phoenix. It still breaks my heart remembering as Cathy asked if she could go in the helicopter with Bob, however the helicopter was configured that night for the pilot, paramedic and a flight nurse so there was no room to accommodate Cathy. I did learn that DPS sent the King Air to Winslow to get Cathy and Bob's daughter Joanie to bring them to Phoenix. I was so proud that they did that.

Chip Brigham – Was called out with the swat team and was at the ranch house. Does anyone remember that the old sheriff of Navajo county took off and left the job to the new sheriff. Did not even bother to help. Glenn Flake was the old and Gary Butler was the new.

PATROLMAN MAC MERRILL
Gary Ciminski #4575

My second duty station was Benson. When I was in the office one day the subject of Mac Merrill came up and Rick Valencia told us how Mac had been run over by the 18 wheeler as he was working that day and helped with scene security or traffic control, I can't remember which. A while after that, I was working a night shift when I stopped a car for a light out. There was a pretty good shoulder to pull over onto, but the car pulled even farther off the road out into the grass. I thought this was unusual so I walked up very slowly and carefully to the passenger side. There was a young man maybe in his early twenties driving and I asked him for his documents. As he was getting them together he said, "Can I ask you a question?" I said sure. He then asked why

I walked up on the passenger side of the car. I told him I didn't want to get run over. He then said, "I can understand that, Mac Merrill was my father." I was speechless and felt pretty bad for the way I had answered his question. All I could think to say was I'm sorry. I cut him loose and wished him a good night. I thought about that stop for a long time afterward. Eventually, enough time passed that I had stopped thinking about that encounter when I stopped another car that pulled way off the road again. I didn't think too much about it and asked the lady who was driving for her documents. As she was retrieving them, she asked why I walked up on the passenger side, and without thinking I again said I didn't want to get run over. She said, "I can understand that, Mac Merrill was my husband." I apologized, we talked for a minute and she left. I felt terrible. The driver of the truck that killed Mac admitted he was playing a game that a lot of drivers played at that time which was to drive close enough to a patrolman to blow their smoky bear hat off their head. This driver came so close to Mac he caught Mac in the duals and killed him. The ironic thing was that Mac was very well liked by many truckers that travelled on I-10. They called him Little Bear and a lot of drivers would call for him on the CB when they came through Benson. If Mac was working he would often go have coffee with them.

PATROLMAN JOHNNY GARCIA
Bill Rogers #3578

I was one of the "lucky" few that was fortunate enough to attend ALETA in Tucson after being hired to DPS. I was hired on March 31st, 1985, which was a Saturday. I always laughed, because my actual first day to report to the Academy was April 1st, 1985, April Fool's Day. Which, at times, was an appropriate way to look over my career. I was assigned with three other cadets to share a dorm room in the live-in academy grounds.

I was lucky enough to be voted vice-president of my class, one of my other roomies was president. The only non-DPS in our room was from South Tucson PD, but he soon got bounced out of the academy for ethics violations. The other DPS cadet in my room was a very solid, positive, just fun to be around person. He had, however, for personal reasons soon left our ALETA class, and my dorm room. Life went on, I graduated, and was assigned to the Globe area.

Soon after, I heard that my former roomie had been placed into a "holding" position, and re-entered ALETA, only to graduate later. I was extremely happy. I heard that he was assigned to Casa Grande, and I hoped that we would meet again, to renew our friendship.

Most officers (Troopers now, still hard for me to get used to that) remember the Special Olympics Torch Run. This is where officers would run distance for donations to the Special Olympics, escorted by a patrol car following behind, since the run was done on the highways. It was, on this day, that I was assigned to follow the running officers. I was to drive to Florence Junction, and meet the officer driving up from Casa Grande, to obtain the torch to be carried during the Torch Run.

My assigned patrol vehicle was a 5 speed Ford Mustang, a fast, sleek, fun car to drive for patrol duties. I drove it with pride and took extremely good care of it. As I traveled down SR79, heading south from Florence Junction, I saw the approaching District 6 officer driving toward me. I saw that his patrol vehicle was also a Ford Mustang. I pulled into an upcoming pullout and awaited the arrival of the other officer to get the torch for the run.

One can only imagine the joy I felt when the officer coming from District 6, was none other than my previous roomie from ALETA, who graduated with a following class. We hadn't seen each other in person since he left, and had plenty to catch up on. And talk we did, about everything we could, to catch up on as quick as we could. We both bragged on our patrol cars, as we both loved them.

And I can still see Johnny, so very young, good looking, energetic, perfect command presence, funny as hell, and excited and proud to be an Arizona Highway Patrol Officer. Those were the days my friend, we'd thought they never end...
And then next month... Saturday, October 14,1989

Officer Johnny E. Garcia died while responding to a report of a drunken driver, whose car was stuck in a right-of-way fence near the Picacho Peak Interchange on Interstate 84 near Casa Grande. While passing a car on State Route 84 near Casa Grande, Officer Garcia's patrol car struck loose gravel, rolled three times, hit a car and then a tree.

OFFICER MEMORIAL MARKERS
Ric Miller #744

In 1993-94 a committee was formed to discuss the need to honor the five fallen officers of District 3. Those on the committee were Officer Ken Hawkins #2873, Officer Monty Long #2484, Officer John Wisner #4738, Sgt. Ric Miller #744, Officer Jim Bee #2044 and Donna Atkinson, District 3 Secretary.

This committee decided each officer should be honored with a permanent marker to be erected at or near the location where he gave his life while on duty. "WE WILL NEVER FORGET".

The first five officers to be honored from District Three were Officer Jim Keeton #310, Officer Don Beckstead #409, retired Officer Bob Varner #438, who was a Navajo County Sheriff's Deputy at the time of his death, Sgt. Dave Zesiger #1848, and Officer Bruce Peterson #3536.

A search for a suitable memorial marker began. Retired DPS Sgt.Tom Gosch #1172 of Flagstaff submitted a sample of a memorial engraved stone, which were obtained from a quarry near Ash Fork, Az The cost would be $400 for each marker.

The committee presented the proposed plan to the DPS Director, Joe Albo for approval. The Director invited the committee to attend an executive staff meeting to allow each administrator see the program for themselves. The memorial marker for Officer Jim Keeton was presented and approved.

The subject of how to pay the cost of each marker was through donations., and that all DPS fallen officers in the state would be included.

Our committee returned to Holbrook and we were informed by the Director's office that the Department would pay the cost of each marker.

ADOT approved the program as long as the markers were placed so as to not present a traffic hazard.

The program was then passed on to other Districts.

Members of the District 3 committee were asked to travel to the sites and provide assistance with site preparation and installation of each memorial.

As soon as Tom Gosch completed each marker they were erected.

This program continues to this day.

WE WILL NEVER FORGET
Tom Gosch #1172

In late 1995, Officer Ken Hawkins contacted me requesting input on District Three's proposal of placing memorial markers at locations where D-3 officers had made the ultimate sacrifice. I agreed that a memorial marker at the exact location would be most appropriate as we felt that to us, the DPS family, these locations were hallowed ground.

Over the next few months, we developed the design and wording to be placed on each marker emphasizing that "we would never forget". The question of what type of surface to put the design on was next; should it be stone or bronze. Bronze looks good and holds up over the years, but is very expensive and tends to disappear into the hands of thieves these days. It was decided that the memorials would be of stone. The question was then what kind of stone; granite, marble or sandstone. Cut granite and marble are great to work with, but once again the cost was a factor. I recommended that we go with a high-quality sandstone quarried out of Ashfork. It was cost effective and should hold up well over the years when properly taken care of. The sandstone was common, but was being called to do an uncommon job, just like officers who had so valiantly served.

The stones were to be set in the upright position against the right of way fence well out of the way of traffic. The stones did not need to be readily observable to the public, they were for the immediate family and DPS family, who will never forget.

Jim Keeton and Don Beckstead's stones were the first made followed by the rest of the D-3 officers. Word got out around the state and other Districts wanted to follow suit.

Unfortunately, the stones to some degree have lost their meaning as they have been placed far away from those hallowed spots; some because of circumstances(e.g. Ranger 29 McNeff and Stratman) and some out of convenience., one more than a hundred miles and a county away. Ken and I had somehow envisioned on day one of a cadet officers' field training experience, his/her FTO would point out these locations to "never forget".

HALLOWED GROUND
Paul Palmer #342

I enjoy Arizona's back roads and Lynn and I are always looking for a back country road we have not travelled.

One day while in the White Mountains we decided to take the back road that runs from SR73 south of Hon-Dah and comes out at Hawley Lake. East of SR73 we came to a faded, broken sign pointing the way to Hawley Lake. We left the gravel road and turned onto a narrower and not as well maintained dirt road. It was not a road that requires a four-wheel drive, but it was narrow and rough.

We were watching for deer and elk and enjoying the scenery as the road dropped down to the north fork of the White River. There was a road across the river that headed east. This was our road to Hawley Lake. But this road was marked R-79 and the road we were on which continued south was marked R-27. These were not on any of our maps! Oh, well, we weren't lost, but I wasn't

100% sure that this was the road to Hawley Lake. We went on, knowing that we could always double back toSR-73 if we had to. We continued on R-79, stopping occasionally to take pictures of the beautiful White River. Lynn and I talked about how isolated we were and that surely out here in the middle of nowhere, we would certainly see deer and elk. With these thoughts, we continued on. Suddenly, out of nowhere, there was a monument with an American flag and behind this was a park bench with the words, "In Loving Memory". We stopped the truck in the middle of the road since there was no place to pull off. To our left was an embankment and to our right, the monument and the White River. As I looked at the polished grey marble monument, I was stunned to see that it was a monument to White River PD Officer Tenney Gatewood, who was shot and killed in the line of duty in December 1999. Officer Gatewood was investigating a report of a burglary at the Hawley Lake store. At this isolated sport in the middle of nowhere, he was shot and killed by two people involved in the burglary. He was later found by a Game & Fish officer.

I can't explain the emotion I felt as I looked at this monument and thought of how he died, alone, so far from help. There were no signs anywhere indicating "monument ahead" or historical monument. All of a sudden you are there, and the impact is unbelievable.

After taking pictures of the monument, we continued on, enjoying this magnificent scenery and sure enough, the road led us straight to SR-473. But for the rest of the day, I could not shake the feeling of isolation and loneliness where Officer Gatewood bravely died. I have thought about it since and it is the same for the monuments for our fallen officers. As was the original plan of Sergeants Ken Hawkins and Ric Miller, the originators of our monument program, these monuments should be placed whenever possible where the officers died. I know that in some cases this is just not possible, but let's not forget how and where these brave officers died, alone and at times far from help. It may be convenient to put them in a rest area "close" to the location of the officer's death, or turn our area offices into a graveyard of monuments, but this was not the thought behind the original plan.

Let's put them where the original plan proposed, at the location where the officer was killed, and in our travels around the state, as we come across one of these monuments, stop and pay our respect and reflect on what happened at this very spot. Let's not become desensitized by multiple monuments that we see daily as we enter an office and they become just stones with words!

PRISON BREAK
Rick Ulrich #182

Not too long after I went to work for the patrol there was a prison break at Florence. It wasn't really a prison break, but a work gang outside of the prison walls got a jump on the guards and the prisoners got away. A work gang was usually watched by one guard on the ground and one guard on horseback who carried a rifle. I don't know the details of how the prisoners jumped the guards, but they did and they tied up or cuffed the guards so they couldn't do anything. Tracks indicated that the prisoners started up Box Canyon East of Florence. Box Canyon runs North and South and there are some ranch houses in the canyon. Going North from Florence the canyon eventually comes out on US-60 between Florence Junction and Gonzalez Pass. The first day of the prisoner escape I was working teletype and trying to help out the best way I could. Patrolmen were called out and road blocks were set up at many locations around Florence. Patrolmen were getting off the state highways and onto county roads and I wasn't familiar with that whole area around Florence. People were asking questions about where officers were being utilized and I didn't have any answers. The person on radio had to eventually answer most of those questions because that person only knew where people were.

There didn't seem to be any real plans for what to do in case of a prison break and in the radio room, we only had highway and milepost maps, nothing about areas not on the state highways. As a new person, I was having a hard time believing that we were so ill prepared for such an occurrence. I asked Jack Monschein if there were any maps on the compound that we could access. He said there weren't any? I asked him where we might get such maps. He said maybe the highway department engineering department might have some maps of roads not on the highway. I volunteered to drive my own car down to the highway department to see if I could get any such maps. Jack gave me permission to do that and I went to the AHD engineering department and spoke with several engineers, explaining what was going on and our predicament. They had some maps, but they really weren't that helpful.

The map thing really ticked me off. Later, I approached Jack Monschein about it and he agreed that the AHP communications did need some maps that were not just highway maps. Over the next few months, Jack did make arrangements to buy some maps and we finally did get some decent maps in the radio room. I mean, I could see this happening many times over, so why didn't we have maps of things that didn't relate to the highway.

Anyway, back to the run away prisoners. They were being tracked up Box Canyon and there was evidence that they had broken into ranch houses for food and anything they could use. It was assumed that they would eventually come out onto US-60 and try to catch a ride to somewhere. Night had fallen and the roadblocks remained in place, but the actual tracking was curtailed until first light.

The next day things resumed and for some reason I was working day shift and I was assigned to work the radio. Yay!! I would actually be involved in what was going on. The missing prisoners had not been seen and they hadn't come out onto highway 60. Things had come to a stand still. For some reason, it was thought that the missing prisoners had separated into smaller groups. I seem to recall that the original number of prisoners was 7 or 8. I learned a lot of things in a very short time. I learned about Box Canyon and where it went. The Kelvin Highway became familiar because it was one way the prisoners might have gone.

Sometime around mid morning, the MCSO called to ask if we could help a deputy who was in a car chase on US-60 headed from around Glendale towards Wickenburg. I used to be able to recall which patrolmen were on duty on Grand Avenue, there was at least one out of Phoenix and another out of Wickenburg. But my recollection of who they were has escaped me. I sent them to help the deputy. The MCSO called and said that their deputy's car had blown up that was following the car. The MCSO had another deputy somewhere around Morristown that had commandeered a semi truck and flatbed trailer and he had the driver put it across the highway to set up a roadblock. Somewhere between Morristown and Wickenburg, the car being chased turned around and headed back towards Phoenix. It wasn't long before our officer saw the car and continued the pursuit. We thought that the chase might end at the semi-trailer road block. Somehow the pursued car managed to get past the semi and flatbed. At sometime during this chase MCSO revealed that they knew that the two guys being chased were two of the missing prisoners. I don't know how MCSO knew this or how the chase got started. The sheriff's office seemed to have a lot of information that was never passed on to the AHP.

As the chase continued, I kept hearing HP-158 Sam Daniels calling on the radio. He was involved in searching for the prisoners around Florence Junction and Superior. I had cleared the radio of radio traffic because of the chase, but Sam Daniels kept calling. I figured he must have some hot traffic so I acknowledged him and told him to go ahead. Sam said that he was Northwest of Superior on back roads and he had Warden Frank Eyeman with him. Sam said that Warden Eyeman wanted me to tell the patrolman in the chase to not hesitate to "shoot their ass off. Well, I knew that Superintendent Hathaway was monitoring this radio traffic and he would not like it if I said that verbatim. I didn't want to tick off Warden Eyeman, so I had to put it out but clean it up. I don't recall exactly what I said, but it was something like, "Warden Eyeman advises that our patrolman shouldn't hesitate to use deadly force to terminate this chase." I think that satisfied the Warden. About this time, the Glendale PD called us and told us to have our officers back off as they got to the Peoria Underpass. Glendale said they would have a large number of officers on top of the overpass and they were armed with shotguns and automatic weapons and they were going to open up on the chase car when it went through the underpass. I advised our units what Glendale said. The car went through the underpass and they did open up on it. The car continued on Grand Avenue for another mile or so and then it turned onto a side street. Then the car crashed into a school yard fence. Our officers were quickly on the scene and the two subjects were taken into custody. I know one suspect had been hit by the gunfire at the underpass, but I don't remember if they both were. But they were taken into custody and they were two of the escaped prisoners. The two escapees were identified as Bobby Favors and Jim Burrell.

The other escapees were eventually killed or captured, but that occurred somewhere other than the highways and AHP officers weren't directly involved.

I looked up this incident on the internet and the Phoenix Police Museum has recorded the criminal history of Johnny or Jimmy Burrell. They have a really good account of his misdeeds and that includes the car chase in 1963 that involved our AHP officers. He was an accomplished escape artist.

Here is the Phoenix Museum website:
https://phxpdmuseum.org/newsletter/every-photograph-has-a-story

PRISON BREAK AND PURSUIT
Heber John Davis #156

Around 1963 I was enroute to Peoria for court on my day off when I heard that 2 of five prison escapees were headed east from Wickenburg and had run a roadblock while shooting at the officers who were chasing them. I knew school kids would be getting on their busses and traffic would be picking up that morning. All I had was my Smith & Wesson .357 Magnum revolver. As they came running by me at a high rate of speed, I fired at them. They almost lost control but continued through Peoria, the underpass and on side streets where they lost control and slid under a chain link fence into the Don Sanderson Ford dealership property. I gave chase and was able to catch one named Borral. When I cuffed him I noticed he had a bullet wound in the back of his neck. About that time my Sergeant, Ernie Johnson arrived and

I told him I had fired at them and he said "You should have killed the S.O.B." When searching the stolen Pontiac, we counted 13 bullet holes in the car. They also had 5 guns in the vehicle. Unknown to me at the time Glendale PD officers had set up a roadblock at the underpass and numerous weapons were fired.

Authorities Shoot, Kill Two Men Following High-Speed Chase
John Fink #683

By Bonnie Walker, Sun Staff Reporter

Two young men in a stolen car were shot and killed by Department of Public Safety officers Sunday afternoon after a high-speed, 110 mile chase ended off the road about 27 miles north of Flagstaff.

Kenneth Lee Gerdes, 18, Tucson, was shot after he reportedly jumped out of the driver's side of the car and opened fire on DPS officers with a .22 caliber pistol. The passenger, who possibly was caught in the crossfire, has not been identified. He was possibly a hitchhiker, according to DPS spokesman Sgt. Allen Schmidt.

The two men in the car reported stolen out of Salt Lake City ran a half-dozen roadblocks in the course of the 100 mile chase, at speeds in excess of 100 mph, which began about 12:51 p.m. on U.S. 89 near Marble Canyon. Schmidt said that the car was stopped by DPS patrolman Keith Judd for a routine traffic check. When Judd walked to his patrol car to call in the license number, the two men sped away.

The men went through a roadblock at 89 and the Page turnoff and through another about 25 miles north of Tuba City. By this time there were several DPS units and Navajo police units in pursuit at speeds of up to 110 mph, Schmidt said.

At 1:30 p.m. the men passed another roadblock - described as semi-physical because patrol cars don't block the roadway but instead try to channel the suspect vehicle off the road.

A few minutes later the car's radiator was shot by DPS officers and Navajo police, but the car continued south.

According to Schmidt, Flagstaff police had been alerted and were in the process of setting up a roadblock north of town.

When the fleeing car reached a point about 30 miles north of Flagstaff the DPS helicopter hovered near the pavement to try and stop it. However, the car continued to come at them at about 90 miles per hour, Schmidt said. At this point the helicopter lifted off the ground and flew to the right of the vehicle.

A paramedic in the helicopter, John Fink, said he pointed an M-14 rifle out the window and pointed at the men in the car to stop. Fink said the men glanced over at him and then back to the road, "just like they were out for a Sunday drive." Fink then shot out the right rear tire, but the car still continued without slowing down. Fink then shot out the right front tire, the car slowed, went off the road to the right and came to a stop.

Schmidt said at this point the six DPS units in pursuit followed the car off the road. The driver then exited with a .22 caliber pistol and fired at least two shots at the officers.

All officers returned fire. In the process the driver was shot and the passenger, who had not left the car also was shot.

Tom Hammerstrom, criminal investigator for DPS in Flagstaff, said that office was in the process of getting a search warrant for the Toyota in an attempt to identify the passenger.

Investigators from the Phoenix and Flagstaff offices of the DPS will be working on the case.

This incident occurred in the early 1980's. This was the first time that anyone had fired from a helicopter. Certainly not something that we had trained on. Due to the extreme circumstances and not letting the fleeing vehicle enter the city limits of Flagstaff, my Pilot, Bill Fry and I decided that the best recourse was to try to disable the vehicle by shooting out the tires. We had the units back off that were in pursuit while we shot the tires out. Finally, with the front tire flattened, the driver lost control and the vehicle headed off the roadway and came to a stop surrounded by police units. Unfortunately the driver came out of the car shooting at the officers and was killed. The passenger who never exited the vehicle was killed in the crossfire. The helicopter crew landed and pronounced both victims.

All officers, including the helicopter crew were cleared of any wrongdoing upon completion of the investigation.

THE TYSON GANG
Heber John Davis #156

While I was stationed in Tucson, the Tyson gang broke out of the state prison and went on a killing rampage across several states, prompting the largest manhunt in Arizona history. With the city, county and Indian police we placed roadblocks in several locations in District 8. We had an emergency response plan in place to call out officers to man the roadblocks. We wanted to prevent them from going to Mexico. Early one morning I received a call about a possible sighting of the gang, so we put a plan in place to man the roadblocks.. At one of the roadblocks they tried to run the block by firing at the officers. The officers returned fire, killing the driver and their killing rampage ended. The movie "Killer in the family" starring Robert Mitchum was based on the Tyson gang.

ARIZONA STATE PRISON DUTY
Frank Glenn #468

In June of 1973 there were at least two prison guards killed at the Arizona State Prison. A lot of officers were sent to Florence along with the SWAT team. Going back that far my memory is a bit fuzzy so I may have some wrong information and incomplete information so just bear with me. I and several others were initially staying at some motel in Florence and I seem to remember Sgt Jim Chilcoat badge 137 being in charge of the squad I was on. Later on, we slept in some big room at the prison where the staff had laid out quite a number of mattresses. We just slept in our clothes.

I along with others on my squad were assigned to Cell Block 2 which is where they housed the worst of the worst. All of the prisoners were locked in their cells when we arrived. I was providing cover for the squad with my Remington 870. The drill was to have the guards open a certain cell then have the prisoners come out and then the squad would search the cell for contraband. In one case one guy had an ice chest in his cell and when they took it out, he was really interested in what was going to happen to it so they took a real close look and discovered there was quite a bit of money hidden in it. When we were clearing the cells two of our toughest guys, I hesitate to name them because I might be wrong, tried to get the prisoner to come out of the cell. Well he indicated he was not going to do that so they went in and got him. He became violent and strongly resisted the officers, during which time he fell down and broke his arm I watched all of this happen from across the way and after that the prisoners seemed to be a little calmer.

The word was that this was the first time that guns had been inside the walls. I believe that we hauled out 27 dump truck loads of stuff that was not supposed to be allowed to be in the cells. I don't remember how long all of us were down there but several days, I am sure.

There was a gun tower inside CB2 and that was accessed from the warden's office through a tunnel.

THE EXTRA MILE
Bill Rogers #3578

My patrol car usually was a very dependable machine. But when it approached about the 40 thousand mile mark, the alternator quit working. I took it to the DPS Fleet shop, where in a budget crunch they replaced it with a used alternator. I drove away from Fleet not knowing this at the time, feeling secure in their repair.

About one week later I was driving along in my super-duper hero patrol mode. You can imagine my surprise when my patrol car started shutting down all the electronics, both the police radio and music radio, air conditioning, power to the engine, power steering, and finally the headlamps. I muscled the car into a nearby "stop and rob" market and called for a tow truck to finish my trip back to Fleet. It was well past 5 o'clock, which meant that I had to go and switch vehicles into a "swing" or replacement car. This is normally a pain in the butt, especially so in the elevated temperatures of the day. It was an exercise that I did not look forward to.

Once the tow truck arrived, loaded my dead car onto its back, and one ticked-off Sergeant into its cab, we headed to Fleet. We arrived at Fleet and the tow truck off loaded its load. Looking across the Fleet parking lot I searched for my assigned swing car in the oceans of vehicles parked there. It was then that I heard the usual noises coming from inside the garage. I expected maybe to hear the janitors cleaning in there, but this was the sound of mechanics working, banging noisy stuff. Being the curious being I am, I decided to look into the unexpected racket.

Going into and past the large bay roll-up doors I found Dave working with his upper body enveloped into the open hood of a sick patrol car. That surprised me since it was now past 7 PM, with Fleet being closed. The last thing I'd thought I'd see was someone working on a car on the rack. I like Dave. He is an older Hispanic gentleman, extremely knowledgeable, quiet, and one of the few DPS mechanics, I like to work on my patrol car. It may sound crazy, but when you drive a patrol car as hard as I do the last thing you want is to worry about the tire falling off.

I greeted Dave and we spoke a few words catching up on times since the last time seeing each other. He told me that he likes to work at night since it's cooler and no one is around to distract him. Being a seasoned police officer I knew exactly what he meant. The "brass" works day shifts. I like working nights, from a work aspect, I am usually the highest-ranking supervisor on the Swing shift and the decisions are mine.

Dave asked what brought me into Fleet and I laid out my tale of disaster. I was speaking to a friend and he was going to help me. On the lift rack next to where we were speaking was a practically new vehicle, which had been a victim of collision. The car was totaled and being parted out, piece by piece. Dave relayed there was an alternator in that vehicle with my name on it. I was pleased thinking that Dave would work on my patrol car tomorrow. I was wrong.

Dave told me to roll my car into the service bay and that he would have me back on the road in no time at all. I hesitated knowing that he had his hands full with the car he had been dissecting. Before I knew it, Dave had talked me into rolling my own car in for repairs. Taking advantage of the offer, I obliged. Within twelve minutes, Dave had the old alternator off the other vehicle and into mine. Truly I was in the midst of a mechanical master. I stood there absolutely dumbfounded and in awe.

Dave didn't have to do this. He went the extra mile, and I appreciated it.

YOU PICKED A FINE TIME TOO LEAVE ME LOOSE WHEEL
Colin Peabody #481

I was sitting alongside RT 66 near Meteor Crater Road west of Winslow in 1968 and a truck lost the spare tire from the carrier rack underneath, then ran over it with the trailer tires, which sent it bouncing. It bounced right over the hood of my patrol car, but no damage was incurred. Needless to say the driver was chased down and cited for an unsecure load.

Many years later, I was on Motors in Phoenix and patrolling the freeway. The cars were slowing way down for no apparent reason, so I was able to snake my way through and found a tire, no wheel, just a tire rolling down the center lane at less than 5 miles per hour. I rolled up next to it and stuck my leg and foot out(heavy leather motor boots) and snagged the tire, brought it in close to my bike and rested my leg on the crash bar until I could work my way to the outside lane. All the drivers honked at me and my expertise(stupidity, actually) but I was able to get traffic moving again quickly. In retrospect, it was a dumbass thing to do, but it worked!

WHICH 58?
Paul Palmer #342

Don't ask me to explain it but during the summer months especially if it was stormy I could sit at the ratio console in Holbrook and hear Kansas Highway Patrolmen talking to their dispatchers. You couldn't hear the dispatchers, only the field units. Our technicians said it was a frequency skip. They went no further, figuring I wouldn't understand it anyway. Patrolman Billy Kuykendal HP58 was stationed in Springerville. A Kansas Highway Patrolman, badge number 58 was stationed in Chanute, Kansas. I don't know how many times I answered KHP 58 thinking it was AHP 58. One night an excited 58 called in and I thought Billy Kuykendal may be in some sort of trouble. But then the voice came across again. "58 Chanute we have a tornado touching down east of Chanute." KHP 58 had his hands full but AHP 58 was sitting in a cafe having coffee.

MY FIRST ACCIDENT REPORT
Richard Richardson #188

During the summer of 1962, my first duty station was District 4, Yuma. My sergeant was Charles 'Chick' Lawwill AHP #717. Being the 'Rookie', I was assigned a 1959 Ford Fairlane 4dr without air conditioning, except for the open vehicle windows. The other officers had air conditioning.

During the first two weeks I rode with various patrolmen and hadn't had an opportunity to investigate any accidents. There was an Area meeting at the AHP headquarters. All the officers attended. Once the meeting concluded, Officer William 'Bill' Algeri #169 left the office. A few minutes later he returned and advised the sergeant that he had an accident in the parking lot. Apparently Algeri was backing his patrol vehicle and the right rear tapped the left rear of another patrol vehicle, resulting in minor damage. This was an opportunity to have me actually investigate my first Code 961 (property damage accident). I went to the lot and checked the two vehicles and proceeded to commence the investigation. Several officers observed me and didn't say a word. Once I completed the report, Lawwill inspected my work. He told me I did fine, considering it was my first accident investigation. I thought about writing Algeri a citation for improper backing. I mentioned that to the sergeant. He laughed and said the minor fender bender was not on a street or highway, but the patrol's parking lot. It wasn't necessary to write out a ticket or finalize the report. It would be Algieri's responsibility to complete an 'Incident Report' that would be sent on to Phoenix Headquarters for review.

The accident report was just for my own benefit to see how well I would do on the report.

10-9?
Jim Chilcoat #137

It was 1960 and I was working the night shift on US80. I was between 75th and 83rd Avenues and I couldn't believe what I was seeing. There was a monkey walking down the centerline! I picked up the mic and said, "Phoenix, 97." Jack "Snoopy" Swartz was dispatching and answered me and I advised him where I was and that there was a monkey walking down the center line.

You could hear roaring laughter in the background as Snoopy asked for a 10-9. "There is a monkey walking down the centerline on US80 between 75th and 83rd Avenue." Snoopy responded with a 10-4 and the laughter was even louder in the background.

About that time the monkey's owner showed up and took possession of the monkey. The owner had a store on the side of US80 and as an attraction had two cages with monkeys on the front porch. When he went to check on them, one was missing. It didn't take him long to find his missing primate.

When I advised radio to disregard, that the owner now had the monkey in his possession, you could hear the other dispatchers still laughing in the background when I got a 10-4 from Snoopy. I think I made their night!

YOU SURE FOLLOW FUNNY
Bob Pierce #355

I was working swing shift on US 60 out of Salome. Jim Taylor (274), also from Salome, was working I-10. In those days, I-10 began at milepost 2 and ended at milepost 30. Toward the end of our shifts, we both wound up at Ramsey Chevron at milepost 34 on Hwy 60. The station was closed but we knew where the key to the back door was, and we knew the dog. We had both finished with fuel, had locked up. and were sitting in the front parking lot swatting flies when an eastbound motorist stopped and told us about a bad two-vehicle accident on I-10 in the westbound lanes close to the east end of the freeway.

As I was parked facing the highway, I thanked the motorist, dropped into drive, hit the lights, and started for the accident scene. Jim had to turn around before entering onto the highway. So when he got out on the highway. I was already a quarter mile ahead of him and running at a high rate of gas consumption. Jim called Yuma radio and reported that he was responding to a citizen's reported accident. He gave the location given by the citizen. By this time, I was approximately a half mile ahead of Jim. I waited a few seconds. Then called Yuma radio and told the dispatcher that I would follow 274 to the scene to assist with traffic control. After receiving a "10-4", I hung up the mike and concentrated on driving. Then a small unidentified voice on the radio said, "you sure follow funny".

IT'S OVER - WELL, MAYBE NOT QUITE
Art Coughanour #3131

For most of my life, I have always felt I was the master of my destiny but when I took a temporary job with the Arizona Highway Patrol in December 1965, little did I know that the Arizona Department of Public Safety would later play such a significant role in my personal and professional life.

I retired from the Department in July 2005 after 24 years of service. I can honestly say I thoroughly enjoyed most of those years as a publications writer/editor/supervisor at DPS despite a year or two spent in agony as Project SLIM forced the downsizing and reorganization of DPS. For a variety of reasons, it was pretty much a personal nightmare as it resulted in a transfer of my unit into a section which my unit didn't belong and the transfer of a close friend (Jack Harrigan) out of my unit into another unit in which he didn't belong. I know I am being evasive, but there's nothing to be gained by naming names but it was a period of agony, not just for me, but for so many others as well.

Anyway, back to my story.

In December 1965, I was a third-year freshman at Arizona State College, Flagstaff, with nothing much to do but to return to my parent's home to celebrate the Christmas holidays. True, I probably could have planned to study for upcoming semester finals, but when you are heading on a fast track towards academic probation, such an exercise certainly would be futile and quite possibly interfere with my educational career path which was very uncertain at the time.

Shortly upon my arrival home for the holidays, my father told me he had accepted a job for me. To this day, I really don't know how this opportunity presented itself other than my dad, a U.S. Customs inspector in Nogales, was a life-long friend of Arizona Highway Patrol Capt. Jaime Teyechea, perhaps at the time the most respected law enforcement official in Santa Cruz County.

At some point just before the Christmas break, Capt. Teyechea asked my father if I would be interested in working two weeks as a janitor at Nogales-area headquarters while the regular janitor burned off some vacation time. Of course, my father to- tally disregarding any type of father-son consultation - remember this was 1965 and my father always knew best - quickly accepted the offer and informed me of my future employment pretty much upon my arrival from Flagstaff.

Amidst occasional snow flurries that December morn, I launched my career with the Arizona Highway Patrol after a short consultation with Capt. Teyechea. I really can't remember much of what was said – similar to how my classes were going at ASC. He did tell me that I would be responsible for raising the flag each morning at sunrise, dusting floors, emptying trash and a few other things. To my relief, this grateful captain told me I would not be responsible for the latrines because his officers would handle that responsibility.

For all I know, those officers may have been retired Sgt. Alan Schmidt or retired Capt. Dick Landis as I learned later both Landis and Schmidt were working in the Nogales area around that time.

Anyway, the Nogales janitorial tour proved to be quite un-eventful although Capt. Teyechea treated me to several "ride-alongs" each morning after my "shift" ended.

In January 1966, I returned to Flagstaff for the second se-mester of educational torture. A couple months later, "spring fever" hit and in late April my future wife, Sally, and I decided we were serious and mature enough to become engaged, after all, I was 21 and she was 19. It was simply something we wanted to do and there was no type of dramatic marriage proposal, nor did we set a date for marriage.

In June, I was back home in Nogales working a summer job with the City of Nogales Recreation Department. My fiancé was working at a restaurant near Roosevelt Lake. Trying to main-tain a relationship via long-distance telephone calls wasn't very effective and fairly expensive. During the first week or two of June, we began arguing and our relationship was quickly deterio-rating to the point where I took a day off in order to drive to

Roosevelt Lake with hopes of mending fences. This moment of détente worked so well that I left her trailer with her engagement ring in my right front pocket.

Yep, we no longer were a couple, but little did I know the Arizona Highway Patrol was about to play cupid the next morning.

As I headed west out of Miami, and I am not lying about this, Roy Orbison was on the Miami radio station, KIKO, singing "It's Over." This simply was too much so I pulled off the road by Bullion Plaza in Miami to gather myself and headed out again shortly after Orbison soulfully reminded me, "It's Over."
As I approached Florence Junction, where U.S. 60 and U.S. 89 intersect, I noticed an Arizona Highway Patrolman had a motorist pulled over. I remember thinking, "Well, that guy is getting a ticket. He's lucky, at least he didn't lose his girl fiancé."

I turned south onto U.S. 89 and had driven only a few miles when I looked into my rear-view mirror and to my shock, here was a Highway Patrol car rapidly closing in on me. I checked my speed which was within the limit and then looked into the mirror again. At about this time, his red Mickey Mouse-ear lights came on.

As he approached my 1960 non-descript white Ford, I thinking again to myself not only have I lost my girlfriend/fiancé, now I am going to get some sort of ticket. Just what I needed to punctuate my misery.

My driver's side window was rolled down as the patrolman approached my vehicle. Bending over, he asked, "Are you Art Coughanour?"

Now, I really didn't have a clue about what was happening so he explained that the Patrol had been asked to locate me and when he handed me a phone number I quickly realized it was the home phone number of Sally's parents. He advised me to call that number collect.

So I doubled back to Florence Junction where there was a gas station, liquor store, and restaurant combo. I called collect and Sally's mother answered.

"That fool daughter of mine wants to see you again," she said.

Now, I was not certain who my future mother-in-law was actually referring to, but I was hoping it wasn't a Freudian slip on describing my character rather than she couldn't believe her daughter set me free in the first place.

Relishing a possible romantic second opportunity, I motored back to Roosevelt Lake and had a sit-down summit with Sally. We patched things up and being so emotionally madly in love and without a whole lot of patience, we decided to get married that summer, having absolutely no clue about the complexities involved in staging a large wedding within six weeks. But, we got it done.

After graduation from Northern Arizona University, I worked for three different newspapers before arriving at DPS in November 1981 as a publications specialist. Within a few weeks at DPS, the Department of Administration hunted me down and presented me with a retirement check of about $16 for my time served with Capt. Teyechea's team.

It's strange how the world sometimes turns. That courteous traffic stop by an anonymous, but vigilant Arizona Highway patrolman on a warm June mid-morning on U.S. 89 (now U.S. 79). It was a traffic stop that changed my life, although it did take a while before that turn south at Florence Junction eventually led to a career at DPS.

Sally and I are still married, having celebrated our 55th anniversary last summer.

THE DAY MY SERGEANT TOOK MY TICKET BOOK AWAY
Gregg Girard #1151

This was another Air Rescue story. It occurred in 1976 or 1977. We had two aircraft, two Bell Jet Rangers, 206B models. We used one as a 24/7 "duty ship" stationed at Falcon Field in Mesa. The other was used for special purposes, such as along the Colorado River during Spring Break, Wild West Days in Wickenburg, similar Wild West Days in Wilcox, or any other happenings around the state where there would be a large gathering of people, which would put a strain on local law enforcement and EMS activities. If nothing was scheduled, the second aircraft and crew was assigned to pull a weekend detail in Tucson. We would be based out of the Tucson Medical Center. They had a helipad, which is where we would park the bird, and the crew would sleep in a hotel across the street. During the day, the crew would hang around the E/R and brush up on medical skills and knowledge. Sometimes it would be busy, sometimes not. The same would occur at night. Sometimes we would catch some shuteye, sometimes not. There are great stories about these Tucson shifts.

One weekend, I pulled the weekend Paramedic shift to Tucson. I can't remember who my Pilot was, but I'm sure that a Pilot will read this and jog my memory. After a preflight, we would takeoff on a Friday and head south. We would follow I-10 to see what activity we could assist at, be it a traffic stop, a pursuit, an accident or two, etc. On this day, we were following I-10 southbound (actually, eastbound) at a couple thousand feet AGL. I noticed a passenger vehicle crossing the dirt median from the EB side to go back WB. Not much was said in the cockpit. I just pointed the vehicle out to the pilot and motioned to put the A/C down. Crossing the median is after all dangerous and a traffic violation. Down we went. You can't sneak up on anyone in a helicopter. The driver heard us but didn't know where we were. He then saw us as we landed about 75 feet to the north. We raised a lot of dust and some of it (a lot of it) went into the violator's vehicle before he could raise his window. When the dust settled, I held my hand up motioning for him to stay there. I grabbed my ticket book, exited the A/C and approached the violator. I advised him who we were and advised him that one should not cross the median. After he presented his driver's license, registration, and proof of insurance, as well as a negative want and warrant check, I issued him a citation. The entire "stop" lasted only about 10 minutes. Both of us were cordial.

Here's the rest of the story. When we returned to Falcon Field on Monday morning, my Paramedic Sergeant, "Doc" Holloway #291, called me into his office and told me to give him my ticket book. I was rather surprised. He told me that the violator complained to the department that it was a waste of a valuable resource just to write him a ticket. I think the words he used were "very expensive." It was no bother, we just happened to be in the neighborhood. The sergeant and I then got into a discussion about job responsibilities. His contention was that I was a paramedic aircrew member, who just happened to be a Highway Patrolman.

My contention was that I was a Highway Patrolman who just hap- pened to be paramedic aircrew member. The Sergeant, who was always a fair supervisor, gave my ticket book back and told me to keep it in my 4-wheeled vehicle.

WHERE WERE YOU IN '72?
Colin Peabody #481

Here is another yarn from nearly 50 years ago, back when the Arizona Department of Public Safety was a fairly new outfit, but still had some of the old west charm about it. There were still some old AHP veterans who grew up on ranches, around horses and cattle and when they weren't in uniform, could be found wearing comfortable Levi's or Wranglers, cowboy boots, western shirts with pearl snap buttons, leather belts with big shiny buckles and a Stetson.

In June, 1972, a new class of patrolmen graduated from the DPS Academy and a couple of those guys were fortunate enough to be stationed in Winslow. Winslow is a nice town, not much on scenery, but with some really nice folks living there. Housing back in those days was hard to find and for a single guy, very difficult.

At the time, I was living alone, had my own house with two bedrooms and word was passed to one of the new guys that I might consider renting out a bedroom and sharing living expenses. I hadn't met this young guy yet, so wasn't sure what to expect.

This guy pulls up in front of my house driving a new Ford F-100 Ranger XLT, top of the line pick-um up truck, gets out and saunters up to the front door. He was wearing Wranglers, boots, leather belt with a big shiny buckle, western style shirt and yep, a Stetson. He even had a neckerchief around his neck! Not a very tall guy, young, about 24 years old. I met him at the door and invited him in.

Once inside, he took off his hat and there was this red headed, freckle faced, smiling guy who looked like Howdy Doody! "Damn, you look just like Howdy Doody." That kinda took him by surprise and he didn't know exactly how to react to a seasoned officer giving him a shot like that. Stuttering, he said, "Uh, sir, my name is Chuck Wright and I just graduated from the Academy and I was told you might have a room to rent."

Now some of you younger folks reading this may not know who Howdy Doody was. He was a ventriloquist marionette and star of the Howdy Doody Show on TV back in the 1950s and into the early 60s. The show catered to kids and the human star was Buffalo Bob, who wore fringed shirts and boots and often a large hat. One of the other marionettes was an Indian maiden, Princess Summer Fall Winter Spring.

A case could have been made that this guy looked like Richie Cunningham on Happy Days, but that show hadn't come out yet and we didn't know who Richie or The Fonz were back then, or maybe even Opie Taylor on the Andy Griffith Show, but nah, it was Howdy Doody.

Well, I offered Howdy, er, Chuck, the room and he took me up on it. It didn't take long to get him settled in, but he had to buy a bed first. Before the day was out, my new roomie's nickname officially became Howdy Doody to not only the rest of the area patrolmen, but to every other cop in town and by the next morning every waitress at every watering hole between Holbrook and Flagstaff knew of this new cowboy/patrolman in town by his nickname. I think they wanted to become his "Princess Summer Fall Winter Spring!"

Now Howdy was a bit jittery, like all new patrolmen, and after just getting out of the Navy, having served on the 5,000 man crew of the USS Ranger, it was understandable. To be honest,

Howdy is still "jittery" to this day. Don't walk up behind him quietly and blow in his ear!

In those days, we covered the new I-40 as well as St. Rt. 87 north and south of Winslow. We had a graveyard guy, the late Officer Bob Varner (R.I.P.). When Bob was on days off, the evening car would cover until 3AM and the day car would cover from 3AM until the start of his regular shift. Howdy, er, Chuck, being the new guy with about 47 minutes on the road by himself, got to work days to get used to the area. One morning about 3AM, Flag radio called for Howdy, to advise that a trucker had reported seeing a nude man with a spear gun about 10 miles west of Winslow. Since I was awake (I had to answer the phone) I woke up the sleeping Howdy and told him what he had. Remember, he had the calls from 3AM on.

After listening to him stuttering and stammering around, I finally agreed to go with him on the hunt for this spear gun wielding nudist who was bothering the late night truckers. We get in Howdy's new 72 Mercury and head west. Code 2 ½ (lights no siren, we don't want to wake anybody up.) About 10 miles out, we see a Pontiac LeMans off the south side of the highway facing east with the headlights on, engine running and the driver's door open. We pull over to investigate and cautiously approach the car as we don't know if we might be the next victim of this spear fisherman or where he might be. He isn't around the car, so we shut it off, lock it and take the keys. We start walking east, and west and we find a shoe in the median west of the car, so now we start looking in that direction, we find another shoe, then socks, then a shirt, Levi's, then some dirty skivvies. "Do you think we are going to find more clothes?" my jittery partner asks. "Well, we have found everything a normal person wears, so I expect not", using my years of investigative experience to guide my young partner.

By now we have covered nearly a mile. We were driving in the median, well I was driving, my inexperienced partner was walking, and we finally see our quarry. He is in the median, waving the spear gun, hollering at every passing vehicle and it looks like he is holding a ham in his other hand. We now approach him very cautiously and we have already taken the blanket out of the trunk of Howdy's car. We are actually able to get close to him, sweet talk him out of the spear gun and wrap him in the blanket. He was now relatively calm. We attempted to handcuff him but he still had this ham thing in his other hand. Only it wasn't a ham, it was his hand that was swollen to the size of a football. There appeared to be the imprint of a large tire tread on the back of his hand, so even my young partner recognized that this guy had tried to assault a semi-truck with his hand and lost. We later found that every bone in his hand was broken in dozens of pieces.

We are now standing in the middle of I-40 around MP 239 and Howdy has the guy's spear gun, cocked and locked. "What do we do with this?" he stuttered. I wasn't about to admit that I had no experience with a spear gun other than to watch Sean Connery shoot them in the James Bond movies. "Fire it down the median, but for crying out loud, don't shoot it across the median and don't shoot it toward your patrol car. I'm not writing a damaged vehicle report for you!" Sometimes you have to explain things to a newbie. I learned that a long time ago when I was a newbie.

Well, Howdy fires the spear gun and we can now see where it went as it is getting very light and we retrieve the spear about 100 yards down the median. We have the guy bundled up in the blanket in the back of the car, and call for a 926. Once the hook is there we head for the Winslow Hospital and have the guy treated. He was from California (Where else!) and we found his sister's contact information and gave her a call. She was surprised to learn where he was but she did tell us he "trips out" once in a while. Not only did he "trip out", but he also "stripped out", giving Howdy's new blanket and new patrol car back seat a breaking in and Howdy an experience he would not soon forget. Me either!

To this day, whenever I see Chuck, I can hear Buffalo Bob asking "Hey Kids, do you know what time it is?" And the kids in unison, "Its Howdy Doody Time!"

A Long Night
Dick Lewis #176

The phone is ringing and I awake from a deep and comfortable sleep. The time is somewhere between midnight and day light. I know before I reach the phone that I am going to have to go. Somewhere someone is in need of help. I need to know where and I have only to answer the phone to find out.

The dispatcher on night watch is apologetic and I am informed of the accident 35 miles east of town. The only thing that is known is that it is a bad one.

I quickly dress, there is a jangling of keys and the stomping of my boots. As I step out into the night my wife calls out, "Be careful." I don't reply, there is no time to waste. The night is chilly and dark. There is no moon.

The powerful engine of my patrol car explodes to life and the radio cackles as it warms up. "Enroute" I report into the mike. Now I realize that 10 minutes ago I was asleep and now I am rushing into the unknown.

I take the shortcut over the hill and come out onto the highway. To my surprise the road is wet. It has been raining out east and is still falling lightly.

The white broken centerline flashes by and the road signs show their colors clean and clear in my bright lights. I count the mileposts as I pass and count off one mile after another. The windshield wipers make their usual little sounds. There is a curve up ahead. I know how fast I can take it in dry conditions but I won't take a chance when it is wet, so I decelerate. It's a sure thing "I cannot help anyone if I wreck!", I think to myself. That would be a fine thing!

The green eye of the radio light shines on in the dark interior of the car. This is my invisible life line and is taken for granted. I can hear other transmissions and traffic from other cars in the state as I gain altitude. It keeps me company.

My headlights are on bright and I am watching for animals and objects far out ahead on the road.

Down at the foot of the grade I can see one set of headlights that are orange. I think, "that car has been sitting there for a long while or the engine isn't running". I'm almost there.

Thirty five miles in a very short time. As I slow, I turn on my red lights. Up to now there has been no need for them. The rain has stopped.

I can't see the accident, but the guard rail is down and there are a lot of marks on the road, and debris. A woman with a flashlight in her hand runs up to the car almost before I get stopped. "Is there an ambulance coming?" she asks. I find out from her how many are injured and I order an ambulance.

The car is down over the deep fill and the woman's husband is done there helping the injured people.

I set flares in the roadway and make sure the road is marked plainly. I don't want another accident right down on top of this one

With my first aid kit and blanket in hand I start over and down the hill. All I can see is a twisted hulk, a tire and personal belongings strewn about. There are boulders as big as a car and hard to get around in the darkness. There are two stretcher cases and they are pretty serious. I must make them comfortable until we can get them out. The time passes slowly. Where can that ambulance be? Another car stops on the road and two flashlight beams show down over the bank. An offer of help, and yes, come on down. I'll need help carrying them out. The ambulance arrives, only we don't have an ambulance in our community, it is a hearse. The driver is alone, but scrambles down with a break down stretcher. It's bulky and he has a hard time getting down.

Finally he is down and a broken form is lifted carefully and strapped down. The form moves but is kindly suppressed.

Now, the task of getting over the rocks and up the incline is started. Five men hold firmly on the stretcher, two men on each side and one in front. We strain and slip and give encouragement to one another. We caution each other about the footage. A woman appears with a light to show the way.

The second trip up wasn't as bad as the first. I reflect as the ambulance is pulling away! I thank my helpers. I could not have done it without them.

The wrecker arrives and gets started. I get out my accident forms and once again start down over and down the fill.
Perhaps an hour has passed since I was in bed, perhaps longer.
The wrecker pulls the wreck up the incline, over the lip and through the broken guardrail just as I realize the increasing light in the east.
Short night I think. I sure so need some coffee.

The sun is fully up and the shadows are retreating as I walk down the steps of the hospital toward my car. The people are hurt really badly but not critical. Lucky, very lucky!

I am only half finished. I have to complete the accident report.

I will go home and get some breakfast, clean up and get back on the road. I still have a days work to do.

I think every patrolman can tell this same story over and over again.

The Longest Day
Alex Carrillo #313

In 1966, I was a fairly new Highway Patrolmen, Badge 284, working in District 3, Holbrook. We were working nine-hour days, six days a week. We were short-handed as two officers were on long-term sick leave and two officers had not yet moved to Holbrook. It was Easter weekend and I was scheduled to work Saturday and Sunday the 5:00 p.m. to 2:00 a.m. shift. My father-in-law, Bob, had been authorized to ride as a civilian observer. Just a little background, in the early 50's, Bob had applied to be a highway patrolman and was accepted. When he found out he had to buy his own equipment, insurance, and the salary, he decided to remain a maintenance supervisor at Hughes Aircraft.

Saturday at 4:45 p.m., I checked on and headed west on U.S. 66 and I 40. There were sections of I 40 that were complete and you would weave from US 66 to I 40 and back to US 66 at Joseph City to Winslow. The section of I 40 between Joseph City and Winslow was complete but not open. I had made a couple of stops and was in Joseph City around 6:00 p.m. when I spotted a new Cadillac sedan towing a second fairly new Cadillac sedan heading east. The driver looked pretty scroungy and was staring my way, appearing to be nervous. I flipped a U-turn and caught the vehicles at the east end of Joseph City. After getting the driver out and running a 10-29, I determined that both vehicles had been stolen out of Los Angeles, Ca. The driver was arrested, hand-cuffed and placed in my patrol car. I requested two wreckers and filled out the tow truck request form. The wreckers arrived and took control of the two Cadillacs. I then took the prisoner to the Navajo County Jail in Holbrook. I booked the prisoner and as it was approaching 8:30 p.m. decided to take my lunch break and drove to my apartment above the mortuary garage in the alley be-hind the Desert Inn. This was one of the nicer rentals in Holbrook at the time and the landlords Felix and Ruby Alcorn were the best.

At 9:00 p.m., I was back on U.S. 66 heading west and stopped a couple of repair orders and a speeder. I was west of Joseph City when I was dispatched to a one vehicle accident just west of Holbrook at Perkins Road. I arrived at the scene around 11:00 p.m. and found a semi with the windshield partially broken out. The Driver had a large head laceration and one eye looked to be bleeding. The driver told me he didn't know what had hap-pened. He remembered being passed by a pickup with a few people in the back. The next thing he knew a huge rock came through his windshield and he did everything he could do to keep his rig under control. I requested an ambulance and tried to clean his wounds and bandage him. Then, I requested a tow truck and filled in all the paperwork. The ambulance arrived and he was taken to the Holbrook Hospital. After finishing at the scene, I went to the Holbrook Hospital to check on the driver's condition. He was stable with a concussion and would probably lose the eye. I left the hospital at around 1:00 a.m. and was soon dispatched to a two-vehicle accident with injuries west of Jack Rabbit on old U.S. 66.

I arrived at the scene, it was lit up with flares, and several truck drivers were directing traffic. The two vehicles were off the north side of the road in the area that was cleared for I-40. Inci-dentally, I-40 had been finished for about six months in this area but was being kept closed by the owner of Jack Rabbit Trading Post, a state senator. I got my first aid kit and extra flares for the people directing traffic. I attended to the driver of the 1964 Oldsmobile and then my father-in-law stayed with him while I checked on the other driver who was driving a semi and was extremely impaired. He admitted to having drunk a number of beers and taken some pills to keep awake. The empty beer cans littered the floor of his truck. He was administered a Breathalyzer balloon test and he blew a .24. (This was when the legal limit was .15). He was arrested, handcuffed and placed in the patrol vehicle.

The ambulance arrived and was driven by a deputy. No paramedics or EMT's in those days. It took three of us to get the driver out of his vehicle as the semi had taken at least a foot off the left side of his car and crushed the driver's seating area. The driver's left side was crushed. The ambulance had a broken tie down for the litter so my father-in-law rode in the back of the ambulance to keep the litter from rolling. A Class D wrecker had been dispatched for the truck and also a Class C for the car. I did my paperwork which took a while, as the owner of the Olds was an auto upholster and had his whole shop packed into the car. I left the scene at about 5:30 a.m.

I went to the Navajo County jail and booked the prisoner. At 6:30 a.m. I went to the Holbrook Hospital to do my follow up and found the driver had passed. I notified radio and asked they advise Sgt. John Consoni the accident had turned fatal. I finished up at the hospital and drove to the Holbrook office arriving about 7:30 a.m. Sgt. Consoni arrived a few minutes later and suggested we have breakfast at the truck stop across the street. As was his habit when you had your first fatal, he would take you out to eat and order something he could totally cover with catsup. Since it was the first fatal I had to investigate, I accommodated him by ordering scrambled eggs and covered them with catsup. We both got a good laugh out of that.

After breakfast I drove us out to the scene and parked on the edge of U.S. 66. Sgt. Consoni asked if I knew how to use his camera, a 35mm box camera. I said yes, so he handed it to me; he hated being the photographer. I placed a roll of 35mm film in it, rolled it up, stood outside and aimed the camera west and clicked off the first picture which many times was no good. Unbeknown to me, I captured two vehicles in mid-air that had hit headlight to headlight in the west bound lane. We heard the crash and saw smoke so we jumped in the car and headed west about a quarter of a mile. We arrived at the scene and the two cars were just settling down and I could see multiple people in one car and a driver in the other. We called it in and asked for ambulances from Winslow and Holbrook. There were five in one car, four with multiple injuries and one 10-year-old boy in good shape. I got the 10-year-old out of the car and grabbed a woman at the scene and asked her to keep the boy away from the cars as he had been begging his mother to be alright and she was obviously deceased. I then went to the other vehicle and the driver had multiple injuries and one hand was stuck under the seat. It was wrapped around a beer can. The passenger was lying on the floor of the car and had a large gash in his forehead. He said he was hitchhiking and the driver had picked him up in Flagstaff. He said the driver was drinking so he tried to get out in Winslow but the driver would not stop. I turned around and saw the boy was back in his car pulling on his mother's arm. I removed him and wrapped him in a blanket and placed him in my car and a women came up and said she would stay with him.

By then there was plenty of help. A group of search and rescue folks from California had stopped to help. They were the Hill and Gully Search and Rescue and had a few people from the medical field. Two ambulances arrived from Winslow and we loaded two injured. There was a Dr with the rescue group and they had their Jeeps set up for litters. They loaded two injured and followed the ambulances. Other members rode in the ambulances and kept all alive till they arrived at the Winslow Hospital and one injured was taken to the Winslow Public Health Hospital. The Holbrook ambulance arrived and took the hitchhiker to Holbrook Hospital. Earlier Sgt. Consoni had come and asked if I had a tow strap and I told him there was one in the trunk. By this time Sgt. Consoni had taken my car and had gone to the Joseph City side of the completed I 40 and ripped out the barricades and opened up I 40. He then went to the Winslow side and opened up east bound I 40.

I had sent the 10-year-old to the Holbrook Hospital in the ambulance to be checked to make sure he did not have any serious injuries. I got the scene cleaned up and drove to the Winslow hospitals. Sgt. Consoni was on the radio explaining to Lt Naval what he had done. He told me he was sure it would cost him but he could not stand by and let another accident happen. By the time we got to the hospitals to do the follow up, all five accident victims were deceased. I got all the information I could from the hospital which was not a lot. With the personal effects, I was able to able figure out that the female driver was traveling with her husband and two sons. The third boy was not related. The only one wearing a seatbelt was the 10year old that survived. We drove to the Holbrook Hospital and found that the 10year old was in good health but emotionally not good. There was no facility where he could be left and the juvenile officer said they could try to find a place to keep him until family could be contacted. I talked to Sgt. Consoni and told him I had room and my wife and I could care for him till family came. At about 7 p.m. I dropped Sgt. Consoni at the office and went home to take the boy and my father-in-law, who was quite tired by this time.

Since I was the only unit on night Sunday shift, Sgt Consoni told me to go to the office and work on my accident reports and take any calls that came in. I got to the office at about 8 p.m. and called the San Diego Police Department and asked for assistance in making the death notification. They were able to locate the next of kin, a grandmother and grandfather. They were not able to find an address for the other boy who was deceased. They said they would go to the house and put them on the phone. About 8 p.m. I got a call from San Diego PD and they put the grandfather on the phone. I made notification advising them their daughter, son-in-law and grandson had been killed in a two vehicle accident on US66 east of Winslow Ariz. Their 10-year-old grandson was well and being cared for by my wife. I asked if they could help with the second 12 year old deceased and they informed me he was a best friend and his folks lived just down the street. They gave the phone back to the San Diego Police officer and they agreed to go down the street and let me make the notification. After 15 minutes I was on the phone with the other parents and completed the notification. This notification stayed with me as it was probably the hardest task I've ever had to do. I then started to work on the scale diagrams and got a great portion of the reports completed before my shift ended at 2 a.m.

On Monday at about 145 p.m. when I checked back on duty I was told to come to the office and call the boys grandparents. I did and was advised they would not be taking custody of the surviving boy. They were 81 and 82 and did not want him to go through another loss in a few years. They had made arrange- ments for the other boy's parents, who lost their only son, to take custody of their grandson and they were having the paperwork being handled so they could come to Holbrook and take the boy home.

The next day they arrived to pick up the boy and asked to see the vehicles and the scene. I drove them out to the scene and showed them where the accident occurred. I did my best to talk them out of looking at the vehicles but they insisted. I took them to the wrecking yard and they saw the vehicles from a distance and decided they didn't need to look in. I then took them to my house and turned the boy over to them.

The truck car accident went to federal court in San Francisco about 2 years later. Also, as an aside, I got my first letter of reprimand for wasting traffic supervision time on two stolen vehicles and was instructed to turn all criminal activity over to the Sheriff's Office. It didn't matter that Navajo county had no deputies available. The good old days

Great men do the right thing even though they know the repercussions of their actions.

Sgt. John was a great man and one who greatly influenced many patrolmen, me especially.

It Wasn't My Time
Don Barcello #515

It was February 1973 and I was patrolling SR87. I had a favorite fishing spot at Tombstone Ridge. I could back into my spot and watch for cars passing over the yellow line.

That day, I had backed into my spot and settled in to watch traffic. I hadn't been there two minutes when a man in a pickup pulls up and the driver tells me there is a large boulder blocking the highway just south of us. I told him I had just come through that area and there were no boulders on the road. He assured me that there certainly was. I pulled out and retraced my route and sure enough a huge boulder was sitting on the highway. I mean a huge boulder! I called the dispatcher and requested that DOT send a crew to remove the boulder. DOT showed up in a pickup. When they realized what they had, they called for a crane and a dump truck. I spent the day directing traffic as they removed the boulder.

I had come through that area just minutes before the boulder came down. If I had come through that area a few minutes later, I would have been history. I was spared that day.

Note:

In our previous book, "That Reminds Me of the Time", we included a story titled "Good News and Bad News" that related a series of events from 1972, when Colin Peabody returned from vacation and was told a story by Bob Varner of how Patrolman George McGuire was using Colin's patrol car one night when he arrested a drunk Navajo woman driving a Volkswagen. Long story short, while George was inventorying the VW, the woman got the cuffs in front of her and took off in the patrol car. George chased after in the VW until he commandeered a Chevy pickup that wasn't any faster than the VW. The woman finally stopped and George completed the arrest about 30 miles from where it started. Now here is the rest of the story

NO HARM-NO FOUL? MAYBE NOT!
Jack Grant #1445

Just reading the book(I am in California and borrowed Frank Root's copy), when I read your account of "Good News/Bad News". Now for the "Really Bad News".

In 1974, my rookie year in Holbrook, the time came around for the "District Party", when all of the officers got together for some steaks and beer, and war stories.

As was the practice, after dinner, Bob Varner emceed the program, which consisted of some short speeches and "awards" to recognize memorable events in which our patrolmen were involved.

As a finale, George McGuire was called up to receive a special award (I don't remember what Bob called it). Bob then proceeded to recount the story of the stolen patrol car.

Everyone in the audience thought the story was hilarious, with the possible exception of George, and Tom Milldebrandt, the Major in charge of the Northern Division. I happened to be sitting across the table from the Major, and I noted that as the story was being told, as only Bob could tell it, the major's cigar was rapidly disappearing, even though it wasn't lit. The major had evidently not heard the story before, since no paper had been filed on it. It seems that while George may have been operating under the "no harm, no foul" doctrine, the major did not agree.

As a result of that and several other incidents which occurred that evening, at least one of which involved a response from Holbrook PD, the following Monday it was very quiet in the District Three office, since several of our folks had been suddenly summoned to Phoenix to have a chat with the Major.

I meant to add, that to my knowledge, that was the last district party held in D-3 for many years. Don't know if the events of that evening had anything to do with that party.

I MISSED THE PARTY
Colin Peabody #481

Great follow-up story!! I believe we were in between Sgts at that time, as I think our new Sgt came on board about the time I came back from vacation, so the story probably never made it to Phx until Milldebrandt heard it in Holbrook. I had transferred to Phoenix the end of 1973, so missed that party!

WORKING ON THE REZ
Dick Lewis #176

One thing about the Apache People, they all take their medicine without complaint. It seems like a fact of life, you get drunk and get arrested, life has to go on.

On the San Carlos and Whiteriver Indian Reservation, we were authorized BIA officers also. This gave us authority on and off the highway.

Often we had contact with Indians who we arrested for DWI. Sometimes women with little kids, sometimes two women with a car load of little kids all under 5 years old.

When we arrested an Indian subject we had to call the Tribal Police. They would bring their wagon out to transport and book. Everybody would go to jail, the little kids and all. No wonder they have an attitude against authority. They had been jailed several times before they were old enough to go to school.

One night I came upon an individual walking down the center line in the dark of night. I asked him, "Are you drunk?" He answered, "Yup, pretty good drunk." It is easier to walk down the white line at night than on the rough shoulder, especially if you are drunk. In those days they drank out of quart bottles, no cans.

I was called out about 2 AM and sent east on US70. A car parked in the road. Between the reservation line and town, I found a dark car, lights out, parked westbound right on the center line.

I approached the vehicle and it was locked and the driver was sitting behind the wheel with his chin on his chest, dead asleep. There was no way I could wake him up, no matter how much noise I would make.

I finally got the windwing open and then the door unlocked. I opened the door and grabbed the persons collar kind of gently. He raised up his head, looked at me and said, "The only reason you are doing this is that I am an Indian", and dropped back into a deep sleep. Needless to say, I put him to bed in the Gila County jail.

YOU'RE NOT GOING TO CUFF ME
Bob Singer #2693

One night, I was working by myself on US-89 north of Gray Mountain on the reservation when I stopped a car going over the speed limit. As I did what I was trained to do, I asked the driver to step out and follow me to the right side of my patrol car and stand in front of the passenger front door while I called Flagstaff dispatch to run a drivers license and warrants check. The driver and only person in the car was a weathered old Navajo man about 6'3" and 220 pounds. We talked about where he was going. He pointed north with his lips and in his heavy Navajo accent, said he was going home to Tuba City, "way ober dare". A minute or two passed by and suddenly the dispatcher said, "2693, 10-38 Mary". I grabbed the mic and said "10-4, standby". Since I was new and out there by myself, I could tell by the dispatcher's voice that she was concerned. I told the driver that he had a warrant for his arrest and I was going to place him under arrest. He looked me square in the eyes and said, "you are not going to put those handcuffs on me". Full of my abilities and confidence that I could handle this, I reached in with my left hand and pulled the long wooden baton out from under the headrest and put it in the ring holder on my gun belt. Still looking me squarely in the eyes, he said in his kind of slow deliberate speech, "you can beat me as much as you want with that stick but you are not going to put those handcuffs on me. Now I was starting to think twice about what was about to happen. Now the dispatcher was calling, "2693, code 20". I answered, "2693 code 4 for now, can you verify where the warrant is out of?" I then told the driver that the warrant was probably out of an off reservation court and that I would not be able to place him under arrest and take him off of the reservation if that was the case. I then told him that just for my safety and his, I wanted to put the handcuffs on him in the front and for him to have a seat in the car and I would leave the back door open while I waited for the dispatcher to verified the warrant and that I would take them off if the warrant was off the reservation. A short time later, Flagstaff dispatch verified that it was out of the Flagstaff J.P. court for failing to appear on a traffic ticket. I told the dispatcher that I couldn't arrest him and take him off of the reservation and that I was "code 4". I let the driver out of the car, took the handcuffs off of him and told him he needed to get to the court in Flagstaff to take care of the warrant. Lesson learned about thinking the long wooden baton would cure everything.

THE GREAT ESCAPE
Tom Ticer #490

Back in the 70's I patrolled I-10 from Blythe to just east of Quartzsite and US60 from Quartzsite to just east of Wenden.

One night while I was working a 6 to 2 shift I had a civilian observer with me. He was Danny Nasca who lived in the area and was a sheep guide to Desert Sheep and one of our wrecker drivers for the area. About midnight that night I arrested a middle-aged man for DUI near Quartzsite. He was handcuffed and placed in the front seat. Danny rotated to the rear seat for the ride to Parker. The handcuffs were secured behind the man's back and once he was secured with the seat belt, we started our trip of about 30 miles to Parker.

After we had travelled about 10 miles Danny poked me in the back and told me the subject was out of his handcuffs and that his hands were in front of him.

As I prepared to stop, the subject started to laugh. We stopped and I took him out of the vehicle to be re-cuffed. I asked how he had slipped out of the cuffs and he said he did not have a thumb on his left hand!

When I re-cuffed him I only cuffed his right hand and put the vacant cuff around his pant belt in front of him with the buckle behind him.

I learned during that arrest that it never hurts to double check the cuffs!

For the rest of my career with the patrol I counted thumbs on all suspects I arrested.

THE DRUNK
Bill Rogers #3578

I don't recall why I stopped his vehicle, I cannot recall the field tests I gave him. These memories dissolve among the hundreds of DUIs that have been stopped over the years. It was probably for weaving in and out of his traffic lane, or speeding, or driving too slow, or lack of control while cornering his vehicle, or a red light violation, or a headlight out, or one of the hundreds of traffic violations drunks commit.

For whatever reason, I know I had arrested a smelly, verbally aggressive, strong young man who had vomit stains on the front of his shirt. I handcuffed him and he was seated in the back preparing to spit through the patrol car cage at me. I listened as I drove the former drunk driver towards the jail to an endless string of foul language, heard explosive burps, and watched spittles of food erupt from his mouth. He continued to try to spit on me. I never saw the picture on the DPS recruitment poster.

I swerved to avoid hitting a dog and my prisoner was propelled forward out of the back seat. He wound up prone, face down in the rear seat floorboard. He was facing the floor, his hands restrained behind his back and only able to split upon himself.

What I did was not exactly following policy. I had not seat belted my arrestee. In this car, I would have had to reach across him to secure the latch. Something I did not look forward to on a spitting, vomit stained person who probably had never worn a seat belt anyway.

For the next few minutes, I listened to mumbled noise coming from the drunk. Then after a few minutes, I realized I could only hear the music on my FM radio, which I had turned up to down out my noisy passenger.

The unmistakable stench of vomit and body order filled my cars interior. I yelled toward my arrestee to try to get a response.

I had a concern for his safety, so I decided to stop my vehicle and check on him. I found a dirt pullout and exited my patrol car. I opened the right rear passenger door away from the traffic side. There, laid facedown and unmoving was my drunk. Yelling and poking at him received no response. My mind flashed back to a recent training video on positional asphyxiation. It had

told how arrested subjects placed in a position not unlike this drunk could possibly choke on their own vomit. Being restrained contributed to the situation, along with their decreased mental and physical capabilities.

There was only one way to find out for sure. I leaned into the rear area and lifted the unresponsive bulk of a man from his current position. Anyone who has ever moved dead weight understands how taxing this can be.

I was sweating and using every muscle I had on this warm summer night. I half lifted, half dragged the drunk man out of my car finally placing him in a seated position with his back against the right rear tire.

I was hot, tired and every pore in my body was sweating, even my toes. But as I evaluated the drunk, a cold chill flashed across my body. His head was slumped over to one side and I lifted his head to check for a pulse. Nothing! No breath were detectable either. I was pretty sure that he had only a few minutes left on earth.

I know how to give CPR but I didn't want to lock lips with him, and once you start you can't legally stop. My mind started to camera roll just how much trouble I was in. I thought I'd always been an alright guy and now it was just over. It didn't seem fair. But then I thought I had a chance to help this guy.

I knew if I could clear his airway, chances were he'd begin breathing again. I guess it would be worth a try. I steadied the drunk to sit against the tire and leaned down on one knee just to the left of him. I drew my right fist and pulled it back behind me to get the most power. I exploded driving my fist as far as possible into his upper abdomen.

The momentum of my fist lowered my shoulder at just the right level for the drunks funnel of projectile vomit to fire past my body.

I watched as the drunk man basically came back to life. After a few minutes I helped him back to his feet and back into the rear of my patrol car, sitting up this time. The remaining journey to jail was uneventful. The man didn't curse or attempt to spit on me.

I never told my supervisor or anyone at work about this drunk. I didn't want to get any lifesaving award anyway. I'd like that the man went out and did something great, win the Nobel Peace or something, but I rather doubt it.

I'm just glad he probably doesn't remember through his alcoholic hazy mind.

HI HO SILVER!
Jim Chilcoat #137

I was working the 1600 to 0100 on Buckeye Road from 51st Avenue to the Cosmos south of Buckeye. MP135 to MP188. I had been on for about an hour when I observed a vehicle that was wandering all over the westbound lane at 107th Avenue and US80. I turned the lights on and they stopped just west of 107th Avenue. That part of 80 had the railroad on the north side and a small drainage ditch before the highway started. The juveniles got out of the front seat from the right front door, but just before they did, the driver traded seats with the passenger sitting in the middle, then tried to tell me he wasn't driving and didn't have a driver's license. There were two more juveniles in the back seat with a case of beer.

At that particular time in history we had been instructed to call juvenile or liquor control officers and turn the juveniles over to them. We were no longer permitted to book them into the juvenile cell at the local police department or sheriff's office. So, I called for liquor control, intending on turning them over to them and let them make the follow-up. Well, it was almost dark before they showed up. But while waiting, a rider on horseback had come down to where we were. But he was on the north side of the tracks. He wanted to know what was going on. I told him to go on about his business and stay on the north side of the tracks. He returned to the west, still on the north side of the tracks.

The liquor control agents finally arrived. Their first question was "where is the beer?" I explained everything to them and was starting to leave the scene when down the middle of the highway eastbound, came the rider on horseback at a full gallop and yelling "Hi Ho Silver!"

I immediately got in my vehicle and did a U turn to head east. The rider immediately turned south on 107th Ave. at a full gallop. I was soon southbound and had gone less than one fourth of a mile when I spotted the rider lying alongside the right edge of the highway. Silver had apparently thrown him.

I got out and after making sure he was okay, arrested him. Then I went to find Silver. He was in his barn and munching hay. I then went to the Tolleson jail to book the lone ranger.

After I had finished the booking and had the rider in the drunk tank, I called my booking to radio as I always did.

It went well until the dispatcher asked where the vehicle was stored. I told him there was no vehicle. He said, "I thought you said it was a charge of drunk driving". I said it was and he asked, "Well, where is the vehicle?" I said there was no vehicle, it was a horse. He then informed the other people in the radio room of what I had said and they were all roaring with laughter. After they had time to regroup themselves, we finished the booking.

And the next morning the judge advised the violator what he was charged with. He pled guilty, was fined $100.00 which he paid, and was released.

A DIFFICULT PHONE CALL
Allan Wright #629

I was the Supervisor for the DPS Criminal Investigations unit that encompassed Cochise County, Graham, and Greenlee Counties. Our primary duties were the enforcement of Narcotics violations, and assisting other law-enforcement departments as requested. The Sheriff and County Attorney of Cochise County had requested that we, DPS, investigate all homicides within Cochise County. At the time two of the best homicide investigators I ever worked with was Herman Flores, out of Benson, and Barney Farnsworth out of Safford.

I had a very good over all team, that I was proud to work with.

In May of 1977, a Saturday, I received a page to call the County Attorney, Beverly Jennings at her office. During our telephone conversation, she explained that a County employee was running a Caterpillar in the Huachuca City land fill when his blade tore open a bag and exposed what he thought was a human breast. He stopped his Cat and looked to see the upper torso of a human body. He called the Sheriffs Office. Beverly wanted my task force to investigate the discovered body.

I told her that the County dump was used by Ft. Huachuca, Sierra Vista, the County and the City of Huachuca, and that I wanted an investigator from each agency so that in the event that this was a homicide the task force would then turn the case over to the jurisdiction agency Officer and then we would support what ever they need. She thought that was a good idea.

I had total and complete support from the Sierra Vista Police Chief, the Mayor of Huachuca City, the Sheriffs office and the Ft. Huachuca Provost Marshalls office who assigned an investigative agent from each Department, except the Huachuca City Dept who did not have an investigator. If the homicide had occurred in Huachuca City or the County, DPS would be the lead investigating agency.

I assigned Herman and Barney as the lead investigators and we decided to use the Huachcua city's offices as a command post. The first huge job was to search the dump for other body parts and any evidence or information that would help us identify the victim. That was a hell of a job to do.

I wanted Barney and Herman to be the only investigators to search the dump so any evidence found would have a good chain of custody. They searched all day and through the night. We brought flood lights out from the County. We were especially searching for the victims head which had not been located.

They called me and asked to meet them at the Huachuca command post that evening. When I arrived, they had a lot of items laid out on several tables with proper evidence identifications marked.. That included bloody clothes, both arms, both legs the upper and lower torsos, but they did not discover the head of the victim. In one of the pants pockets they discovered a drivers license and a civilian dependent ID card in a cut off pair of pants. The identification was of JLC age 20.

The Provost Marshal investigator (can't remember his name) immediately went on Post to see who she was. He came back and told us that she was married to a PVT. Michael B Cagle, age 20, an Army nurse at the Post hospital and that he had one of his officers covertly locate, but not disturb the husband and said he was presently working, and his POV motor cycle was at the hospital.

We established a surveillance team consisting of our team, DPS Dan Barns and DPS Bob Boyle, a Sierra Vista investigator (can't remember his name) and I think DPS Mike Cass out of Bisbee, along with the Army investigators. That way, if he went off base, we would have both jurisdictional agents involved with the surveillance.

We also obtained the couples living location in Sierra Vista a 14' wide mobile home they were renting at a mobile home park.

The dump search team, DPS Herman Flores and DPS Barney Farnsworth, wanted us to find a cadaver search dog, so we located one at the Tucson police De- partment and they sent a team to the dump.

Believing that the homicide probably occurred at their mobile home, I contacted Lt. Jim Moody, my supervisor in Phoenix and requested they send down a lab team via Queen-Air to assist with the evidence search of the home involving blood and tissue.

Meanwhile, the suspect, M. Cagle, was on the move. He went to the Army's Psychiatrist Office for awhile then to the Post's drinking establishment. Then he left the Post and returned to his home in the trailer park. The only vehicle he had was his motorcycle. We did not have enough probable cause to arrest him yet, so I had a surveillance team sit on his house all night, while Herman and Barney worked through the night at the dump site. Pvt. Cagle did not leave the house that night, but he did return to work at the hospital the next morning.

All the evidence was packaged and labeled, body parts put into a refrigerator at the command post and the Sierra Vista investigator along with Herman and Barney went to the County Attorneys Office in Bisbee to get a search warrant for the house.

The DPS lab technician arrived at the airport and one of our officers picked him up, and by this time it was late evening the next day. All the officers were dead tired, so I relieved them from the house surveillance and I took over that job as the Army's team kept track of him on Post.

Late that evening, while Herman, Barney and the Sierra Vista detective were still in Bisbee getting a search warrant, Cagle left the post and arrived at his house. I decided to arrest him for illegally disposing of a human body, to keep the arrest out of the homicide part and to try and preserve any evidence inside the house, as we had enough to arrest by that time.

When I arrested him, I placed him in my Blazer while the team was coming with the search warrant. They had advised me they had the warrant plus an arrest warrant, as the County Attorney said we had enough to prosecute, even without the search of the house.

I asked Mr. Cagle if he needed anything, as I did not want to formally question him about the homicide until we could get the Sierra Vista detective involved with the interview. He asked me if I could find someone to take care of his dog.

When the team arrived at the house to do the search, I left with the suspect and went to the Sierra Vista P.D. office. The Sierra Vista detective arrived and we started the interview.

I received a phone call from Herman Flores who told me the first place they started to search was the bedroom. They opened the closet door and on the top shelf was the head of the victim. The lab technician passed out.

During our interview, we advised him of his rights, again. It was obvious we had to go easy with Mr. Cagle as he would just stare at the table and talk with a low voice. He told us that he and his wife would fight over money all of the time, and he had stashed some money in his sock drawer and she found it. They argued, and she picked up a pool cue and struck him with it. He had been taking drugs that day and drinking and just snapped and choked her to death before he knew it. When he realized she was going he tried to give her CPR and revive her, but she never did respond.

He further stated that he did not know what to do. He could not take her out and bury her as he only had his motorcycle. He did more drugs, drank more alcohol and then decided to cut her up and put her in the trash. He placed her in the bath tub and dismembered her body using a steak knife. Then, I asked what was he going to do with the body part in the closet? He looked up from the table and said he loved her very much and was going to take that part and bury it under a tree where they had made love in the Chiricahua Mountains.

We took photos of his person, there was a bruise mark where she struck him with the pool cue and scratch marks to his neck and arms. He was booked into the Sierra Vista City Jail.

The evidence was obtained from the house search, the lab tech swabbed the bathroom and sinks, and they found a steak knife with serrated edges that appeared to resemble the serrated parts of the body.

All of us were dirt tired and the rest of the work could be done the next day, as officers had worked non stop since the first body part was found at the dump. I went to my condo and tried to relax. At about 10 pm I got a phone call from a man that identified himself as the father of the deceased woman. He said he was Vice President (as I remember) of American Airlines and wanted to fly her remains home, so he contacted the funeral home to make arrangements. The director at the funeral home told him she could not be viewed. When he wanted to know why they gave him my home phone number. I was shocked and really didn't know what to say to him, but he kept insisting he know. I finally told him his daughter had been choked to death and then Mr. Cagle dismembered her body. He screamed and the phone went dead. About a half hour later, he called again. He was composed, but wanted to know more information. That was the most difficult phone call and death notification I ever experienced, and was not happy with the funeral director for giving out my home phone number. If I remember right, he was also the Mayor of Sierra Vista at the time.

Mr. Cagle was convicted of second degree murder and sentenced to the State Prison.

My hat is off to all of the team that did a great job. That is the way it is suppose to work.

ALIVE AND WELL
Ron Cox #1101

This story was told to me about Larry Landers, #1075, by his son Travis. I am submitting it for Travis with his permission. Larry was working graveyard by Gila Bend. It was a cold, wintery night and traffic was slow. He decided to back up by an overpass, out of sight, and just wait and see what might come by. After a very short while, a long limousine went by at a fairly high rate of speed and he decided to give chase. He caught up to the limo and the driver obediently pulled over. As Larry is walking up to the limo, he shines his flashlight in the rear window and to his surprise, sees a cadaver stretched out in the seat! He became quite excited, pulled his revolver, and starts ordering the driver to get out, then starts putting the handcuffs on him. The driver is frantically hollering and asking why he's being cuffed? Larry says, "What the hell are you doing with a cadaver in your back seat?"

The driver says "it's not a cadaver! It's DAVID BOWIE!" Larry answers..........oh. That was the night that Larry got to meet DAVID BOWIE, alive and well.

JUDGE AL BOLLMAN
Gary Ciminski #4575

I started out in the Willcox squad and the JP in Willcox at that time was Al Bollman. Judge Bollman was a retired Border Patrol station chief and was pretty famous for running a strict court. I went into his office or chambers once and hanging on the wall next to his desk was a hangman's noose. I never saw it myself, but the deputies swore up and down that whenever Judge Bollman was holding court he had a Colt Peacemaker on his belt under his robe. The Cochise County attorney allowed us to write tickets for personal use marijuana and I found out pretty quick that Judge Bollman was a lot less lenient with marijuana charges than if you filed felony charges. I asked him once why he always issued the maximum sentence for personal use when other judges were so lenient and he told me in his slow drawl, "The law doesn't say you can have some marijuana, it says you can't have any." One day I stopped a young guy from back east and immediately smelled marijuana when I walked up to the car. I got him out and found out his license was suspended in Arizona so I hooked him up. The only dope I found on him or in the car was the last bit of a joint in his shirt pocket. So I buttered him up telling him this was a felony in Arizona, but I was allowed to cite him with a misdemeanor that was a lot less serious etc. Then I took him in to see Judge Bollman. The judge read him his rights and the charges and when he got around to asking how he wanted to plead, the young man (thinking he would get off easy) said, "It's mine your honor, I want to plead guilty." Again in his slow drawl, Judge Bollman said, "Very well, this court sentences you to pay a $1,000 fine (to which the young man eagerly said yes sir), and 30 days in jail." I couldn't help chuckling to myself as the sentence was pronounced, but I almost laughed out loud when I looked over and saw the young man at the defendant's table crying. I sure miss Judge Bollman.

THAT'LL BE $100.00
Tim Hughes #793

While I was stationed in Salome, Kerry Nelson chased but couldn't catch a speeder westbound on US60. At Quartzsite he noticed the vehicle getting gas at Stuckeys. Kerry approached the driver and learned that he was Dan Gurney of professional racing fame involved in a cross country road race of some kind.

Kerry cited him for 100+ MPH into Judge Hagley in Quartzsite. Several days later we were at the judges residence which also doubled as a courtroom and the judge was trying to decide what to fine Gurney. Someone suggested to the judge that Mr. Gurney was a race car driver and that he needed a drivers license to race so he would certainly pay any fine the judge levied.

At that time, Judge Hagley grinned and pounded the table and said, "$100.00." Of course in those days $100.00 was a pretty severe penalty and as it turned out Mr. Gurney paid the fine and was never heard from again in Quartzsite to my knowledge.

THE DOWNFALL OF JUDGE DAVIS
Bob Pierce #411

In book one, I read two stories mentioning that Judge Davis from Salome had been removed from office. That was true and here is how it happened:

In 1967 when I graduated from the academy, I was assigned to Salome as my first duty station. Judge Davis was the JP and had been for years. As time went on, I found that a lot of citations issued to out-of-state drivers were coming back OJ (out of jurisdiction). This was happening with more and more frequency. In reviewing these out-of-jurisdiction citations, I found they were issued to out-of-state drivers working for major truck lines. I began stopping trucks from these truck lines looking for those drivers. My intentions were to arrest these drivers and to have their trucks towed, explaining to the drivers why I was stopping them.

After about a week of this, a truck from one of the truck lines stopped behind me as I was dealing with a violator. When I was finished with the violator, I walked back to the truck to see why he had stopped. It turned out, he was one of the truckers I had been looking for. He had his canceled check to prove he paid his fine and it was signed by Judge Davis. Within about three weeks, I had over 20 canceled checks all made payable to, signed, and cashed by Justice of the Peace Davis.

REMOTE DUTY AND RURAL JUDGES
Tom Gosch #1172

I had the privilege of living and working in remote duty stations over the years, namely Ash Fork and Salome. The officers were tightly knitted together as we lived in close proximity and our families interacted. We were often called out in the wee hours of the night to back each other up; it was a life style.

Another advantage was getting to know the locals. There were those who became life long friends and those that only Jesus could love. Getting to know the Justice of the Peace was a definite advantage and most often a real treat.

On one evening in the early 70's, Judge Hank Blanchard of the Seligman Justice Court was riding with me as he did on occasion. He was a short balding guy in his 60's, on the heavy side with a patch over one eye. On this particular evening, I stopped a car between Ash Fork and Seligman and the driver proved to be DUI; while frisking and cuffing the driver near the right front fender of my car, he looks over and loudly inquires as to who "that little one-eyed son of a bitch" was and assured me that with that goatee he looked like a little one-eyed billygoat. I advised him that he was Judge Blanchard and that he would be seeing him in the morning; he would be well-advised to control himself. Needless to say, my advice was not well taken and the violator continued to berate the Judge until the steel door was closed on the jail cell. Now the cells at the Seligman jail were steel boxes approximately 8x10 feet with a steel door, wire mesh window with a cot and a blanket. I can't help but think that many an offender changed his lifestyle after experiencing those accommodations. At any rate, this one stood before the Judge the following morning with a very apologetic, guilty plea.

After Judge Blanchard retired, Judge Biggins was elected to replace him. I was familiar with Judge Biggins as I had previously arrested him for DUI. I figured my conviction rate was about to take a dive. On the first DUI defendant I took before him, he looked the defendant in the eye and stated that if Officer Gosch arrested you, you were DUI, "guilty". Assume nothing.

In the early 80's, I was stationed in Salome. It was evening and Judge McCaw was riding with me. We happened to be sitting by the post office and across the street was Donaldson's gas station (pretty much the whole town in those days). At any rate, a Porsche pulls into the station, a young guy and his apparent girlfriend are in the car. I note a radar detector sitting on the dash. I told the Judge, watch this. I turned on the radar unit and the guy quickly reaches up and clears the detector; I wait for the guy to about get out of the car and hit him with the radar again. We do this a couple more times while the Judge laughs heartily. This time, I let him get out of the car and walk away. I hit the radar again and the girl grabs the radar detector off the dash and throws it on the floor...need I say more.

YOU CAN'T MAKE THIS STUFF UP
C.B. Fletcher #923

In 1962 I was going through some type of training at headquarters in Phoenix. I lived and worked on the east side. One afternoon on the way home I was on US60 which at that time was not a freeway and it went through Mesa. I was near the US60 - SR87 junction when radio advised of a bad accident north of US60 on SR87. I offered my assistance and headed to the scene. When I arrived, it was a 3 car accident partially blocking the highway.

I asked what the officers on scene needed me to do and they told me to put out traffic cones to direct traffic through scene and to direct traffic. All went well until a car with California plates came roaring through the scene at about 50 miles an hour, scattering traffic cones everywhere.

Sgt Louie Hudson was the supervisor at the scene and he jumped in his patrol car and took out after the vehicle.

One of the officers at the scene told me to follow Louie because Louie was steaming mad and who knows what would happen.

I took off after Louie and he was just getting out of his patrol car after stopping the vehicle when I pulled up behind him. Louie was a little on the heavy side and as he got out of his car he took off at a run, well, maybe a fast waddle towards the violators car. Louie had the old style holster and with every step, his sidearm would slap his leg. I can still see it to this day.

I stood and watched as Louie approached the drivers door, reached in through the window, grabbed the violators shoulders and pulled him out through the window. Louie stood there with a stunned look on his face when he realized that the man had no legs. After a quick recovery, Louie put the driver on the roof of his car and commenced to lay down the law. Louie raged at the guy for a bit and then told him that if he ever saw him in Arizona again, he would never leave the state because he would put him in jail forever. Fuming, Louie turned and walked back to his patrol car got in and drove away.

I was still standing there in shock not believing what I had seen. The man on the car roof said, "Excuse me officer can I ask a favor?" "Sure" I responded. He then said, "Can you out me back in my car?"

True story. You can't make this stuff up!

A LIFE SAVED - A FRIENDSHIP FORGED
Terry Johnson #2479

After graduating from the Academy, I was assigned to the remote duty station of Robles Junction (Three Points), which is about 20 miles west of Tucson on State Route 86. Toward the end of April, 1981, I had just come off a month of swing shift. On swing shift, our area Sergeant allowed us to be very flexible with our 10-8 time; some days we checked on at 1600 hours and other days we would start our shift 1800. If we had reports to write, to have a faster response time to an emergency in our area, our Sergeant would allow us to write reports at our remote housing also known as the Three Points 103.

Being assigned to this remote duty station, with more than 150 miles of three, remote, two-lane highways, we had our share of serious injury collisions in desolate areas and we relied heavily on DPS Air Rescue to assist with medical rescues and other missions. If I was on duty and a serious injury collision occurred, it seemed Denny Welsh, #1608, was always the on-duty Paramedic and because of this, Denny and I became good friends.

On April 25, 1981, I was attempting to get caught up on a back log of reports when I received a call from a DPS Dispatcher who said there were reports of a one vehicle rollover "accident" near Ryan Field. The Dispatcher asked if I wanted Air Rescue to respond. Initially, I thought let me get to the scene and determine if Ranger would be needed or if a ground ambulance would suffice. Something in the back of my mind said send "Ranger." I went with my gut feeling and requested Ranger to respond.

As I approached the scene, Ranger had landed moments before my arrival. I noticed a pick-up truck with heavy rollover damage blocking the roadway. A male child (Shawn) was sitting in the roadway, an injured woman (Cindy) who I assumed was the mother of the child in the roadway and I noticed Denny was with a female child (Misty) in a car seat. I first checked on Shawn. He was confused about what happened, but seemed to be uninjured. I then went over to where Denny was located and noticed he was intently tending to Misty. It was obvious she was seriously injured or even possibly deceased.

Soon after a ground ambulance arrived at the scene. With Misty in his arms, we began loading Cindy and Misty into the helicopter. The medic on with the ground ambulance told Denny they would transport "the mother". When Denny heard that comment, I thought there was going to be a fist fight between Denny and the medic. There was no way Denny would allow Cindy and Misty to be separated. As we were loading them into the helicopter, the husband/father (Marvin) arrived. Understandably, he was frantically seeking information about his family.

Cindy and Misty were transported to the University of Arizona Medical Center. After I completed the collision investigation I responded to the hospital for follow-up. As Cindy was being treated for her injuries, she explained what had occurred. She had reached toward the passenger side of the vehicle to retrieve something. When she looked up, she had run off the road, over steered the vehicle back on to the road and the vehicle started to rollover.

I asked if the child seat had been secured, Cindy told me it had not. The investigation revealed, during the multiple rollover action, the car seat Misty was strapped in to was thrown forward. She impacted the windshield and then went through the windshield. Soon thereafter, I talked to the tending physicians, they were not hopeful, Misty, a two-year-old, would survive her injuries. At the time of the collision, both Denny and I had two-year-old daughters. To say this collision had an impact on us is a gross understatement. Later that day I attempted to call Denny to give him an update on everyone and learned he had left work soon after he finished this call. I called his home and it became very apparent Denny was very upset about Misty. As we were talking, Denny told me, Misty had died at the scene; while being transported to the hospital she went into cardiac arrest and he did CPR on her all the way to the hospital.

A couple of months later, I was washing and waxing my patrol car, when I noticed a vehicle pull into my driveway...... it was the family from the collision! Marvin and Cindy step from the car first and started talking to me. I asked how Misty was doing, they opened the right rear passenger door and out stepped Misty. Needless to say, that was a very emotional meeting with Misty. No one expected her to live. I had completed the fatal supplement to my report and was waiting for the date of death to finish that supplement. Soon after Misty stepped from the vehicle my daughter, Nicole, came out of our house to see what was going on. The two of them instantly became friends.

I was transferred to Tucson, and unbeknownst us, the family moved approximately one mile away from us. Misty and Nicole went to grade school together and their friendship grew.

Denny retired from DPS on August 31, 1994 and went to work for the Tucson International Airport Authority as a Police Officer. After his retirement, periodically, Denny and I would talk or we would run into each other. Every conversation we had would turn to questions about Misty and remembering that day.

I am unclear of the exact date of when Denny was diagnosed with Leukemia. As his health began to deteriorate, he asked if I knew how to get a hold of Misty and her family. We planned for Denny and Misty to meet on May 10, 2016, some 35 years and 15 days after the collision occurred. With it being such great story, with the help of the DPS Public Information Office, a story of their meeting was covered by a Tucson television station. Ten months and eleven days later, on March 21, 2017, Denny passed away. After his passing, it became very clear the meeting with Misty was his dying wish and I am thankful I was able to play a small part in granting his wish.

Many times, I have reflected on that day. I know if it was not for Denny, his quick actions and his abilities as a Paramedic, Misty would not have survived that collision.

Recently, I posted on Facebook a photograph of Nicole and Misty I took of them as teenagers. That caused a flurry of comments and prompted Nicole to search the Internet for the story about Denny and Misty meeting, 35 years after the collision.

Nicole and Misty's Facebook comments about the photograph:

Misty: 'Awe, I love this picture!! Life long best friends!!'

Nicole: 'Holy cow! Look how young we were lol. Is it

wrong for me to mention that she's older by 18 days 14 hours and 3 minutes?' 😜🩶 "

My wife Kallie's comment about the photograph: 'Who would have thought one day I would be Nicole's step-momma and another day I would sign Misty's marriage license and be at her wedding in my court. Love you girls so much!!!' 🩶"

Nicole's Facebook post: 'Since my Dad shared a picture earlier of Misty Heard and I, it prompted me to find and share one of my favorite stories ever, about how we became friends.'"

Misty: 'That was such an amazing day!!!! My family and I were so excited to finally meet Denny!! He was such an amazing man and I'm so glad that our families became friends!'"

THE FIRE AND THE PAPERBOY
Art Coughanour #3131

It was a sunny breezy Flagstaff summer afternoon. My wife, Sally, was out front watering our sprouting grass lawn while I was in the house meandering in a back room behind our kitchen gathering what was needed to cut some firewood that mid-June evening.

At the time I was the assistant managing editor of *The Arizona Daily Sun*, Flagstaff's afternoon daily newspaper. After fetching what I needed, our telephone rang as I headed for the front door. This was long before we had robotic phone solicitations, so it was important to answer phone calls in those days. On the other end was one of my reporters who had planned to go wood cutting with me that evening.

Before answering the call, I placed my chain saw and related equipment on our kitchen counter next to a gas range. My friend, Rick Velotta, informed me he was running about 10 minutes late.

After hanging up, I looked at my chain saw and checked to see if it needed gasoline. With another 10 minutes to spare, I decided to refuel my chainsaw. So I picked up the gas can and began refueling. I set the can down and screwed the gas cap back onto the saw. I then reached for the gas can's lid at which point I knew I had a serious problem as the pilot light on our range had ignited the gas can.

This two-gallon gas can sat on the counter lit like a giant candle leaving me pretty much undecided on what to do next. Being the brain trust I thought I was, I decided I could pick up the can, carry it back through the kitchen, through a back room and out the back door where I could toss it into our backyard.

The first two or three steps went according to plan, but reality hit and adrenalin vanished as I entered the back room. My hand began to feel that severe burning sensation which strongly informed me that Plan A had to be scuttled very quickly.

So on to Plan B. Being a capable athlete at the time, I thought I could heave this "Molotov Cocktail" through a glass window in the back room. Just as I entered this room, I was about 6-8 feet from the window when I let go. This air-born can never made it to the window, falling about three feet short, resulting in a raging fire ball.

Plan C had me running back through the kitchen, through the living room and out the front door where my wife was. However, Plan C also quickly fell apart. When I entered the living room, I heard my 2-year-old son, Aaron, scream. Unbeknownst to me, Aaron had wandered into that inferno. By the grace of God, I was able to race through the flames and grab him.

With Aaron in my arms, I sprinted out of the house and yelled at my wife to go next door and call the Flagstaff Fire Department. For whatever reason, my wife thought I was joking until I threw Aaron at her and grabbed the garden hose she was using to wet our burgeoning lawn endeavor. After grabbing the hose I proceeded to break a window into the back room.

I don't know how long it took Flagstaff fire to reach the scene, probably no more than five minutes, without a doubt the longest five minutes of my life.

While sitting with the fire captain explaining to him what had happened, a number of Flagstaff fire fighters were busy saving my house while Flagstaff police officers cordoned the area. It was pure chaos.

While these 15-20 first responders went about their business, I looked out the window of the fire captain's truck and saw our newspaper courier walking down our street with a bag full of newspapers stuffed in his canvas bag strapped across his shoulder.

As he approached our house, he stopped to survey the situation. To my surprise, he walked down the drive way through the firefighters and then onto the sidewalk to place my copy of *The Arizona Daily Sun* next to the front doorstep. He then cautiously retreated along the same route before heading towards his next home delivery.

Now, you may be wondering what does this have to do with the Arizona Department of Public Safety.

That newspaper boy was David Denlinger, the same David Denlinger who joined DPS as a highway patrol officer before retiring as a captain a few years back. Ironically, before he retired, Capt. Denlinger was my supervisor for a short time in the Criminal Justice Support Division. Under his command, I always made sure when I had to deliver paperwork to him, I placed it very neatly on his desk if he wasn't there. To me, it was a form of professional courtesy.

POT ROAST
Doug Kluender #363

I came across this article in the Arizona Republic under the heading "Pot Roast" that appeared on 8-11-82.

Electricity provided today by the Arizona Public Service Co. may be of a "high" grade.

The Department of Public Safety is giving APS about 33,000 pounds of marijuana for fuel for its Cholla Power Plant near Joseph City.

"We have the stuff to get rid of, and we might as well get some use out of it", said DPS Capt. Doug Kluender, who suggested the idea after learning about similar burns in Florida.

The burn, dubbed the "pot roast" by the DPS will destroy marijuana valued at $35 million that has been accumulating for four or five years. The pot will be mixed with coal, crushed, pulverized and fed into one of four steam generators.

Coal produces about 10,000 British thermal units of heat per pound, and a government study says marijuana can produce about 86 percent of that amount.

This will be the largest marijuana burn in Arizona history, the previous largest being 6,000 pounds. Before, it was burned in incinerators or isolated pits.

Kluender said people downwind probably won't feel any different during the burn because the smoke will be filtered through the plants anti-smog devices.

He said that the burn won't violate the state's new law banning the sale and use of drug related paraphernalia.

"We're under court order to dispose of it," he said. "I don't know if you can consider a power plant paraphernalia."

THE BIG BURN
Bernie Gazdzik #1930

While sitting at my desk one quiet January morning contemplating the lineup for the softball game later that evening, I was interrupted by a phone call that led to a historical event in narcotics history for the state of Arizona. Now mind you as the Assistant Commander of a narcotics task force in Tucson called MANTIS, I had no idea that I would have to go out in the field to make a decision that would bury the task force for months both figuratively and practicality.

The story goes that I had just sent off the street squad sergeant on training in another state when I got a call from the acting supervisor. Vince informed me that they had received an anonymous tip that there was a large quantity of drugs in a warehouse in the south Tucson area. He informed me that they had tried to talk to a gentleman on the premises that was stating he had hurt his head recently and he could not remember anything. He could not provide any information on who was the property owner or any documentation as to his right to be on the premises. He did not have any lease agreement or rental paperwork identifying anything about the property. He again told me he had a "brain injury" and could not remember anything. Finding this as odd to say the least I turned to my officers and told them to go on in and check out the place for any improper entry indications. Within seconds I heard officers that had entered the front door yelling "Hands Up Police" multiple times. At this point I drew my weapon and went inside myself to find a subject laying on the ground with officers over him. I could see a rifle had been pushed aside and secured. Additionally, a female subject was also prone on the floor with officers over her.

Officers continued inside the warehouse but within minutes came out and said to me "Bernie we got dope, a lot of dope." Little did I know at this point just how much dope! I proceeded inside further and was directed to a room that appeared to be filled with a considerable pile of wrapped plastic material. I can remember poking at it with my finger to see how soft it was. I assumed it was marijuana. But it was firm and was quickly informed it was cocaine. It was a mountain of cocaine. My first thought was we would need additional officers and a lot more help.

I stepped outside again to see the three subjects cuffed and secured and I started making phone calls. I started calling Tucson Police for immediate perimeter security, placed a special weapons team on call, and called out every other officer in the task force to get there as quickly as possible. I knew I would need an army. I even started calling Chiefs of Police in the task force, the Sheriff, and of course my chain of command at DPS. I knew it was going to be a long night. I would not be playing softball that evening.

Without going too much into detail of the investigation there was considerable evidence of load vehicle preparations with vehicles being modified in the warehouse. Auto Trader magazines were on the floor, and it was clearly apparent this was a stash house and transitionary port for the cocaine. Search warrants were served, as necessary. The investigation became a complex case involving city, county, tribal, state and federal authorities. That is a story in itself.

But the bigger issue was how do you process all this cocaine. Initially I ordered officers to go get a U Haul truck by any means possible. And after one truck was being loaded by what we approximated were 20-pound bundles it became evident that one truck wouldn't be enough. A second was acquired and it too was overloaded. Now the question was where to take it. As per procedure with MANTIS all evidence was processed by Tucson PD. So, there it went and ended up overwhelming their crime lab and literally was stacked in the hallways on the first floor. There was cocaine everywhere. After this outstanding work by task force officers and the Tucson evidence personnel a final tally was found that the total amount seized was 11,868 pounds of cocaine. I called it 6 tons to be simple.

Again, not wanting to get too specific on the case investigation, the following day I was buried in phone calls from Federal agencies wanting to claim the case and the cocaine. Each Federal agency claimed jurisdiction and wanted to take the dope into their possession. I had to call a task force board meeting the next day to get direction on these matters. Again, that meeting is a story in itself but the final decision was to share the information with all Federal agencies inquiring and hold on to the cocaine. As I mention I was the Assistant Commander of the group, the Commander was on vacation in Europe, so I was pretty much making decisions on my own. Holding on to the dope did not please the Federal agencies......

After some time and working with Federal and County prosecutors, we received permission to destroy the evidence. But what to do with 6 tons of cocaine. I don't remember who suggested it but ultimately it was decided to take the dope to Winkelman copper smelter. We were to dump the dope in boiling metal caldrons where it was vaporized.

On that fine day I again assembled the army and two Special Weapons teams. We commandeered a tractor trailer placing an officer as driver and passenger and proceeded to take the dope north. This was quite a sight of a parade of police cars unmarked and marked heading down the road. Ranger helicopter was also above.

Finally at the smelter, the truck was backed up to a position where the caldron could get close. Officers began throwing the bundles into it and it swung inside to the immense fire where it was dumped. Officers were positioned to observe with two up in the control center who would operate the machinery. Of course, this was done with close oversight of the factory personnel. I believe it took a few hours but all I can remember was I was extremely happy when it was completed. We all were extremely proud of what we did and to be part of history in what could be the largest narcotic seizure in Arizona history.

THE PURPLE FLAME
Paul Palmer #342

I remember the cocaine burn Bernie wrote about. The cocaine was brought from Tucson to the Phoenix compound under heavy guard. I recall seeing the semi tractor trailer on the compound with all kinds of heavily armed serious looking officers around it.

The video unit was informed that we would be going with the load from the compound to the smelter in Winkleman to video tape the operation.

Since I would have to video tape the convoy at different locations and get shots of the helicopter overhead, I was assigned to ride with Bob Stein and Pete Borquez of our PIO office. Bob would be driving.

I knew we would be going into mountainous terrain and I began having flashbacks of riding with Bob on a trip back from a video assignment in San Diego. We had stopped in Yuma and got some burgers to go. Enroute back to Phoenix we barreled down Telegraph Pass and I looked over and saw Bob with a hamburger in one hand and a wad of fries in the other as he steered with his knees. Anyone who has been down Telegraph Pass knows that this is quite a feat! I've never been so glad to get back on flat ground in my life.

But I digress. I shot video tape of the convoy and Bob would get us in position to get ahead of the convoy at various points so I could get video of the convoy passing by, then speed off to catch up with the convoy. We also stopped several times so I could get video of the helicopter overhead. It worked out great even in the mountainous highway between Superior and Winkleman.

I had made sure that Bob had eaten before we left Phoenix.

When we arrived at the smelter there were officers armed with automatic rifles guarding the entrance and the property around the location where the cocaine would be burned. They were all wearing dual canister breathing apparatus. As we got out of the car we were each given the same type of breathing apparatus and told to put them on and not take them off.

They backed the semi up to where the big smelter was already shooting orange flame. The officers began loading the cocaine into a large steel bucket that looked like it came from a huge front end loader. The bucket was suspended by huge chains and when the bucket was loaded with bags of cocaine, the operator would lift the bucket and swing it over to the flame and dump the cocaine into the fire. When the cocaine hit the flames, the flames turned the most beautiful purple you have ever seen.

It was really difficult to shoot video with my breathing apparatus on. I had been watching Pete and noticed he had taken off his mask. I watched him for a while to make sure he wasn't going to fall over. He seemed ok so I took off my mask. It made running the large camera a lot easier.

What a day, watching six tons of cocaine burn. Bernie estimated that the cocaine was worth approximately $540,000,000.00. You can bet there were some unhappy drug dealers somewhere.

OPERATION BIG MAC/ MORENCI COPPER STRIKE
Frank Root #1089

First of all, the way our troops preformed at Morenci was a tribute to the quality and training of the men and women, both sworn and civilian, that worked at DPS or were associated with DPS. These occurrences took place almost on some details. One of my main duties was to see to it that we had the logistics support the troops and civilians needed, in an area hundreds of miles from the Phoenix compound. My second job was to write orders to place into action the directions of Bill Reutter and Norm Beasley.

Timeline

Aug 1983 National Labor Relations Board (NLRB) declared a 10-day cooling off period for the striking factions.

Early Aug 1983 Reutter, Beasley and Root are assigned to develop a task force and take control of the problems in Morenci, AZ. The Task Force, would later become known at Operation BIG MAC. The 10 day cooling off period allowed DPS to organize, move into position and train for the conflicts that were to follow.

An operations plan was developed that involved DPS sworn and civilians, the Arizona National Guard and several Sheriff's Offices. This plan resulted in the assembling of largest collection of DPS personnel in one place to date.

It took everything and everybody at DPS to make it happen.

It started on a morning at 0630 hrs. when I was notified to contact Captain Beasley. I was the Intelligence Division Commander at the time. After we met with Captain Reutter the task force concept was developed. By the time we were done with the initial meeting, it was decided that Agent Hawley was now the Intelligence Operations District Commander and was to stay behind to protect the women and children. God only knows what he did to change things while we were gone to Morenci.

We staged in Safford, and it was like a Battalion of GI's invading their city.

First we had to quarter the officers and civilian support in Safford, which was south of Morenci. This required someone, I still don't know who, going to all the hotels and motels that were livable and having them cancel all their reservations. Which we did, and of course that made for some unhappy folks who were coming to visit Safford that summer.

The striking miners were also in Morenci. The mine had hired replacement miners to work the mine. That was not well received by the regular miners, so the striking miners would line up outside the gates to the mine, standing along the highway. The mine had chartered busses to bring the working miners in and out at shift change. If there was anything the striking miners could do well it was throw their slag tailings. They threw them at the vehicles as they went in and out of the gates. And when the miners didn't have busses to throw at, the miners would skip the slag material off the pavement and hit the officers in the shins. The edges of the slag were very sharp, and the striking miners were very accurate with their throwing techniques.

It was decided that DPS would line up outside the gates and keep the peace. Great idea, but we were going to need more troops, a lot of troops and the civilians to support them.

Having a military background, the first thing we needed to do was come up with a name for the operation. Kind of like the invasion of Normandy using 'Operations Overlord". After giving it some serious thought as I ate my lunch at McDonald's, I came up with "Operation Big Mac". Big MAC stood for <u>Big Mob Activity Control</u>. I thought it had a nice ring to it. Director Milstead didn't object, so it was officially adopted.

What seemed to be a bit of riot control humor was not so funny when I was on the stand testifying during the civil trial 2 years later. You cannot believe how offensive the attorneys for the miners found the name. It was even more offensive to them, when during my questioning, they discovered I was the one that came up with the name. Amongst other things I was criticized for being insensitive and inconsiderate of the miner's plight.

As we were setting up operations in Morenci and developing our plans, Governor Babbitt arrived in Morenci to observed what was happening. I did not expect much in the form of overt support from him as he was a Democrat. It would not be politically expedient to support a law enforcement action against a union strike.

That night the governor arrived at the intelligence center we had established at the mine complex. He appeared to be reviewing the large charts and maps we had posted on the walls. He then asked a number of questions regarding everything that was happening. Then there was moment of silence as we all watched. You could see that he was about to do something that may not be politically expedient for his future career. He then said, "I will not have terrorist running my state, what do you need to address the problem". Those were the magic works. We knew what we needed, and now we had the support we needed. We covered a few of the basic items with the governor, the expensive ones. He responded, "fine let's make it happen" or words to that effect. He then turned and left the intelligence center.

The Governor authorized the use of the National Guard as support troops and the use of their equipment, in addition to whatever else was required. Our first action was call back to the districts to alert their officers as to their deployment to Morenci. Initially they staged in Safford, and later moved in a convoy up to Morenci.

Fortunately, many of the troops and some civilians were ex-military or in the National Guard and Reserves. The billeting problem was solved by the Guard provided General Purpose Medium tents. These are large, heavy canvas, nasty smelling tents. The troops set about erecting the tents, under the guidance of those who had the misfortune of living in them in their prior carriers in some faraway places. So now we had our hotel accommodations solved.

The female officers had their own set of tents, but due to the high temperatures and high humidity, they slept with the side up. Modesty was out the window at Morenci. Oh, I forgot to mention, it was August in Morenci, and the tents did not come with air conditioning. Hell, we didn't even have fans. They were toasty.

The male officers used the mine showers, which were giant gang showers. There was a small motel which the task force commanders were assigned. At about seven AM the commanders left their room, and left it unlocked. The maids brought in a stack of towels and that is where the female troops showered.

Due to a lack of Restaurants, the National Guard sent out a mess unit (mobile dining facility) to cook our meals. We were usually so hungry, everything tasted good. For many of us it helped us remember why we left the military before we joined DPS. Restaurant problem solved.

We requested Technical Communications to set up an Intelligence Center communications system in one of the rooms at the mine facility. Next thing I know we had full access to all our intelligence files online and everything else on ACIA and NCIC back in Phoenix.

We started having multiple problems with dehydration amongst the troops. It was determined by the paramedics we needed electrolytes for the troops. Phoenix Supply was never one to let us down. Mike Baird, head of supply, went to the local Costco (then Price Club) with a State Purchase Order and a large U-Haul truck. Costco promptly refused the purchase order as they advised the State paid too slow. So as Mike related to me, he wrote a personal check for approximately $5,000 for multiple pallets Gator Aid.

Costco placed the pallets in the U-Haul and off someone from supply went to Morenci, to be available the next morning. Mike then reportedly, that same afternoon, went to our Business Office and explained that he needed $5,000 ASAP to cover a hot check. And you guessed it, the Business Office made it happen. Mike did reportedly ask Costco to not be too quick in cashing the check.

We were very concerned regarding injuries to officers anticipating an escalation in the conflicts. We kept one and sometimes two DPS helicopters in the Morenci area for medivacs and observation platforms. At one point we contacted the Clifton Hospital for planning assistance. Since we felt the nurses in Clifton would be married to or associated with the miners, we did not think it safe for their nurses to care for any of our injured officers. Needless to say, this was not received well by their nurses.

We planned to medivac the officers, as soon as possible to Phoenix or Tucson, if necessary. We then requested three trauma nurses from St Joseph's in Phoenix. We requested that they bring whatever they felt was necessary medically, which they did. Our nurses now set up in the Clifton Hospital with the understanding that our nurses would take care of our troops and they could take care of the miners. This was only done during the height of the conflict.

Feeding the troops was going to be a major challenge before we moved from Safford to Morenci. We planned on a morning arrival in Morenci, to allow the troops to take in the beauty of the area. Sgt. Edward Slechta, #323, who was also ex-military, was sent up from Tucson, to take over organizing and setting up (messing) dining that morning when we were getting ready to deploy to Morenci. Slechta arrived in Morenci, and I explained that I needed approximately 500 troops and civilians fed, starting at 0400 hrs. and loaded on the trucks to go to Morenci by 0700 hrs. Ed contacted a local steak house in Safford and had them open at 0400 hrs. They were to serve one specific meal, bacon, scrambled eggs, toast and whatever else for even money. The restaurant decided it would cost $4.00. They went overboard, to include serving coffee in copious quantities while the troops were dining. The way they treated DPS, you would have thought we were leaving to go overseas.

THE RIOT
Rick Ayars #457

Morenci, June 30-July 1, 1984. After a full year of striking the Phelps Dodge mine and smelter at Morenci, The United Steelworkers union was facing an election to decertify it as a representative union. DPS had begun the previous year to be the buffer between the strikers and the replacement miners that had been hired and were bussed daily from Safford , through the town of Clifton and to the mine in Morenci. To prepare for the potential of violence during the last day of the strike, DPS had gathered 120 officers in Safford motels two days in advance and conducted riot control drills. The front line troops were issued side handle batons and shields. The detention team was issued arrest reports, pens and flex cuffs. On the morning of June 30th, the 120 boarded busses and were deposited in the Morenci Civic Center to await and be ready for whatever happened.

My name is Rick Ayars and I was a captain assigned command of the detention team. My team consisted of Lt. Joe Slama, sergeants Bernie Gazdik and David Gonzales with two squads of officers and a detention bus. We were to take charge of anyone arrested by the front line troops and prepare the paperwork.

The day proceeded without incident until the busses left with the replacement miners at 5PM and drove down through the canyon that separates Morenci from Clifton. The canyon is narrow but contains several businesses including a medical clinic and a tavern in a strip mall configuration along the state highway. The striking miners had been partying in this area during the day with access to alcoholic beverages. The busses received a hefty barrage of rocks and were beaten by sticks during their transit of the canyon. DPS Deputy Director Sam Lewis and operation commander Captain Bill Reutter observed this melee while in their vehicle following the busses. When their vehicle was similarly accosted, the radio call went out "bring down the troops". (I believe an expletive may have left my lips).

Into the busses and down to the canyon we go. The front line troops form a line from the steep bank on the left of the road to the parking area in front of the businesses on the right. My troops were arrayed and ready right behind. Did I mention the tear gas? By now all troops had on gas masks. Tear gas specialists headed by armory Sergeant Ed Teague were equipped with canisters, a fogger and launchers for tear gas distribution.

HARDENED CARS
Frank Root #1089

Then we started having a problem with the Gas Teams shooting gas from the cars. The teams were unable to deliver gas forward of the vehicles. We ask Rad Kirchner at the Phoenix Auto Shop to give us vehicles with roof openings. The next thing I know we had cars arrive with moon roofs installed backwards so they opened up to the front. They were great. I'm sure they were a little noisy inside when the gas teams sent the gas out, but did they look good while they were doing it.

Later we had to ask the auto shop to cover the side windows with a heavy plastic, to keep the rocks from coming through the windows. Apparently, the striking miners did not like the gas teams or their new vehicles. Next thing you know we had plastic on the windows. The only problem was that you could not roll down the windows for air when the AC quit working.

And you guessed it, that is exactly what happened one day. As one of the gas teams came back from making a gas delivery run, the gunner yelled out the moon roof, "We need a medic". I observed as they opened the driver's door and the officer rolled out onto the ground. I must have been all of five seconds before a DPS Paramedic had the driver's sleeves up and hit him with an IV line with another officer holding the saline bag high in the air. Ten minutes later the driver was back on his feet.

CLIFTON
Rick Ayars #457

Our front line troops (and some of us behind) immediately began being pelted by flying rocks. To counter this, Ed Teague and his team utilized a gun loaded with wooden pellets that was designed to be shot into the ground in front of rioters and cause contusions to lower extremities. These tools along with the tear gas were employed and the front line began marching at the half step down the road. The tavern became a focus of interest when the door would open and rocks would be thrown and the thrower would jump back inside and close the door.

The first arrestee was a naked streaker that ran head-on into the front rank of troops. Several more were received from the tavern area after some tear gas "leaked" inside. The tavern owner, a woman that was 6 months pregnant, was one of the last of 20 arrestees and I decided to release her on her own recognizance. After several minor contusions to the troops and a major leg injury to their commander, Captain Ron Hoffman, it was decided that we would withdraw back to the busses and return to the Civic Center in Morenci. It was starting to get dark down in the canyon and we were woefully short of tear gas. When I loaded the detention bus and I looked back down the canyon, I saw a barricade 4 feet high entirely across the highway. Did I mention that it was on fire?

BACKUP TROOPS
Rick Ayars #457

Meanwhile, back at the Civic Center the front line troops were tired and hungry. My team however had to arrange to bed down our prisoners in the cloakroom and try to sort out which officers of the front line had first initiated the arrest. Requesting information from the front line troops resulted in nothing. It was now 9:30 pm and I was notified to report to Director Milstead at the headquarters office. I was asked to get on the helicopter, fly to Safford, and organize the 80 DPS officers that had been ordered to respond immediately from their duty stations. Captain Frank Root advised that the National Guard would supply transport at 4 a.m. and the Department of transportation would supply a skip loader and operator from Clifton at 4:30 a.m. I was to have my newly formed company in the barricaded canyon by 5 a.m. and clear the road.

FOOD CONCERNS
Frank Root #1089

Feeding the troops became an issue. Someone came up with a State Purchase Order that was to be taken to Colonel Sanders in Safford. Duke Moore, #1045 (RIP) and I loaded up in one of the Rangers and departed Morenci. The Safford Police Volunteers had cordoned off a landing zone in the shopping center parking lot in front of Colonel Sanders. We landed in Safford, and it must have been quite the attraction for the locals. We waited while the Colonel cooked and boxed each individual drumstick and thigh for the dinner. We should have requested the large buckets of chicken, it would have been easier to load.

One of the things the military trains you to do is to calculate the cubage and weight of your load. You start with the size of the individual item and multiple it by the number of items you are going to have in the load. This had not been done. I cannot recall the number of meals we loaded, but it was in the hundreds. We had meals on the rear floors, seats, tops of the medical equipment, and on top of the pilot's seats, wedged in every conceivable space available in the Ranger.

After loading the Ranger and getting the doors closed, Duke Moore who could fly anything and the box it came it, fired up the Ranger and brought it up to a three foot hover. At that point he advised me, I think we are going to make it. I don't know if they ever got the chicken smell out of the Ranger when it was over.

THE CLEAN UP
Rick Ayars #457

I turned over the detention team to Joe Slama with advice to book the prisoners for riot even though we didn't know the arresting officer. The arrests would result in a large civil suit that played out over the next several years and is for another story. I grabbed Lt. Chuck McCarty and we headed for Safford. We left Safford on busses that morning so the motel rooms were still available. We commandeered a large conference room and started to get organized. One of the first responders was Captain John Pope, who is one of the best organizers in the department. He was followed by the "old gray fox", my OJT coach, Sergeant Ray Carson. With that base of officers, we put together an organization chart and filled it with approximately 60 troops (20 less than was promised) arrived. We gathered at the guard armory and loaded onto about 4 deuce-and-a-halfs for the ride to Clifton. I went ahead to meet the DOT at the Clifton maintenance yard. The maintenance supervisor advised me that his skip loader operator refused to respond to work because he had many friends among the strikers. I asked the supervisor if he knew how to operate the loader and when he said yes, I told him to take my bullet proof vest and get moving. After a slow drive behind the loader through the completely empty streets of Clifton, we arrived in the canyon to find five barricades of large boulders and one of burned railroad ties and railroad tracks. My troops disgorged from the trucks and arrayed themselves along the side of the road behind the loader and it went to work. As we approached the burned out barricade, the loader began to stir up the leftover dust from the tear gas, (another little unexpected pleasure).

As we cleared the last barricade, the detention bus with my former crew rolled down the hill headed for the Greenlee County Jail. It was followed by the Director and the rest of the 120 officers headed for their motel rooms and a shower in Safford. My newly formed and very tired crew went to dorms in Morenci and crashed but were told to be ready if more problems erupted. As for me, after a short nap, Captain Reutter came to get me to go with him to meet with the heads of the Steelworker Union. They were complaining about the wooden bullets, the tear gas and that Phelps Dodge bulldozed their huts off the cliff during the night. They had built the huts for shelter during the year of the strike. We explained it was Phelps Dodge property and not State of Arizona right of way... so tough! We offered to show them the situation in front of the front gate to the smelter so they followed us and we were describing our highway right of way when Bill Reutter got a page to meet the director at the Phelps Dodge Headquarters about 300 yards down the highway. He drove away leaving me with the now decertified union officials. Immediately a 4-door pickup with 4 rather large security guards descended on us and they began to threaten to throw us off the cliff just as the huts had been done away with. I was in civilian clothes and I was just able to get my ID out and play like a NFL Referee between feuding linemen. Both sides eventually went their separate ways and I was left to walk the 300 yards and express my dismay to Reutter. With the exception of the lawsuit, that was the last altercation that I know about during the Morenci Strike.

A MORENCI LOONEY TUNE
Jack Bell #1777

In late July 1983 a three year old girl was shot in the head as she slept in her home in Ajo, Arizona.

The little girl survived, but this act of violence was the trigger point for the Governor to deploy the Department as peace keepers during a miners strike with Phelps Dodge in both Ajo and Morenci.

The Yuma District was tasked with supporting the Pima County Sheriff's Office in backing up the local deputies stationed in Ajo. We trained and drilled for riot control and eventually had a show down with the striking miners on State Route 85 near the Ajo Fire Station. The situation was best summed up as a standoff or show of force by both sides. Fortunately cooler heads prevailed and the miners dispersed. In all I believe we had a presence in Ajo for about nine weeks before being tasked with responding over to Morenci, Arizona.

In Morenci, it was same strike situation as in Ajo. The Phelps Dodge plant was experiencing a labor strike and was using non-union workers to keep the mining operations going. The union miners were upset and violence escalated as the strike negotiations were stalled.

Initially a handful of officers (roughly 5) were sent into Morenci. We stayed at the Morenci Inn and were assigned to cover the morning and afternoon shift changes at the mine's main gate from the state highway. During the rest of the day, we simply roamed around and stayed visible along the highway. I wasn't in Morenci for the major riot with the miners; but I was sent up with the Yuma District the next day to help clear the state highway and support the policing effort in the event of another showdown with the strikers. After a few days things calmed down and we were able to withdraw.

Before the big DPS deployment and violence I think I spent about four weeks in Morenci. Our presence in Morenci protecting the mine's gate and keeping the state highway opened, was best described as a Warner Brothers Looney Tune. In the cartoon that came to mind there was a sheep dog and coyote meeting

240

each day at a time clock to log in. They were cordial to each other and then went about the day with the sheep dog protecting his herd and stopping the coyote from harming them. At the end of the day they would meet again at the time clock, punch out and say good day.

Each day we would drive up to the main gate and park just off the highway. The striking miners would park on the other side of the main gate and establish their picket line. As in the cartoon we took on the role of the sheep dog protecting the herd while the miners played the part of the coyote trying to menace the herd. Prior to shift change everyone was friendly, the strikers were in lawn chairs and relaxed. It was so friendly, we were even offered baked goods and refreshments the picketers were sharing. But when the whistle for shift change blew and the non-union workers began driving in or out of the gate it was very adversarial. It was mainly a lot of noise and gestures from the picketers, but I'm sure our presence kept it from escalating at that time. After shift change the strikers would return to being civil and we would all leave only to repeat the same scene at the next shift change.

SMOKEY BARE
Tim Hughes #793

During one of our numerous times in Morenci, we played volleyball on the lawn at the Morenci Motel between shift changes. Normally, there were some locals who watched the play. This one day, Bill Kramer went up for a spike or block and as he jumped Ken Hawkins gave his shorts a tug. Unbeknownst to Hawk, Bill's wife, from what I understand, had split his shorts up the side to allow for a cast that he had after an accident. She had put Velcro down the side so he could get the shorts on over the cast.

When Ken tugged on the shorts, they just dropped to the ground as the Velcro gave way. There stood Bill for a split second in nothing but a jock strap and it was painfully obvious that his backside had never seen the sun. As I recall, the game ended at this time as everyone was laughing so hard that play had to be halted. I often wondered what the folks watching thought.

PATROL CARS I HAVE HAD
Tom Gosch #1172

I started with DPS in September 1972. There had been about 90 new officers hired that year between Classes 19,20 and 21; this put quite a strain on transportation to get out new cars. Senior officers would get the new cars and new officers, their hand me downs. In those days, new cars were issued every two years or fifty thousand miles and they came in all colors.

My first car was a beige 1971 Dodge Coronet, as was my second, but the third was blue. My Sergeant finally advised me that I would be getting a new car and that he would go to Phoenix and get it. At that time, they were issuing AMC Ambassadors or Matadors; also Dodge Coronet and Polaris'. My hope was for a '73 Coronet.

Many colors ran through my head; blue, green, white and brown, certainly not red as I didn't want to look like a fireman. The day finally came and Sgt. Jones, #95 went down to get it. He brought it back and parked it in front of the old weigh station on the west end of Williams. (Even though it didn't have any heat or electricity that was our "office". It didn't make much difference as all reports were done at home on our own time.)

I was working the swing shift and very busy as snow had been falling all day. When I finally was able to drive to the office, I saw the new car all covered with snow. I got out of the car and wiped some snow off, only to find that it was a chicken poop yellow Dodge Polaris, not only was the outside ugly, but the interior was a putrid dark green and yellow in a plaid pattern. No doubt headquarters was wanting these cars well out of Phoenix and the new officers were the lucky winners. With six new officers assigned to the area out of Classes 20 and 21, two were assigned yellow Dodges, myself and Bill Hopkins, #1152.

Besides not winning a beauty contest, the car consistently threw the fan belt any time the speed approached 100 mph. I found that if you popped the hood to the safety latch and kept moving you could make it to McMahons Texaco in Ash Fork where Paul kept a good supply of belts. Sometimes there were bigger problems and the car couldn't run, another officer would push you to where it could be fixed. Let me tell you that it is a long way from Seligman and Ash Fork to Flagstaff when you are pushing or being pushed with the push bumper.

The car did have a couple of advantages. You could be driving at the speed limit and have a car pass you at a high rate of speed, it was kinda like a freebee contact .The drivers excuse of "I just thought it was a taxi cab" was kind of humorous especially since there was a big banner across the back saying Arizona Highway Patrol not to mention a set of double bubble gums on top. Then again, out of staters' weren't used to multi colored patrol cars. Another advantage was when you arrested a DUI and put him in the car, they would take one look at the interior and figure they had to be drunk as no car could be that ugly. Your only hope was that they wouldn't blow their groceries as the upholstery was so ugly.

I'll always remember, though not fondly, old D-138 my first patrol car. I had many good patrol cars in the years that followed, my favorite being a 89 Mustang, T-216, wish I still had it. Those are the only two car numbers I remember.

THE DPS AMBASSADOR
Brian Frank #1148

My first patrol car was a new 1972 AMC Ambassador. This was unheard of for a brand new officer to have a new car! But, I soon found out why none of the other officers wanted it. The Ambassador's had a series of mechanical problems, which included: a very weak front end, electrical, transmission, exhaust and most troubling of all- major engine failures. In addition, the exhaust kept blowing out gaskets, which made car sound like it didn't have a muffler. You get my drift.

My very first week on the road, with this fine piece of Detroit engineering, the number seven piston separated, which I later learned was very common problem. Not to fear, AMC replaced the engine. I soon found myself driving it on patrol and on my days off having to have it repaired at the local AMC dealership., This went on for sometime. One memorable day while stopped, the engine back fired and you guested it- it caught on fire! Once again, it was fixed...rats. Another time I recall one Sunday morning parking in front of the Chandler Police Department, in a space which had a slight rise to it for drainage purposes. Having placed the gear selector in park I locked the doors and exited this fine ride and while walking away from it, I noticed to my horror, that it was now rolling backwards and headed for certain rear end damage. At this point all that I could do was to grab the front push bumper and try to stop it with all 145 pounds of me... this while working my way to the locked door so that I could open it up to engage the parking brake before it crashed into something expensive, all to the entertainment and delight of people walking into the police department to visit their relatives that had been arrested Saturday night.

OLE YELLER
Greg Eavenson #680

It was a 1973 Ambassador. It was yellow. I got it new, looked sharp, blew 8 engines (6 patrolling @ 45 mph). Had to take it Gila Bend upon transfer in mid '74. It began stalling out at idle. Replaced everything electrical to no avail. Got new Merc in late 75. Ole' Yeller went to shop for strip out. Shop couldn't get it started, pushed it into lot where tires finally went flat. Had approx. 35,000 miles after almost 2 years of use.

A NASH FOR A MERCURY?
Jay Atwater #1434

Upon graduation from the academy in 1973 I was assigned to my first duty station ion District 3. I was to transport a chocolate brown "Nash" (AMC Rambler) to Holbrook for Patrolman Bob Varner #438. In return, I was assigned his 1972 chocolate brown Mercury with around 42,000 miles. When Bob and I met to switch vehicles, I was greeted with "You son of a b——ch!" He never forgot to remind me every time he saw me.

HEY SARGE, NICE RIMS
Dick Lewis #176

I was the sergeant in Payson with a five man squad. We all got along pretty good. Our watering hole was the Knotty Pine Cafe in Payson. I would check out there and two guys would usually show up for coffee and shop talk. It was a very pleasurable time.

Steve DesJorden had procured a set of beauty rims for the wheels on his patrol car. We all had good cars and were proud of them. He called my attention to them and I thought they looked pretty good.

One day, unbeknown to me, or Steve, Dean Baker took those pretty beauty rims off of Steve's car and put them on my car. I didn't notice until Dean called my attention to them. We left them on my car and no one paid attention to it for some time.

One day we were having our coffee at the cafe and Steve was there. I could see our cars out the window parked in the lot. I said to Steve, "How do you like my new beauty rims?' He said, "They look good, I have a set just like them." Then he looked at his car and said, "Hey, those are mine!"

It was a good joke and we all got a big kick out of it. We still talk about it today.

I DON'T KNOW! I JUST DON'T KNOW!
Paul Palmer #342

Remember when we first came on the department and we thought all the brass were smart? Well, I did at least. Then when we had been on for awhile we began to see the chinks in their armor. By the time we retired, it became what the hell were they thinking!

I came across an article from the Arizona Republic from August 10 1965 written by Paul Dean. seems even back then, the brass just didn't know.

Here is that article. I think you will enjoy it.

Patrol Official Drives In Comfort
It's Such A Pleasure to Take The Thunderbird...

Arizona Highway Patrol Lt Jim Phillips polices in comfort at the wheel of a Ford Thunderbird that cost the state taxpayers $4,367.00.

Registered to the patrol as an unmarked undercover car, the 1965 power equipped, white hardtop was issued to Phillips by patrol Supt Greg O. Hathaway.

I understand it originally was bought for Supt Hathaway's use, Phillips said yesterday.

I asked him if I could borrow it several months ago because I thought it would be nice to drive, added Phillips, a 14 year patrol veteran and once highway patrol aide and chauffeur to former Gov. Paul Fannin.

Phillips users the car on his 5,000 mile a month tours as commander of the patrol's eastern Arizona district, which includes Tempe, Mesa, Apache Junction, Globe-Miami, Safford, Clifton-Morenci and another cities between Phoenix and the New Mexico border.

As an officer who is "on call" 24 hours a day, Phillips keeps the Thunderbird at his Tempe home and drives it back and forth to work.

The patrol's six other district commanders drive unmarked Chevrolets or regular Fords which costs $2,000.00 less than the Thunderbird and are part of the patrol's active fleet of 289 vehicles.

In addition the patrol maintains a surplus squad of 100 1966 cars, now gathering dust in the Phoenix yard of the patrol. Some have been there for months depreciating without being driven a mile.

The patrol also uses 19 expensive Oldsmobiles and Ford LTDs to ferry lawmakers and VIPs in and out of the state.

But only one Thunderbird is registered to the patrol and that is HLW 635 driven by Phillips.

Asked why he drove a Thunderbird, or why the patrol needs a luxury vehicle, Phillips said, "It could be an experimental undercover car, I guess....I just don't know.

Maj Jim Hegarty, the patrol's business manager said the Thunderbird was bought from Paradise Ford, Scottsdale, last year and "the superintendent drove it when it was first purchased."

Hegarty was unable to give a specific reason behind the purchase, but said, "A lot of cars are bought for their special features, generally speaking for evaluation purposes."

"We have Ford Mustangs being used around Globe, I think, to check the suitability of a short wheelbase car," he said. "We also have a Pontiac that we are looking at."

Asked what special features a Thunderbird has for patrol work, Hegarty said, "I just don't know."

Maj Walt Sheets, the patrol officer in charge of purchasing and specifications and Supt Hathaway were not available for comment yesterday.

(The article was also featured a photo of the Thunderbird parked on the DPS compound)

Jim Phillips must have had pretty thick skin, because he didn't let some newspaper article keep him from patrolling in comfort. In the summer of 1966 Jim stopped by my apartment in Holbrook for a visit during one of his swings through the state. He took my picture standing by the Thunderbird. At the time I didn't know exactly how famous that Thunderbird was.

I could have been one of the brass cause at the time I just didn't know!

A SPLIT SECOND DECISION
Charley Ruiz #1267

In February of 1977 I was working undercover in Narcotics. I had two subjects who were going to make a buy of heroin from dealers in Somerton, just south of Yuma for $600.00. I drove them to Somerton for the deal. They knew I had $500.00 in my pocket. The deal did not materialize and we drove back to Phoenix.

We arrived in Phoenix and drove to a motel with Sgt Vic Ruiz, Officer Jim Stevenson and officer Dick Richey near by acting as backup.

We sat in the car and talked for a bit and the two suspects got out of the car. One walked away and the other knocked on a motel room door. A suspect came out and the two subjects walked back to the car. One subject opened the right rear door and slid across the seat to a position behind me. The other subject walked to the left side of the car and stood there by the driver's door.

My senses went into high gear due to their actions and I attempted to lock my door to keep the subject standing by the drivers door out, but the subject in the back seat reached around and grabbed me around the chest and placed a pair of scissors to my neck saying he would kill me.

I reached around with my left hand and grabbed the scissors and at the same time drew my weapon and threw myself down on the front seat pinning the subjects arm. I pointed my weapon over my shoulder and told the subject that he better drop the scissors or I would shoot him. The subject outside the car reached in and was trying to get my weapon. The subject with the scissors continued to say he was going to kill me.

I made the decision not to shoot the subject and instead fired two rounds through the windshield knowing that it would get the attention of my backup team. They responded immediately and we took the subjects into custody. The third subject who walked away from the car then returned and he was also taken into custody.

There are those who say I should have shot the guy but I believe my decision was the correct one. We took 3 subjects into custody with no one being injured.

It is strange how the mind works in a crisis situation. In a split second I decided to shoot through the windshield and looking up through the windshield I aimed at a palm tree thinking that if I hit the tree, the bullet would not come down and possibly injure someone.

The department issued a letter that stated that my actions were justified and proper within the guideline of General Orders.

GOING THE EXTRA MILE
Don Uhles #2092

It was January or February 1978 and COLD! I was patrolling US 66 just east of Winslow, there was still no I-40 Bypass around Winslow. I was between Winslow and the old wooden RT 66 bridge; anyone who worked this area will remember that old bridge and how narrow it got when working an accident on it.

I noticed an individual waking in the traffic lane and decided that we should visit. This individual was small in stature, wore a heavy full length outer coat, multiple layers of clothes under the jacket, and heavy boots. As I interviewed this individual, I quickly learned that he was 10-16. He showed no signs of intoxication but he was not mentally present. In spite of his clothing, it was obvious that with his mental condition and the looming sub-zero temperatures he would not fare well tonight. I booked him into the Winslow City Jail for the charge of Pedestrian in The Roadway in hopes that he would receive some needed counseling the next morning.

A day or two later I saw Don Williams (#1096) parked at the West Winslow City Limits. At that time, I worked Winslow to the east and Don worked Winslow to the west. I pulled in behind Don and as he walked back to me, he had a perplexed look on his face. As I looked closer, I could see the top of a small head in his back seat. Don leaned in my window and said "I got a real nut on my hands". I asked Don "is his name Lenio?" to which Don replied "as a matter of fact it is!". I told Don of my encounter and my actions and he described his encounter. Don was conducting a violator stop on I-40 and during this stop he caught sight of something in a nearby culvert. After finishing the stop, he went to the culvert and ordered who-ever was in there to come out. A voice from within the culvert said "OK but I'm not responsible for this mess." Don asked "what mess" to witch the individual replied "the mess in this hotel room, I told them not to mess the room up but they wouldn't listen to me." Don told him to get on up here. Now you member his dress when I first encountered him, well he was now barefoot, no jacket, and was wearing only pants and a light shirt.

While Lenio showed no signs of intoxication he told Don that he did have a history of alcohol abuse. Because of his history Don took Lenio to the local LARK Center. They were hesitant to accept Lenio but finally agreed to admit him.

In the mean time Don started doing some research. As a reminder, back then there was no Google, no cell phones. Research meant you made multiple interviews, coordinated with dispatchers, and made lots of phone calls. As we didn't have access to make long distance calls, we were required to call an 800 number that rang at the state capital. You would tell the capital operator who you were, the number you wanted to call, and they would patch you through. Don learned that Lenio was once a Sergeant with a police department in the Midwest. A respected Officer who left his police career and bought a bar. His partner in this venture ran out on him leaving Lenio with nothing. His drinking increased, his life spiraled downhill, and he eventually wound up on the streets in Winslow, AZ. Don was able to make contact with Lenio's family, who were worried sick for him. Lenio's family was then reunited with him and he returned home.

Don and I reshared this story many times through the years. Don and I recanted how you're a pillar of the community and with just a few untoward events you're like Lenio and on the streets. Over the years Don's recollection varies slightly from mine but he's not here to defend himself, so my version goes and, in my mind, Don is the Hero .

It would have been easy to simply leave Lenio on the side of the highway and he would have likely become another winter statistic in Northern Arizona. Instead, Don went Above and Beyond and reunited Lenio with his family.

CHOPPING WOOD AND BRINGING DOWN A CARTEL
Ron Cox #1101
Paul Palmer #342

A lot of our old time patrolman who helped to make our department great had roots in Arizona. None more so than Frank Gillette.

Frank was born in a cabin on Haigler Creek at the base of the Mogollon Rim in 1918. The general area was known as Pleasant Valley. Pleasant Valley is most known for the Tewskbury-Graham feud known as the Pleasant Valley War which took place during the years 1882-1892.

The war involved cattleman associations, sheepmen, hired guns, cowboys and Arizona lawmen.

Frank grew up on the Haigler Creek ranch with no close neighbors and no friends to play with. A big event would be when his parents would ride into Young on occasion and get their mail and a few supplies that they might need. It was a custom that whoever got their mail would also get mail for other families on nearby ranches and deliver the mail to them.

Frank tells of his father riding his horse each year to Young to pick up his Christmas present, sometimes in terrible weather. There were no roads in the area and few automobiles in Gila County. The present would have been ordered earlier in the year from the Sears and Roebuck catalog. His father would leave early in the morning and not return until nightfall.

His parents worried when Frank neared his eighth birthday because state law required that all children at age eight had to attend school. There was no school for Frank to attend. Frank's parents and other parents on ranches in the area who had children, needed to have a school for their children that was closer than Payson. They lobbied the state and a school was started in a one room school house in Gorden Canyon. The school was still far enough away from Haigler Creek that Frank was sent to live with friends during the school year.

This was the life of Frank Gillette. Frank joined the Highway Patrol in 1951 and was given badge number 65 which became number 25 when the badge number system changed. Frank spent most of his time working the Globe area. After retirement Frank wrote two books, Pleasant Valley and Cop's Diary.

Ron Cox continues the story:

Along with Frank Gillette's truly interesting life history, there lies another story about him that I don't believe many of the DPS/AHP folks are aware of. I'd like to tell it, if I may.

I had heard stories about Frank, but had never had the pleasure or opportunity to meet him. I'll leave some names out, for obvious reasons. While I was in CI, I was sitting in the office one morning and answered the phone. Frank told me who he was and related the following: " the wife and I was cutting wood by the airstrip by Young. We had a load and we're pulling back onto the main road and this vehicle pulled broadside in front of me blocking the road. I told my wife to hand me my thirty-eight from the glove box. I was fixing to have a talk with this guy. Before I could get out of the truck, a purple, twin engine airplane took off right over the top of us, and two more vehicles came out of the airstrip, and all 3 of them took off heading towards Globe. I just thought you guys would like to know about it."

He then gave me a very good description of all 3 vehicles. This was in August of 1984. My squad was working constantly with the US Customs Air Support folks, and I called them immediately. It happened that they had a Cessna 206 flying around the Globe area. I gave them the info, they contacted the Gila County SO, who set up a roadblock on the Young road. The 3 vehicles were stopped, and two of them had large suitcases in the pickups with camper shells. They were filled with what turned out to be over 1200 lbs. of cocaine!! Bill Reutter told me to fly up to Globe in one of our aircraft and see if I could help in any way. Off I went.

When I got to the Sheriffs Office, I went to the County Attorneys office, as instructed, and knocked on the door. I was told to come in. An attorney was sitting at his desk writing out what I assume was a search warrant. He asked who I was and what did I want? I told him who I was, that I had received the initial info, and told to come to Globe and see if I could help. His exact words were, " I don't need a F_ _ _ ing thing from you!!" He then put his head back down and continued writing. I took that as a signal that I was dismissed from his presence.

I called Capt. Reutter, we agreed that I probably ought to come back to Phx.

To shorten things up a bit, a monthly meeting was set up between myself, a Gila County deputy, and......a DEA agent. We were supposed to share gathered info with each other. After about 3 meetings, I told Capt. Reutter that it was going nowhere and he agreed. DEA subsequently took over the case. Which turned out to be a good decision. I think it was a couple of years later that DEA ended up disrupting a major cartel through this case. Several high dollar aircraft were seized, and the main player got a life sentence here in the US, and is still in Federal Prison. I checked online periodically, and that individual is now in deteriorating health. You will read more about this in Charley Ruiz's story about Kiki Camerena.

Not long after the initial bust, my Sgt and I, along with Customs personnel, flew to Young in a Huey helicopter and met Frank Gillette, face to face. We presented him with a bit of a reward and thanked him profusely for what he helped do by simply making a phone call. Not bad for a country boy/Arizona Highway Patrolman!!

Note: As you read in the above story, Patrolman Frank Gillette was an Arizona Pioneer who later became an Arizona Highway Patrolman. In 1959 Frank wrote and published a book titled Cops Diary. The following story is from that book and is reprinted here with permission of Franks family.

THE REAL MCCOY
Frank Gillette #25

One night one of my buddies was riding with me. Traffic was thin. We'd patrolled for a couple of hours and hadn't seen anything worth bothering about. We'd only stopped a couple of guys with headlights out and given them repair orders.

Presently, we were driving along directly behind a convertible with out of state plates. One of those premonitions that I sometimes have prompted me to say,
"What do you think of that convertible?"

From the silhouette of the headlights we could see a woman driving and a man sitting by her side. She was driving on the speed limit and was obeying all the traffic rules, but still some little voice kept saying, "That car just doesn't look right."

"She seems to be driving all right", my buddy said. "Yes, but somehow they just don't look right," I said. "Well, let's look 'em over."

I hit her with the red light and she pulled to the side of the road and stopped. I approached with caution , playing my light over the interior as I walked up. The woman had a big bag in her lap, rummaging through it, in search of a driver's license. The man was a somewhat wild-looking character. A small child slept in the back.

"What's the matter officer? We speeding or something?" the woman said.

"No, you're driving pretty good", I said "I'm just stopping you at random to check your driver's license.

The woman had found the driver's license and handed it out to me. The man seemed very nervous. The atmosphere was rather tense, and I couldn't tell just why. But it felt like there were ants crawling up my back.

I glanced briefly at the license , then glanced into the car again. The woman had set the bag in the seat between herself and the man. Her right hand was resting on the seat. In her lap, I caught the glimpse of a gun. I looked more closely. It was a nickel-plated revolver with a pearl handle. The seconds seemed hours long.

There are times, when a man is in a spot, that his own speed amazes him. Such was the case with me. I was watching the woman's hand. She raised it slightly. In a flash I had plunged into the car, made a grab and came out holding the gun and a piece of her dress. She jumped like I'd poked her with a hot iron. My buddies eyes popped as I made the play.

I felt about six inches high when I looked close and found it to be a cap pistol. It belonged to the child in the back. The woman for some reason was carrying it in her lap.

ENRIQUE "KIKI" CAMERENA
Charley Ruiz #1267

In 1982 two U.S. Customs Agents were doing a surveillance on two known smugglers. The two smugglers were known only as Bill and Chuck. The

Agents called our Air Interdiction Unit and Bill Roller, Bill Dailey, Ron Cox, Mike Stevens and I responded to assist.

The smugglers were preparing a motorhome for a trip. "Bill" left in the motorhome followed by the customs Agents and our Interdiction Unit joined the surveillance. We followed the motorhome to a sugar plant at Riggs and McQueen Rd in Chandler and drove to an area where a truck and trailer were parked. We noticed the motorhome was riding high and the curtains were open.

Later the motorhome left the plant riding low with the curtains closed. We followed the vehicle to Ray Rd and Arizona Avenue (Country Club at that time) where it parked on the corner and appeared to be waiting for someone.

A second motorhome arrived and I noticed a station wagon driven by a Mexican male wearing a cowboy hat. He parked and never got out of the vehicle. This vehicle seemed out of place. I had a feeling that this was the one "Bill" was waiting for. After about an hour "Bill" got back in the motorhome and drove out to Arizona Avenue and headed north with the surveillance units following. I stayed behind and watched the station wagon that then followed the our units out. He would follow the units and then pull up alongside them and check them out. I drove up next to the station wagon and got a good look at the driver. I continued to follow the station wagon which then took a different route than the motorhome. I was then called and told to break off my surveillance and rejoin the unit. Both RV's were followed west on I-10 to MP82 where it pulled into a rest area.

The drivers were observed transferring boxes from one RV to the other. We then followed them back east where one RV was lost in Apache Junction area and the other continued east followed by Ron Cox.

With the assistance of the Superior PD a stop was made east of Superior. After consent was given approximately 1,500 pounds of marijuana was found. The other RV was later located and was found to be transporting 45 pounds of marijuana.

A search warrant was executed at the plant in Chandler where the RV's were first observed and 8,000 pounds of marijuana was found in a furniture truck. The owner of the plant said that Mexican males rented the place. A propane tanker truck arrived with marijuana hidden in the tank and the marijuana was transferred to the furniture truck.

Dave (Buck Savage) Smith had been called in along with other officers to assist and he and I were in the office at the sugar plant when the plant employee answered his phone and unable to understand the caller and knowing that we were looking for Mexicans males he handed the phone to Dave. Dave attempted to converse in broken Spanish and I took the phone and was told that the Mexicans that were involved in this operation were staying in bungalows in the rear of the San Marcos Hotel.

Agents in three vehicles headed to the hotel. When we arrived we observed the suspects walking away from the bungalow with their suitcases. When they saw us they all took off in different directions. Dave and I chased one suspect into the restaurant. Dave ran behind the suspect through the customers yelling "Alto! Policia! Alto! Policia!" That was quite a sight.

The suspect, later identified as Roberto Silvas Leo, gave up and the remaining suspects were captured and all were transported to the Chandler Police Department.

I interviewed them and proceeded to start a conspiracy case against them. They all refused to admit they were involved and they were released to the MCSO for deportation by the Border Patrol.

I continued my investigation and learned the driver of the station wagon was Samuel Leo. The suspects had a room at a motel in Chandler where I found numerous Mexican IDs and documents. I seized and recorded all of this evidence for the conspiracy case.

In reaching out to other agencies both local and federal, I got no response. Then one day I got a call from DEA Agent Ray Cuevas from San Diego. He was surprised that no agency in Arizona had contacted me. One suspect, Robert Felix Beltran was considered a major heroin dealer. His sister had been arrested in possession of 76 pounds of heroin in Tijuana.

Agent Cuevas took it upon himself to fly to Phoenix and meet and give me a run down on this group. It was at this time that I received a teletype from Jim Kuykendall, a DEA supervisor in Guadalajara. Agent Kuyukendall advised me that our seized 8,000 pounds of marijuana was probably sent by Ernesto Fonseca (Carrillo). I then called Agent Kuykendal in Guadalajara and gave him a list of the suspects.

Kuykendal connected me with one of his agents that knew the Fonseca clan. This agent was none other than Enrique "Kiki" Camerena. He gave me the real names of who the suspects were. Sorting it all out was mind boggling and time consuming. One was a suspected money man for Fonseca.

I stayed in contact with Kiki for over 3 years. With Kiki's and Ray Cuevas's help we were able to identify cartel members. The only suspect I had trouble identifying was Samual Cortez.

One day while visiting my brother-in-law at the Phoenix VA, I started a conversation with his sister who was visiting from Tucson. I knew she travelled in Mexico to some of the areas where the suspected cartel members lived and I told her about some of the guys I was trying to identify. She said I should be looking at a guy named Samuel and she described him. It was the suspect Samuel Cortez who was driving the station wagon in our conspiracy case. She described him to a "T" and said his real name was Samuel Cortez Gil.

Due to supervisor changes it took over 3 years before I

sent the conspiracy case to a federal grand jury and got a true bill on the co-conspirators and warrants were issued. Most were arrested and pled guilty and received a light sentence. The two hard core ones were Samuel Cortez Gil who was arrested in Payson and Roberto Silva Leos who was arrested in Calexico, California.

I got a call from Calexico DEA supervisor Robert Hernandez. I had worked with him previously when he was working undercover for the Phoenix PD. He advised me that they possibly had one of my suspects in custody that was caught trying to cross the border at Mexicali. He advised me that I would have to make a positive identification. I contacted Ken Sul who was pilot for DEA and we flew to Calexico.

I met Agent Bobby Hernandez who took me to meet the suspect. When I entered the room I addressed him in Spanish calling him by name. At first he didn't recognize me but as we talked he finally admitted to being part at the crime scene. He pled guilty and was given a light sentence, but at least all those involved had a criminal file attached to their name.

Over the following years I received bits and pieces about some of the suspects. I was told that Robert Silva Leo owned a ranch at the southern tip of Baja California, Mexico. On one occasion he roped one of his workers and dragged him to death behind a horse because he suspect him of stealing from him.

It was also said that he was a bookkeeper for Ernesto Fonseca and closely associated with Rafael Caro Quintero (Rafa). Both these men were connected to the kidnapping and murder of DEA Agent Enrique "Kiki" Camarena.

From 1982 to 1985 I stayed in constant contact with Kiki sometimes just shooting the bull about our family members. We talked about his sons who're about the same age as my boys. Although we never met in person we became close friends over the phone.

On Feb 8 1985 Mike Stevens and I were assisting Randy Nations, Mike Mauser and Lynn Smith with a Pop Warner football team. DEA supervisor Dick Johnson met with Mike and I and asked if we had informants that could go into Mexico, It turned out that we did have two informants that at one time flew loads for Quintero.

When we asked why he said that one of his agents was kidnapped and when I asked who the agent was, he said, "You probably don't know him. His name is Camarena, I said, "Kiki?" and he replied, "So you do know him."

(It was later learned that Kiki had been kidnapped by the cartel. They tortured him for three days prior to killing him. His body was found a month later.)

The following day we met with the informants and DEA where they were given instructions on what to do while they were in Mexico, and who did they think was capable of kidnapping the agent. They mentioned Rafael Quintero, Michael Felix Gallardo and one crazy one called El Coche Loco. the crazy pig. They named a few others whose names I do not recall.

When the informants returned they reported that everything was crazy in Mexico and all the cartel members that they knew are suspicious of anybody and anybody asking questions. They were accused of working for the DEA. They flew back the first chance they had or otherwise they would have wound up missing.

To this day I can recall the conversations with Kiki, and meeting his mother and wife at the National Latino Awards Banquet in Phoenix. This gave me some closure.

THE LONG LEGGED DRUNK
Ralph Shartzer #220

I received a call about a non-injury accident about 5 miles south of the Utah/Arizona border on I-15. I had a reserve trainee officer riding with me. When we arrived at the scene, I observed a passenger car Northbound off the right shoulder of the pavement with a male subject standing at the rear of the vehicle and another person, apparently passed out, sitting in the driver's seat. The standing male advised me that the person in the drivers seat was his brother and they had been to Mesquite Nevada at a casino.

The vehicle had very minor damage to the right front due to contact with the embankment. I asked the passenger if there were any injuries and got a negative reply. A visual check of the passed out person behind the wheel, I detected no obvious injuries. The passenger said the driver was his brother and they were going home to the Papago Indian Reservation at Pipe Springs Arizona. The passenger was obviously intoxicated and the driver had a very strong odor of alcohol about his person. I advised my trainee that I was going to remove the driver from the vehicle and for him to be ready for anything in that quite often a person under the influence might become combative. I placed my hands in his armpits from behind and began removing him from the vehicle. As his feet hit the pavement, I observed his right foot at a very unusual angle and his boot was about a foot longer than his other boot.

I thought 'oh crap, he has a broken leg' and I about did a number in my pants. His brother saw the look on my face and started laughing and said: Ha - ha, he has a wooden leg!

Needless to say, after the arrest and booking, I did do a uniform inspection.

THE DOCTORS
Lee Patterson #2733

As a Criminal Investigations Bureau (CIB) Detective in the Special Investigations Unit (SIU) from 1988 to 2000 , I have many "on the job" memories which come to mind. Due to the nature of the assignment, which frequently involved the investigation of major departmental critical incidents, officer involved shootings, and homicide cases, it's inappropriate to discuss the majority of these memories due to public dissemination restrictions.

Obviously the cases and crime scenes we worked in SIU were generally very stressful and demanding on many different levels. One of the ways we dealt with the environment we worked in was with the introduction of a little levity amongst our unit detectives when appropriate. This "cop humor" was manifested for a while when we were at the various scenes around the state, by each of us referring verbally to each other as "Doctor".

The reactions we garnered from various individuals who were not part of our unit was priceless. Since we typically were attired in business suits and ties, the people who overheard us were seemingly either impressed and/or mystified that DPS had the resources to utilize investigators in that capacity! Anyways, my fellow SIU Detectives and I always got a little chuckle out of it, and it made our tasks just a little less stressful. Fortunately for us and the department, the news media never got wind of our discrete humor!

ARIZONA MEXICAN BORDER LIASON UNIT
Larry Thompson #148
Martin Marquez #2938

A "fluke" beginning with a sound result.

Early in 1983 the Mexican Federal Highway Patrol did patrolling and enforcement work on the highways of Mexico and in the ports (airports and seaport). Among their extra duties was the responsibility to assist the Mexican Presidential Protection unit with some logistics, to include transportation and communications. When there were events in the Mexican "outback", the communications gear would need to be transported and installed in that location.

During this time (and earlier), there was little interaction between lower level agencies and officials in the US and Mexico. Most of the attention was focused on the DEA and drug problems across the border. Occasionally the officials in Mexico would invite their US equals across for a "goat barbecue" and the destruction (bonfire) of seized marijuana. These happenings improved the rapport across the border but further cooperation was still limited.

It was in the early part of 1983 that the Mexican Presidential Protection unit requested assistance with communications at a remote location in Mexico. This assistance included the transporting and installation of a rather large radio tower. One of the officers from the Mexican Federal Highway Patrol was Arturo Jimenez. In the process of erecting this tower, it became entangled with some high voltage transmission lines. The result was that Officer Jimenez was badly burned. Treatment for this kind of injury in Mexico was limited and Officer Jimenez was transported to the Maricopa Burn unit in Phoenix. During this time, his wife accompanied him and stayed in Phoenix for the entire time. We were (AZ Highway Patrol) contacted by the Mexican officials and asked to look in on the Jimenez family and assist in any way possible. This we did with pleasure. The wife visited our offices several times and various of our officers would look in on Officer Jimenez. His treatment was completed in late May or early June and he returned home to Mexico.

A short time later, we were contacted by the Federal Highway Patrol Comandante Jorge Cabrera Luna in Mexicali. We were invited to come to Mexacali to visit the Comandante and be thanked for our efforts on behalf of his man Arturo Jimenez. We accepted the invitation and a date was set early in June. Lt. Max Welch was the district commander in Yuma and he was invited to attend with me. I flew to Calexico, California where Lt. Welch met us and provided transportation into Mexicali.

While visiting the Comandante, we were interrupted when three members of the California Highway Patrol entered. This was a surprise to us but it appeared that there was no surprise for the Comandante. As this meeting evolved, it was revealed that the Mexican authorities and California had a working arrangement.

The CHP contingent consisted of Ben Killingsworth, Border Division Chief, Lt. Ralph Limon, and Sgt Joe Ortiz (Border Liaison Unit). It was learned that this unit had existed for some time and was enjoying success across the border. This was totally new information to us. We continued to discuss how this arrangement worked and what it would take for us (DPS) to initiate something similar in our state. Lt. Welch continued the conversation thru and after lunch and got their contact information so that he could follow up. Lt. Welch stated that he had "just the right officer" to initiate such an assignment. As it turned out, Lt. Welch was able to put together the beginning outline and did initiate it on August 1st. 1983.

The just the right officer"turned out to be Martin Marquez currently in District 4. The qualifications of Officer Marquez were outstanding. Martin was born an American citizen but had grown up in both Mexico and the US. He was actually born in Mexico but his mother was a US citizen thus making Martin a "derived" US citizen. His birth place was Rancho Las Bocas Huajucar Jalisco, Mexico. The family later located in San Luis Rio Colorado, Sonora where they resided for 5 years. In 1967, they moved to Somerton, Arizona. Martin not only understood the Mexican culture, he had experienced it. As he moved into his Liaison Officer assignment, he was able to use this knowledge to his advantage and allow it to help him succeed.

As Martin proceeded toward his DPS career, he served as a sworn officer in the city of Somerton at the age of 19 yrs. (the minimum age was 18). Martin's family is a whole other story. He is a twin and one of 13 siblings. His dad still lives in or near San Luis, Arizona as do most of the other siblings. Lt. Welch and I , discussed this new unit and assignment for Martin. He was found to be totally enthusiastic about the new duties.

Having gained rapport with the CHP officers in Mexicali, Lt Welch contacted them about the beginnings of his new unit. It was suggested by Lt. Ralph Limon that Martin participate in a two week ride along (OJT) program with the CHP. Officer Rudy Parra out of El Centro, Cal. was to be the coach. The time spent with the CHP illustrated the value of developing numerous contacts with US and Mexican officials at all levels. On August 1, 1983 Martin started his assignment as a Liaison Officer in Yuma and was assigned to the Southwest Border Alliance with Sgt Roger Boddy (1198) as his supervisor. (temporarily in CIB).

After the period of OJT, Martin took on the task of meeting with all the local, state and federal law enforcement agencies along the border in Mexico. These agencies are all encompassed in San Luis, Sonoyta, and Puerto Penasco areas of Sonora. We also met with representatives of the U S Consulates in Hermosillo and Tijuana Mexico. All of these agencies played an important role in the detection and recovery of US stolen vehicles. Another important agency in this operation was the Mexican Consulate office in Calexico, California. The recovery process was outlined in the "CONVENTION ON THE RETURN OF STOLEN OR EMBEZZLED VEHICLES AND AIRCRAFT" signed by the US and the Republic of Mexico.

On July 1, 1984 the Vehicle Theft Interdiction Unit (VTI) was formed and placed in the Highway Patrol Bureau. The new unit consisted of the sergeant, Terry Conner, and three officers to assist in the three divisions with auto theft investigations. The first officers assigned were Dale Doucet, Rick Williams and Bill Hansen. Officer Marquez remained the "liaison officer" in Yuma. In November of that year a second "liaison officer", Gerry Navarro, was brought on board and stationed in Nogales.

Officers Marquez and Navarro began to expand their contacts throughout the states of Sonora and Baja California. Due to all the networking, the liaison officers began to see a huge increase in the numbers of stolen vehicles being located and identified. The vehicles were identified by the Mexican authorities through the VTI unit. The originating agency (US) would be contacted by the liaison officers. This was a telephonic process between the Mexican officers and the DPS liaison officers. Written confirmation of the stolen status was sent to the Mexican officers which would give them the legal grounds to seize the vehicle(s). The liaison officers would follow up with the originating US agencies to include instructions for the owners that they needed to return their vehicles to them.

The task of identifying and locating stolen vehicles was the beginning of much cooperation between the authorities in the US and Mexico. This became the conduit to work together on many types of investigations (except Narcotics). This cooperation increased daily day by day and it expanded to all levels in Mexico and Arizona.

This cooperation resulted in many visits with Arizona officials visiting Mexico and the reverse of this with Mexican officials coming to Arizona. On a local level, the executives of the CHP and Az DPS began a series of meetings to compare things that they were doing that might contribute to more and greater success. California's Border Liaison along with Arizona's

Mexican Liaison were the beginning.

(side note) Not pursuant to the liaison program but during this time of cooperation, the Director of the Mexican Federal Highway Patrol, Director Antonio Arizpe Mireles attended the mid year meeting of the International Association of Chiefs of Police (IACP) Highway Safety committee in New Hampshire. The Director was hosted by the National Highway Traffic Safety Administration (NHTSA) and was accompanied by DPS Liaison Officer Martin Marquez. This let a lot of people see that cooperation can occur on the local, national and international levels.

DO YOU UNDERSTAND THE WORD JAIL?
Jay Atwater #1434

I'm not sure of the timeline, it was probably in the 1980s, I was working traffic on I-40 west of Flagstaff. A traffic stop was made on a vehicle for a speeding violation on I-40 eastbound in the Belmont Flats around MP185.

As I approached the vehicle I noted two males in the front seat and two females in the rear seat. All were dressed as if they were going out for the night. After explaining why I had stopped them, the driver responded in French. Being a courteous and vigilant patrolman trying to explain the need to slow down, even pointing on the speedometer at the speed limit.

Doing this, I spotted the two ladies in the rear seat smiling at each other. I then asked the driver, "Do you understand the word jail?" The driver responded in very clear English, "Yes Sir, I do."

The citation was then issued, the driver then stated they were leaving the country in a few days, did that matter? For whatever reason, I said, "He may not be able to leave the country if the citation has not been taken care of." I had no idea if that citation was addressed or not.

YOU'RE SITTING ON A SNAKE!
Randy Strong #1295

In May of 1979 the Department sent the motor training staff to the CHP Motor Training School in Sacramento, California for a refresher course. Sgt. Gary Fitzsimmons # 574 organized the trip which also included Rick Williams #897, Bob Haliday #1255 , Johnny Sanchez #1463, Dave Johnson #689 , and me.

Each morning, as we were prepping the trainer motorcycles, the CHP training instructors would have one of us take the "chase vehicle" around to the gas pumps and gas it up.

One morning one of the instructors killed a rattlesnake on his way to work and brought it with him. Bob happened to be in the office when he got there and got an idea when he saw the snake. He asked the instructor if he would have Rick gas up the "chase" car

Bob then took the snake and coiled it up on the driver's seat and stuck the stump (where the snake's head had been) into the crease of the seat. Bob, knowing that Rick was afraid of snakes, made sure that everyone knew except Rick what was going to happen.

When the instructor asked Rick to gas up the car, we all thought he would open the car door, jump back and scream like a little girl. We were all ready for that moment. But that didn't happen. To our surprise Rick opened the door, sat down on the seat, and drove off to the gas pumps which were on the other side of the building. We waited for a big scream coming from the gas pumps. No scream. Nothing.

Pretty soon here comes Rick. He drives up, and pulls in front of us while we're working on our motorcycles. He gets out and leisurely walks back to his motor. We all just stood there dumbfounded. Bob's big joke was a bust.

Now Bob takes Rick over to the car and opens the door. "Rick, did you even see this?" as he points to the snake on the seat. Rick jumped back and squealed. We all finally got the laugh we intended to get earlier. But Rick didn't believe that it had always been there until Rick pointed out the blood spot on the back of his Levi's. Rick said he thought it was one of those cool cushions that people used to use. We all laughed even more.

To this day Bob is known as "snake man," and Rick is still afraid of snakes!

When the pandemic hit and everyone was quarantined at home, Paul Palmer contacted Colin Peabody, Chairman of the Coalition of DPS Retirees, and talked over having retirees submit stories about their careers. The original thought was to collect them and then Colin would send them out to retirees in the CDPSR e-mails for our officers to enjoy as they were homebound. It was such a success people began saying the stories should be in a book. The book "That Reminds Me of The Time" was born.

In our first book, "That Reminds Me Of The Time", the retirees of the Arizona Highway Patrol/Department Of Public Safety shared stories about their time with the department. As we read the book, we laughed, we shed a few tears, and we thought, I've never heard that story, but that reminds me of the time...

In "That Reminds Me Of The Time Volume 2", we hear more stories, some from retirees who didn't think they had a story to tell until they read the first book and found that yes, I do have a story.

In volume 2 you will read about snowstorms, floods, rescues and shootouts, some in remote areas with no radio communications with the dispatch center. You will see the humor, the fears, and the bravery of dedicated officers of the Arizona Highway Patrol/Department of Public Safety.

Once again, Paul Palmer and Colin Peabody enjoyed putting these stories together. Not only does it record the history of our department, it provides some fantastic reading.

ISBN 978-1-0879-0270-8

90000

9 781087 902708